JIM & RACHEL BRITTS

TO SAVE A LIFE

A NOVEL BASED ON THE MOVIE

JIM & RACHEL BRITTS

TO SAVE A LIFE

A NOVEL BASED ON THE MOVIE

To Save A Life

DEDICATION

To all the teenagers we've had the privilege
to work with over the past ten years. We pray this story
can inspire you to change the world.

HOW APPROPRIATE, Jake thought darkly to himself as he reluctantly stepped out of his truck into the somber drizzle. The tiny drops of water tingled on his skin, and he shuddered. *Why did I come here?* he wondered. *What good will it do now?*

He forced himself to walk toward the tiny group huddled ahead. They whispered and hugged and stood with their hands in their pockets, trying to warm their numb hearts as much as their bodies. There was Roger's mom, trying to look okay, but not succeeding so well. Roger's little sister stood close to her, just staring blankly ahead. There was Jake's neighbor, Mrs. Jones, looking sweet and kind as usual, but her eyes were red and puffy, and her ever-present smile was absent today. There was Clyde Will, tattoos peeking out of his dress shirt.

Just as Jake got close, a guy maybe thirty-five years old stepped apart from the group and started talking. He looked almost as awkward and unsure as Jake felt.

"Well, today we come together to remember the life of Roger Andrew Dawson." He paused, breathed in, and then continued,

"While we know there was so much life left in him, we thank God for the eighteen years we did have with Roger."

Roger's mom started shaking uncontrollably as she tried to hold back her sobs. Suddenly Jake's tie started choking off his air supply. *Why am I here?*

It's the summer before fifth grade—a hot July afternoon. Jake and Roger cruise slowly up and down their neighborhood on their bikes, listless and barely talking.

Suddenly, Roger turns to Jake with one of his mischievous smiles. "I got an idea," he grins. "Oh, yeah. I've hit the gold mine. We're going to be rich!"

Familiar butterflies flutter in Jake's stomach. Roger's craziest ideas always came out of nowhere. "Is this going to get me grounded again?" he protests.

"Jake, that's a risk I'm willing to take. Anyways, who can say no to this smile?" Roger flashes his pearly whites.

Jake chuckles back another ripple of apprehension. But the lure of an adventure draws him in, and his curiosity wins.

Minutes later, Jake and Roger are sprinting down the street, each wearing their best effort at a costume: capes and masks found crumpled at the bottom of Jake's closet, and two of Jake's mom's pillowcases. The boys' gleeful shouts echo through the neighborhood. All inhibitions gone, Jake flaps his arms, bobs his head, and prances like a choking seagull, which sends Roger into a fit of laughter. He playfully shoves Jake, whose black cape tangles around his legs and sends him tumbling to the ground. Roger pounces on him, but Jake headlocks and pins Roger in a maneuver worthy of the WWF. "IIIIIII am the chammm—piooooon!" Jake belts out, arms lifted high in victory. He helps Roger up, and they adjust their capes and masks before racing up the neighbor's lawn. They pound on the door urgently.

Mrs. Jones appears in the doorway, a woman of natural beauty whose smiling face makes her look much younger than her fifty years. But before she even says a word…

"Trick or treat!" Roger and Jake announce.

Mrs. Jones chuckles at the ragamuffin superheroes on her doorstep. "Boys, it's the middle of July!"

Roger delivers: "I love what you did with your hair!"

Mrs. Jones instinctively runs her fingers through her newly dyed, flame-red hair and succumbs. "Let me see what I got."

With Mrs. Jones' back turned, Jake and Roger give each other a silent high-five. This is easier than they expected!

Mrs. Jones returns a minute later with a granola bar and juice box for each of them. Before the loot hits the bottom of the pillowcases, Roger pulls a daisy from behind his back.

"And this is for you!" Even with the cheesy wink, his smile could not be more charming. As she accepts the flower with delight, the boys take off down the street, yelling, "Thank you!" over their shoulders.

At the corner, Jake looks back at Roger. "Hey, where'd the flower come from?"

Roger grins and points to the flower patch in Mrs. Jones' front yard.

"You're crazy, man!" Jake admires, and takes off sprinting ahead to the next house across the street.

"JAKE!!!"

Roger's scream jerks Jake's head up just in time to see an SUV speeding right toward him. His eyes connect with the absent-minded driver, who slams on the brakes too late. Jake freezes in panic as the car skids right at him.

"NOOOOOO!!!" he hears Roger scream again.

The next thing Jake remembers is being tackled from the side, falling to the pavement inches from the braking car. He hears the sickening crack of breaking bones. Dazed, with a small trickle of blood oozing from his skinned knee, Jake looks back into the street. His best friend lies motionless under the bumper of the car, his right leg bent in the wrong direction, his red cape covering his face like a shroud.

Jake shuddered at the memory of that day eight years ago and just stared at Mrs. Jones, standing across from him in the rain. The guy who must have been the minister was still saying something.

"None of us know the pain Roger was experiencing or the demons that raged in his head. We don't understand why God allows these things to happen, but we do know His heart. And we trust Him in the midst of our pain."

Why am I here? Jake thought again.

It's the beginning of seventh grade—a crisp autumn morning. Junior-high Jake dribbles the soccer ball down the field with incredible control, racing by the much-slower defenders. Parents yell like maniacs on the sidelines as he splits the defense. Sports have always come naturally to Jake; he is the resident first-pick for whatever game the kids are playing.

On the sidelines, attempting to match his best friend stride-for-stride, Roger cheers at the top of his lungs. He runs with a noticeable limp, dragging his right leg behind the rest of his body and falling farther behind Jake with every awkward step.

Jake attacks a new pair of converging defenders and kicks the ball just out of reach of the diving goalie. Jake throws his hands up triumphantly, and everyone on the team surrounds him—almost everyone. Roger remains off the field, his jersey white enough to star in a laundry detergent commercial. He jumps up and down alone.

The referee blows the whistle to end the game. One of Jake's teammates, Doug Moore, pulls Jake and a couple of the other players over to his dad.

"Good game, boys!" Mr. Moore hands each of them a snow cone fresh from the snack bar.

Jake reaches for the icy treat and notices Roger standing just a few feet away. He smiles at his buddy through the bubble-gum flavor and starts toward him. But his teammates envelop him first and, distracted by their chatter, Jake starts rehashing his game moves at the crowd's insistence. *It was pretty amazing, after all,* he thinks. *Anyway, Roger's got his mom.*

Jake stared at Roger's mother, tears mixing with the raindrops rolling down her cheeks. *Where has she been?* Jake thought. *How could she have allowed this to happen?*

The young minister finished his speech, and Roger's casket sunk slowly into the ground as if it bore the weight of everyone there. Family and friends shuffled to the edge to drop in a handful of soil. Jake just looked at the clump of dirt in his hand. Every muscle in his body begged him to run in the opposite direction. At last, Jake stiffly tossed his clod in as well. The thud of the dirt on the casket echoed in his ears. This was his final insult: posing as one of Roger's faithful friends.

Yeah, friend.

A camera crew had set up equipment less than thirty yards away. For the first time in his life, the press repulsed Jake. He turned to slink back to his truck.

"Jake."

The familiar voice stopped him mid-stride, and Jake slowly turned to face it. Roger's mom threw her arms around him before he could respond. His arms couldn't hug her back.

"I'm so, so sorry. It means so much that you came. You two—" Mrs. Dawson broke into sobs. Jake feebly patted her back, relieved when a relative walked up and squeezed her shoulder to signal that it was time to go.

Mrs. Dawson broke out of her desperate embrace, wiping her eyes with an already soaked tissue. "Where did we go wrong?" she begged. "Had you two spoken lately? Did he give any indication?"

Jake just shook his head and stared at his feet. Mrs. Dawson finally gave Jake a wistful look and trudged to the waiting car.

What am I doing here?

It's the middle of freshman year—a fabulous Friday evening. The Pacific High School gymnasium is a zoo of cheering students and parents charging the air with anticipation and rivalry, hormones and sweat. As the announcer practically sings the starting lineup, each player's name prompts a new roar from the packed house.

"And starting at guard, averaging fifteen points and eleven assists, the Freshman Phenom...JAKE TA-A-A-A-YLOR!!!" Jake flashes a smile and jumps off his seat, pumps both fists in the air, and joins his teammates in their pre-game chant.

From the opening tip, Jake leads his junior and senior teammates in hustle and determination. He dives for every loose ball and bangs around in the paint, somehow coming away with the rebound against much bigger players. In only his tenth game wearing varsity colors, Jake's valiant efforts quickly prompt the crowd's undying, screaming support.

With four minutes to go in the game, Jake has led his team to a five-point lead. His four sweet nothing-but-net three-pointers, ten assists, and handful of rebounds have brought both fan and foe to their feet. Every vein in his body pulses with adrenaline; every nerve tingles with focus. His movements flow unimpeded by conscious thought.

Jake dribbles down the court, eyes scanning and evaluating each option in a nanosecond as it develops. He fakes to the right wing, then tosses a no-look pass to a wide-open teammate under the basket, who dunks the ball with authority. The next moment, Jake steals the inbound pass and takes it in for an uncontested layup.

Oh, life is good. Jake's nimble feet back-pedal to play defense, and his glance drifts toward the cheerleaders standing along the back wall. His eyes lock with a cute blonde freshman, also moving instinctively with her squad's routine. While the tumult in the gym thunders all around him, Jake's world stands still, his heart pounding in his chest. Amy Briggs. The very thought of her makes Jake shiver under his sweat, but only for a second. His focus shifts back, and he powers on down the court.

The opposing point guard rifles a pass up the court to his open teammate hustling down the right sideline, and he races past Jake toward the basket. He threads a perfect pass back to Jake's man, who finishes off the give-and-go with a layup that goes unchallenged. Jake swears under his breath at his momentary lapse of concentration as his coach yells at him from the sideline. The in-bounder flings a half-court pass to Jake, who dribbles three steps and pulls up for another three-pointer, this time from four feet behind the line. Swish!

Jake takes no time to celebrate, stepping up to his man for a full-court press. There will be no more easy baskets on his watch.

After the game, Jake strolls out of the locker room where parents and friends wait for the players. He scores plenty of congratulations and high-fives, but as usual, his parents aren't there. The sight of Amy Briggs, however, helps him forget it. She's leaning casually against a pole, surrounded by a cluster of guys from the freshman team vying for her laugh, but her attention is riveted on Jake.

"Twenty-two points, eleven assists. You make us freshmen look good," she smiles as Jake walks by.

"Uh, thanks." That pounding in his chest starts up again.

Amy deserts the crowd of boys to walk with Jake, and her bare shoulder brushes his arm. She motions to his sports bag. "Why do you have a little bird on your bag?"

"It's the mascot for the University of Louisville. I'm going to play hoops there someday." Somehow, it doesn't sound as cool spoken out loud as it did in his dreams. But Amy doesn't seem to notice.

"Oh," Amy giggles. "Well, are you going to the party tonight?"

"Okay." Jake pauses. "What party?"

Amy giggles again. "You are so funny. So, we could kind of go together?" She stops walking and faces Jake, catching him playfully under his arm. Her touch sends a current through his body. "Give me your phone," she whispers, stepping closer.

The cool confidence Jake commanded on the court earlier evaporates, and he fumbles in his pocket before his fingers find their target. He finally hands the phone to Amy, hoping she doesn't notice his sweaty palms. As she punches her number into his phone, Jake glances over her shoulder and sees Roger limping toward them.

Jake cringes. As Roger hobbles past the scattered chattering pockets of people, their conversations lull, and their stares follow him. Jake even hears a few snickers. Why can't Roger just fit in? The limp isn't nearly as defined these days, but it is still unmistakable, a continuing and annoying reminder of that fateful day three years ago.

Since middle school, Jake's natural ability to excel at any sport put him on the fast track to popularity. Unfortunately, "the accident" had eliminated Roger's chances of athletic success, and he just couldn't keep up with Jake's new and growing group of friends. Jake and Roger still hung out from time to time, but it was always Roger who called. And to be honest, Jake enjoyed his new "cool" reputation and some-times feared losing it by being seen with Roger. Still, there was always a nagging guilt that he couldn't ignore.

"My friend, Roger—we were going to hang out. Is it cool if he comes too?" Jake asks reluctantly as Amy hands his phone back.

Amy follows Jake's gaze to Roger. "The car only has room for one more," she shrugs. "You know what I mean?" She squeezes Jake's fingertips before skipping away to her girl-friends waiting by a hot red Mustang with its top down.

Jake's eyes follow the enticing bounce of her little skirt—until Roger's voice brings him back. "Am I seeing things, or were you just talking to Amy Briggs?!" Roger beams.

Jake grins, still star-struck.

"Well, let's get out of here. My mom already ordered the pizza." Roger lightly punches Jake on the arm, just inches from where Amy had rubbed it.

Jake drops his eyes. "Rog, I can't come."

"What? We just talked before the game."

Jake glances up. How can he pass up an opportunity like this? "I kind of told Amy I'd go to this party."

Roger's shoulders slump and his smile fades. "Um, okay, cold pizza's still good. Where's the party?"

Jake takes a deep breath. "You can't come."

Silence. Roger falls back as if the words are a physical blow. After a moment, he growls, "I get it. Things are different now." He turns and limps away.

"Rog!" Jake calls out, half-apologetic, half-irritated that his friend doesn't understand. With a sigh, Jake starts after Amy, but he hears Roger punch a locker before dragging himself around the corner.

Jake stood anchored to the manicured cemetery lawn, watching Roger's mom walk away. The rain was still falling relentlessly.

"Freshman year, Mrs. Dawson," he finally mumbled under his breath. "That's the last time I spoke to him. Freshman year."

MRS. DAWSON and her relatives had left at least an hour before, and the few friends at the funeral had departed with them. The news van packed up shortly after getting some uncouth shots of the mourners and filming a brief statement by a reporter. And still Jake remained.

He now sat leaning against the tombstone of some Harriet Wesson, who had succumbed to this resting spot back in 1932. The showers had finally stopped, and the coolness of the dark granite chilled his aching body, but it didn't slow the frenzied whirling of his mind. Jake stared numbly at the cruel hole that marked Roger's life and wrestled with the events of the past week.

How did I get here?

It's the middle of senior year—a fresh, early spring day a little more than a week earlier. Jake walks to his usual lunch spot in the middle of the quad where the basketball team hangs out. On his way, three stunning freshmen girls, showing more skin than clothes, walk by and wave at Jake. He has no clue what their names are, but they sure know his. He flashes his customary smile and nods, but keeps on walking as they giggle in response.

Matt McQueen, the six-foot-seven center, and Tony Henderson, the only junior in the starting five, are playing one-on-one with a wad of paper and a trash can. They are surrounded by the normal herd of twenty or so girls and guys, all trying to be associated with something cool. Matt, also known as the Mouth, keeps a running commentary for the onlookers.

"McQueen backs the poor lad down. He fakes right, fakes left and…Kareem-style skyhooks right in the back of the—!"

Jake jumps in and swats the wad of paper away. "Not in my house!" he yells, arms flexed like a bodybuilder. Matt and Tony bust out laughing—not the response Jake is hoping for. "What's so funny, homies?"

Matt calls on the groupies for support. "This man just admitted that he lives in a trash can!"

They groan. Jake rolls his eyes and puts Matt in a playful headlock. "You boys just remember who gets you the ball!"

Shaking himself free, Matt consoles, "Just playin,' superstar." He straightens his shirt, then pops his collar with fresh attitude. "You just remember, the trash man comes on Wednesdays." He ducks to avoid Jake's pseudo punch, which morphs into a chest-bumping man-hug.

Doug Moore, starting power forward and Jake's closest sidekick, leaves a cluster of hotties and pushes his way into the action. On the way over, he grabs an apple out of the hands of a poor unsuspecting freshman and claps it like a basketball.

"Let's run it again," Doug orders with a cockiness that inspires Tony and Matt to take off their letterman jackets and start throwing elbows. Doug tosses the apple to Jake.

"Clock's down to 5-4-3." Jake sets the scene, crouching into triple-threat stance. His rocker step sends Tony flying. Doug spins around Matt, and Jake throws a perfect pass to Doug's outstretched arm. He slams the fruit into the trash can, to the horror of the unfortunate freshman. Doug looks down at the mashed apple and shrugs at the helpless kid.

Jake raises his hands for high-fives. "A team effort."

Doug puts his arm around his friend's shoulder. "Leave that for the reporters. Louisville's already paying your way."

As Doug turns to the other guys, Jake secretly winks to the freshman and throws him an apple from his own lunch, then quickly turns back to the group. "It is a team sport and I'm telling you...we are sweet!"

"You're sweet." Amy's moist breath tickles Jake's ear as she surprises him from behind with a kiss and a steaming Styrofoam cup. Amy Briggs' freshman cuteness has blossomed brilliantly into a full-blown gorgeous body. Her arms wrap snugly around Jake's torso and he doesn't resist. Jake raises his cup and inhales the mocha vapor to say thanks, then he twists to put his arm around Amy and pulls her closer. "Where's mine?" Doug pipes up.

"Why don't you get your girlfriend to get one for you?" Amy smiles, coyly sipping her drink.

"You know I don't have a girlfriend," Doug argues.

"Hence you have no coffee either," she smirks, twirling her cup right under his nose. This elicits a chorus of "oohs" from the other guys.

Matt sidles up beside his friend and pats him on the back. "She got you, man."

"Whatever," Doug retorts. "Your mom got me last night." Again, a chorus of "oohs".

Matt purses his lips and taunts Doug in a baby voice. "Ah, the big ugly said something funny!"

Doug, no longer smiling, turns to Matt and looks him in the eye. "And I'll kick your ass if you keep calling me that." All eyes suddenly are on him, so Doug's smile slowly returns, and he slaps Matt lightly on the cheek.

Jake turns to Amy and whispers, "Wanna get out of here?"

She entwines her fingers in his. "You know I don't need much to skip calculus."

The bickering banter continues behind them, but Jake and Amy ignore it. They're off to much better things.

Jake has actually been planning this little escapade for a while. The destination isn't new to them—it's their private little ocean bluff where they shared their first kiss. That was the summer after ninth grade, long before he had his truck and a license. He had told all his buddies about his smooth moves and how she had practically melted in his arms. But the truth was that Amy had been the initiator, and he had been so nervous that his retainer popped out. He was so embarrassed, but Amy had never told anyone.

Jake shudders at the memory, but today is different. He opens Amy's door, leads her around back, and whips off the tarp covering the truck bed to reveal a picnic complete with a layer of sod, scattered wild flowers, and a basket on a red-checked blanket.

"Oh, Jake!" Amy gushes, cupping his face in her hands. "You are so romantic!"

"You're right," he shrugs with a grin, swinging her into the truck. "Let's eat!"

They settle down to eat. Jake inhales his sandwich; Amy picks at hers. After eating, they relax in each other's arms watching surfers tackle the waves.

"Eighty school days, and then you leave for Louisville." Amy rests her head on Jake's shoulder.

"Gonna feel like eight hundred with my folks," Jake groans.

"Your mom's not that bad."

"My dad just won't stop riding me."

Amy nestles closer and whispers in his ear, "Don't worry, I'll protect you."

"You know him. He's still trying to live out his own failed dreams..."

"Jake."

Jake stops his rant mid-sentence and looks at her. She musters up the toughest face in her arsenal and flexes her biceps like a blonde boxer. Jake bursts out laughing and squeezes her muscles.

"Oooh, yeah, you are pretty tough. I bet you could take him."

Her stern façade melts into a smile, and their laughter entwines. Jake kisses Amy softly on her forehead.

"Let's be cool parents," Amy murmurs as she snuggles in next to him.

"Who said I wanted kids?"

"I did."

Jake furrows his eyebrows in mock disapproval, then yawns and slowly stretches his arms up over his head, then around her shoulders, under her arms, finally resting on her supple waist. His fingers crawl up under the edge of her lacy tank-top. "Great point," he concedes, and unleashes an ambush tickling.

"Stop, stop. Stop!" Amy squeals. As she catches her breath, she pulls an envelope from her back pocket and waves it in front of Jake. "I got you a love letter."

Jake grabs at it and leans over to peck her on the lips before opening the envelope. His eyes scan the typed page.

"What? You got accepted to Louisville? Early admission!" Jake is genuinely shocked. In all their conversations about the future, he had never once asked her to follow him to Kentucky. For every inch of beauty, Amy doubled it in brains, and her dream had been getting into Stanford.

Amy grins. "Now we can be together," she answers simply.

Jake leaps to his feet and stands in the truck bed facing the preoccupied surfers. He throws his arms up and shouts at the top of his lungs into the salty breeze, "My girl's AMAZING!"

After watching the sun dip below the waves, they slowly drive back into reality. Jake knows that homework, nagging parents, and silent tension await him at home, but for the next few minutes, he savors the bliss of playful chatter and inconsequential gossip. Jake is fully engaged in Amy's story about their teacher, Mrs. Denison, when he notices a kid walking alone under the glowing street light ahead. The load of books he carries seems heavy. As the truck draws closer, Jake recognizes Roger by the obvious limp. Unpleasant reminders flicker into Jake's mind, so he tries to refocus on Amy's tale of Mrs. Denison's great-great-uncle who was a serial killer and ran for president. But then Jake sees a group of neighborhood skaters whiz by Roger. One of them bumps Roger, and he stumbles. Several of his books tumble to the ground. The kids don't stop to apologize or even look back. Almost instinctively, Jake moves to pull his truck over, but then a sudden warmth on his leg compels him to look back at Amy. She is sliding her hand along his thigh; then she waits. And whatever happened back there on the sidewalk suddenly doesn't seem so important. Jake folds his arm around Amy and pulls her close. She's the only thing on his mind now.

After Jake finally drops Amy off, he rolls his truck into his driveway and floats into the house, an elegant two-story custom in an exclusive neighborhood. As he opens the front door, he hears it: the muffled arguing of his parents from the bedroom upstairs. I should have known, Jake growls to himself. He doesn't even bother to turn on the lights, and his good mood dissolves as he starts up the stairs to do his homework.

Jake shoves his bedroom door open, sending a basketball flying across the room into a corner. He flips on the wall switch and slumps down on the bed, reaches for his backpack and yanks out a notebook, a pencil, and a worn math text. He bites down on the pencil and flips through the pages of the math book, but when he finds the page, he just stares at it. He takes the pencil out of his mouth and doodles around the quadratic equations, then stares a little longer into space. He flips over on his back and gazes at the ceiling, his head lying in the open book on his bed. The dark house is so heavy with frustration and the echoes of angry shouting; it's even seeping under the bedroom door.

Forget this. Jake rolls to the floor, grabs his basketball from the corner, and bounds back down the stairs, leaving the math book open on the bed with the pencil in the binding. He jumps over the last two steps and lands hard on the wood flooring, adding a cynical thump to the hostility in the air.

While many of the other guys enjoyed the popularity more than the game, Jake had truly lived and breathed the sport since he could remember. The soft worn leather of his ball is a caress nearly as sweet as Amy's. Its bounce is always true, always predictable. Jake savors the power of its response as it springs through his legs, behind his back, and around his body down the street to the neighborhood court.

With no one around to hear him, Jake becomes his own commentator under the lights. "Louisville's down two with ten seconds to go...They inbound to Taylor who brings the ball up the court...As always, he's double teamed..."

A mere fifty feet away, a light shines from an upstairs window in the house across the street. Roger Dawson sits at his bedroom desk, typing intently on his MySpace page.

In times past, that lit window would have served as a beacon, calling Jake to its source. How many practice sessions had ended with Jake crashed on Roger's floor, tossing his ball in the air while complaining of the hardships of his young life. Since middle school, however, Roger's room had ceased being a sanctuary as much as an awkward reminder of Roger's accident. These days, the basketball court is all Jake needs to escape, and tonight he never even notices the light beyond.

Jake's reverie continues: "...There's no doubt in anyone's mind. Taylor is taking this shot...5-4-3...Taylor spins along the baseline. He elevates...2-1...Taylor throws up a three from downtown!" The ball swishes through the net. Jake's hands shoot up in celebration with the cheers in his head.

Far beyond Jake's concern, and in a much less celebratory mood, Roger, too, responds to voices only he can hear. He slips into his mother's room and searches through her night-stand drawer. When he finds what he's looking for, the cold metal touching his skin sends shivers through his heart.

As Jake inhales the freshness of the evening breeze and shivers as it chills his sweaty body, Roger exhales as he finishes up his writing and shuts down his computer.

Jake dribbles home right past Roger's house, never noticing the bedroom light, even when it goes out.

Nine hours later, Jake and 2,500 other students converge on Pacific High for another day of the school routine. Jake strolls

down Senior Hall, stopping to joke with some football dudes on the way to his locker.

"Senior Hall" wasn't actually an official title, but for as long as anyone could remember, this was where the cool upperclassmen hung out. Those who weren't could just pass by. Everyone knew that stopping to "hang out" in Senior Hall was by invitation only, and the moment you scored one, your status climbed to new heights. Jake had been invited his sophomore year, as had Amy independently.

Jake and Amy are now the very foundation of this esteemed part of campus. In fact, the table where Jake pauses to relive the highlights of last night's SportsCenter is the current collection center for prom court votes, but he has no concerns. He and Amy are already a lock for this year's king and queen. While he always denied caring, secretly he's loving it.

And so, Jake reenacts Kobe's buzzer-beating fade-away jumper while his buddies interject their commentary, oblivious to Roger's limping entrance to his right. It's not like Jake would have acknowledged him anyway. Roger's leg drags behind him, and his forehead is beaded with perspiration. A few inches more and Jake and Roger's paths would collide, but instead, they pass without interference or recognition.

CRACK! CRACK! CRACK!

People scream, scramble like disturbed ants, and drop to the ground for cover. Light fixtures shatter, spraying the hall with glass. A girl shrieks from behind a bank of lockers, "He's got a gun!"

Jake finds himself face-down on the hallway carpet, partially barricaded by the tipped-over prom table. He peeks around the edge, and his eyes dart from face to face, searching for the source of all the chaos. He shifts his body to scan the rest of the room for the shooter. Or shooters? All around him is a cacophony of terror, but inside Jake's head, the deafening rush of blood drowns it out. This is so surreal, he thinks— something that happens on TV, on the six o'clock news, in other cities, other schools, not right here, right now.

But it is indeed happening, and Jake cannot find the perpetrator. Where are Clyde and the rest of school security?

And then, Jake sees him—in the middle of the hall, pointing

his gun in the air, black hoodie pulled over his head. Even with his back turned, Jake immediately knows it's Roger. The pulse in his ears quickens.

What is Roger thinking?

Jake's stomach lurches, and he forces himself to his feet, inching toward the hunched, black-clad figure of the boy he grew up with and had once called friend. Ten feet away, his shaking legs quit on him. He doesn't fully recognize the cracked voice coming from his own mouth.

"Roger! Dude, what are you doing?"

Roger spins around, bitter hurt in his eyes. "You."

"What are you doing?" Jake tries to hide his fear.

Roger's face twists into a sardonic smile. "What does it matter?"

"We're friends."

"Yeah," Roger repeats with a smirk. "Friends."

"So put the gun down," Jake begs as he inches again toward Roger. "Rog, you don't have to do this."

Roger gazes into Jake's eyes and utters four words that will haunt Jake for months afterward.

The pounding in Jake's head overwhelms him as he watches four security guards, Clyde at the front, crash through the doors behind Roger and rush the shooter. With a trembling arm, Roger raises the gun to his own chin.

"NOOOOOO!" Jake yells, deafened by the final crack.

A sobbing groan escaped Jake's throat as he banged his head against the unyielding grave stone. *What now?*

THE SHARP MORNING SUN blazed into Jake's eyes, and he squinted as he turned into the Pacific High student parking lot. He pulled his truck into his usual spot, turned off the ignition, and took a deep breath, yet the strength to get out evaded him. So he remained crumpled in the driver's seat, gazing at the scene with detached interest, as if he was watching it on television.

Sitting on a hill a mile away from the ocean, Pacific High School was like any other campus, except for the killer view. The only explanation for how the school had scored such a prime piece of real estate was its hundred-year history—a century ago, there wasn't much else going on in town. But despite the daily view of breaking waves and dazzling sand, the hordes of crapping seagulls reminded everyone that living close to the beach wasn't always as fine as an episode of *Baywatch*. Jake had been lucky so far, but he knew other "experienced" students who carried an extra shirt in their backpacks. Today, however, seagulls were the least of the students' problems.

Everyone was returning to campus for the first time since Roger Dawson's shooting spree two weeks before, and Jake was dreading it. He stared at the students clustered around

campus, greeting one another with hugs and exclamations. Most seemed to have enjoyed the unexpected time off and appeared tanned and relaxed. But for Jake, it had been anything but a vacation. He had nearly suffocated from the tension at home, what with his parents' fighting and thoughts of Roger raging in his head. And instead of catching up on sleep, he'd spent each night tossing and turning, replaying scenes from his childhood, from the shooting, from the funeral. The same question kept plaguing him: *Could I have done something?*

But sitting in his truck all day wouldn't help, so Jake finally pushed himself out, taking one last survey of the scene. Even if he could ignore his troubled thoughts, the caution tape surrounding Senior Hall, metal detectors at the front gate, and camera crews and reporters clamoring for student interviews served as a hideous and unavoidable reminder.

Surrounded by all the chatter, Jake wondered how everybody would respond. Would it be OK to laugh at a funny joke? Would all the teachers insist on doing a quick-write or discussion on what had happened? Would it ever be possible to hang out in Senior Hall again? And why did they wait two weeks to reopen the school, anyway? Was that how long it took to fix things, or how long it should take to forget?

Jake didn't think he'd ever heard of a school shooting where the student had only shot himself. If other students had been killed or even injured in the process, there was a clear protocol to follow. And if Roger had just killed himself at home—well, schools had dealt with suicide in the past, too. But had any campus ever had to address it so traumatically and publicly? *Besides, most people don't even know Roger anyway,* Jake thought. So there they all were, stumbling around in an attempt to just move on.

Jake trudged toward the new line of security in front of the school. He passed a reporter wrapping up her story live on the air.

"We're here live at Pacific High School as students arrive for the first time in two weeks after senior Roger Dawson opened fire in the school hallway, then took his own life. Security has been heightened at the school with police presence, metal detector searches, and ID checks. Grief counselors are available to meet with students dealing with post-traumatic stress. We will keep you updated as this story..."

"Hi, Jake!" Some freshman hotties broke into his trance, wiggling their fingers at him and giggling from a few places behind him in line.

"Ladies," Jake acknowledged with a head nod, falling naturally back into old patterns. Another kid waved at him, and Jake smiled back. As he slowly folded into his old routine, the tension he'd been carrying for the past two weeks started to melt away. Each step forward brought him closer back to his life before the tragedy, and it felt good.

Once he got through the metal detectors, Jake headed toward his locker on the other side of campus. A couple of JV basketball guys standing by the chem labs knocked knuckles with him as he walked by, as did some of the water polo dudes by the pool. At the art quad, even the emo-goth crowd acknowledged Jake with a tip of the chin. A strut started to fill Jake's step. He was Jake Taylor, after all—captain of the basketball team, homecoming king—and in only a few short months he would leave all this behind to start his new life at Louisville.

He passed the band room, behind which the usual group of potheads were puffing away at one last joint before the school bell rang. Band wasn't a popular class at Jake's school, so the area was pretty empty, plus the first-floor stairs and the breezy hallway tended to hide the group from the security crew. But today, Jake was kind of glad to see them—just one more sign that today could be business as usual. The gang nodded his way and offered him a puff. Jake had actually joined them once or twice in the past, but since accepting the Louisville scholarship he wasn't taking any chances. So he winked and waved and kept on walking.

Passing by a group of girls, Jake couldn't help but overhear part of their conversation.

"I was so scared," the short one with dark hair gushed. "I mean, did you see him?"

"I know!" her curly headed friend chimed in. "He was like, so evil. I thought I was going to die."

A third one questioned, "Did you even know who he was?"

Jake was out of earshot before that question was answered, but it didn't matter. Instantly all of the frustrations he'd carried since the day of the shooting came flooding back. Jake winced, and he found himself wanting to shout at them, *"He was Roger Dawson. He was a senior, and he was my best friend!"*

But he didn't. He didn't even slow his pace. Instead, his legs moved faster, trying to outrun the voices crowding back into his head. *Maybe these feelings will just go away,* he tried to convince himself. They had to—he couldn't live like this forever. He'd just made it five minutes without thinking about Roger. That was progress. So Jake just kept smiling back at everyone who sought his attention, maintaining the picture of a guy who had it all together.

He stormed the glass doors of Senior Hall, teeth clenched but head held high. He marched through, trying to stay focused, but the fateful hallway whispered to him. He couldn't help wondering what final thoughts went through Roger's mind as he walked through those very same doors. Now the scene replayed itself more vividly in Jake's mind, and his head ached with all the scenarios of how he could have stopped it, how he should have stopped it. Jake's fingers squeezed his temples to stop the throbbing, and his eyes closed. Suddenly he sensed he was about to run into something, and his eyes popped open just in time to avoid the head security guard, Clyde Will, standing two feet away.

"Taylor!" Clyde barked.

Jake was pretty sure he'd heard all 756 rumors about Clyde circulating Pacific High: ex-con from somewhere back east, former UFC fighter, played a stint for the Harlem Globetrotters, retired Navy Seal—the list was endless. Jake (and many others) had asked the buff, six-foot-five, tattoo-covered security guard numerous times to reveal the truth, but it seemed

Clyde enjoyed the mystery. Jake didn't know what to believe. Maybe the big man was simply a security guard who actually cared about the kids he was always prodding to class.

"Hey, Mr. Will." Jake tried to sound casual.

"I saw you at the funeral. Didn't know you were a friend of Roger's."

"From a while back," Jake mumbled, dreading where this was going. He thought about asking Clyde how he knew Roger, but he really didn't want to get into it with so many people walking by. *Maybe another time.*

"You doing OK with this?" Even Clyde's gruff voice couldn't mask his concern.

"Yeah, yeah, it's cool," Jake lied, looking around at the craziness that was typical for Pacific High two minutes before the tardy bell. Students hurried to unload their backpacks into lockers, couples gave goodbye kisses that would help them survive a whole hour apart, and teachers stood by their doors trying to break the couples up. Jake's eyes lingered at the far corner of Senior Hall; already all his buddies were there hanging out like nothing had happened. He shuddered.

"You sign up for a counselor yet?" Clyde motioned to a sign-up table a few feet away.

Jake caught a glimpse of the nearly blank page. "Nah, I'm good."

"You should," Clyde replied, his eyes piercing Jake's soul.

"I'm cool, man." Jake brushed him off. This conversation needed to be over.

"There you are, dawg! You hear they're finally opening up the gym?"

Jake spun around to see Doug strolling up, showing off his hand where a girl he'd just met had scribbled her phone number. His swagger and infectious smile screamed coolness—even the three-week-old goatee he sported looked like it belonged there. And as he rolled obliviously over the very same spot where Roger had stood two weeks ago, a realization flashed before Jake: *Doug is everything Roger was not.*

Jake's friendship with Doug had always revolved around sports. They first met on their sixth-grade soccer team. Doug was the all-star goalie who, thanks to an early growth spurt, was able even as an eleven-year-old to fill the entire goal. In Little League, Doug was catcher to Jake's fiery pitches, and their team almost made it all the way to Williamsport. Pop Warner was another field where they triumphed together. But for both of them, their first love was basketball. They dominated the local basketball leagues all through junior high, and it was always understood that they would someday co-captain the Pacific High Pirates.

In addition to his athletic prowess, Doug's other self-proclaimed expertise was women. He bragged he could get any girl's phone number in less than five minutes. While Jake had been with Amy for three years, Doug had jumped from blonde to brunette to redhead every couple weeks for most of their high school career. Pacific High had a long list of broken hearts, thanks to Doug Moore. Jake had challenged him many times to just try and settle down, but Doug always playfully responded with a smile and a "Come on, now, that wouldn't be fair to the ladies."

Jake enjoyed their friendship, and right now it was a welcome relief. The thoughts whirling around in his head—well, they were definitely not something he wanted to talk to Doug about. Jake stepped away from the counseling table and knocked knuckles with his buddy.

"Wait. You? Signing up to see a shrink?" Doug joked.

"Are you kidding me? No!" Jake wondered if his grin was convincing enough. Out of the corner of his eye, he saw Clyde shaking his head.

"Good. The team doesn't need you wiggin' out on us." Doug slapped Jake on the chest.

Keeping up the grin, Jake reassured him, "This...right here." He pointed to his head. "The wig-free zone."

Clyde placed his strong hand on Doug's shoulder, but his eyes burned through Jake, and his somber voice was clearly intended for Jake's ears. "Nothing wrong with seeing a counselor."

"Chillax, Clyde," Doug coolly mocked the security guard, putting his own arm around him. "No one's going loco."

"OK, amigo." Clyde began to move away with a shrug, but his stare pleaded with Jake one last time.

Doug's hands pointed like six-shooters at his hips. "Palabra." Then his attention was suddenly distracted by a passing sophomore wearing a tight shirt that revealed every detail of her petite frame. Forgetting all about the present company, Doug side-stepped into the path of the unsuspecting girl, causing her to run right into him. "Hola, Stacy!" he crooned.

As Doug exchanged witty repartee with his new target, Clyde called out to Jake and motioned toward the counseling table. "Just think about it, okay?"

Jake barely nodded his head, and the security guard went back to work herding students into class before the late bell rang.

Doug turned back to Jake, one eye still on Stacy as she flounced away. He was scribbling out the old phone number on his hand and inking in the new one underneath.

"What about the other girl?" Jake pointed at the crossed-out number.

"Who?" Doug laughed, kissing his hand with a flourish.

Through the glass doors, they watched as scurrying students trampled over the caution tape as they hurried to class.

"This place is creepy," Jake remarked under his breath.

"That kid was just lucky I wasn't there."

"I was. It wasn't like that."

Doug softly slapped Jake's cheek. "Why are we still talking about this? That freak made us give up three games."

"Dude, shut up." Jake brushed his hand away, annoyed. "It was intense."

Doug stared at Jake. "What's intense is the El Capitan full-court press." He gave a cocky smirk to end the subject.

The late bell rang, and they knocked knuckles one last time before parting to go to their first-period classes. Jake turned toward the English building where Mr. Gil awaited him. Showing up a few minutes late to class was just one of the privileges of being a star athlete.

As Jake turned a corner, a copy of the Pacific High Enterprise lay on a nearby bench. There, on the front page, was a giant picture of Roger. Jake stared at the picture. If he hadn't known better, he would have sworn Roger was staring right back.

4

THE PACIFIC HIGH GYM was full beyond capacity for the final game of the season. Students overflowed onto the floor and along the walls. Normally, the administration would have stopped selling tickets due to fire codes, but even they were making exceptions tonight, allowing whatever it took to help the school move on with life. The Pirates each wore a black wristband in memory of Roger, but even the principal had admitted she didn't know who he was.

School spirit was high, erupting like a long-inactive geyser. Green and black pompoms fluttered everywhere, and air horns blared. The marching band filled the air with a riot of crashing cymbals, burping tubas, and strident trumpets, all of which melded into the sea of bodies and reverberated off the walls. Some juniors started a wave that surged around the gym fourteen times before faltering. At the top of the bleachers, seven chanting senior guys danced shirtless with the letters P-I-R-A-T-E-S painted across their chests. A visitor would have never guessed what had transpired just weeks before.

Unfortunately, while the Pirates had previously been on the cusp of making the section playoffs, three forced forfeits de-

stroyed that dream. Still, this game was against their cross-town rivals, the El Capitan Wildcats. EC had already locked up the No. 1 seed for the section, but Jake and the rest of his senior teammates couldn't think of a better way to end their high school careers than with an upset win.

The intensity of the game was a great escape for Jake. He was in the zone, his private world, where the only thing that mattered was that sympathetic orange ball. His troubles from the past few weeks were left in the locker room; nothing was going to disturb his concentration. Besides, he had something to prove tonight: The last time these teams had met, it was an El Capitan romp which Jake remembered like an old injury. Sitting alone in the locker room after the shellacking, Jake had promised himself that next time the teams played, the outcome would be different, no matter how poorly the rest of his team played. So tonight, in his gym, he only had one thing on his mind: revenge.

Jake waged his private war with ferocity. He was the only player on the court who had already signed to play Division I college ball, and his ability to find the open man and consistency in knocking down fade-away jumpers kept the Pirates in the game, even when the other guys struggled. The Wildcats shot out to an eleven-point lead in the first quarter, but the Pirates crawled their way back by half-time, thanks in part to strong play in the paint by Doug, but even more to Jake's above-average seventeen points and eight assists.

Jake's ability to create success out of nothing had snagged the scouts' attention as early as his sophomore year. Since then, he'd been interviewed by more college coaches than he could remember. At six-foot-one, Jake wasn't as big as most college-level players, but what he lacked in height, he made up for in hustle and hard work. Jake always seemed to see what others missed. He executed what he saw like an artist, making the others look good. He was every coach's dream. Still, there was only one school Jake ever dreamed of playing for. When the full-ride offer came from Louisville (a juggernaut in the world of college basketball), Jake easily made the fated choice.

With three minutes to go in the fourth quarter, the game was close, both teams swapping the lead back and forth. The gym had grown steadily louder with every Pacific basket until now, the noise was deafening. Of course, Jake heard none of it, remaining safe in the steady realm of his head. He sensed his guys were being buoyed by the wave of cheers, so he just kept pushing it. But while Jake was the heart and soul of his team, he still couldn't win the whole thing alone, and time was running out.

With just nine seconds on the clock, the El Capitan power forward stepped to the foul line to shoot his second free-throw, which would give the Wildcats a one-point lead. SWISH.

Since the Pirates had no timeouts left, the ball was immediately inbounded to Jake, who raced up the court. He single-handedly broke the full-court press but couldn't shake his defender. Oblivious to the 1,500 fans on their feet screaming at the top of their lungs, Jake checked out his options, then locked eyes with his opponent.

"Four high! Four high!" he yelled to his teammates.

He head-faked right, crossed-over left, and flew by the sticky El Capitan defender toward the basket. The entire El Capitan defense collapsed on his attack. Then, out of the corner of his eye, Jake spotted his open man.

"6 – 5 – 4..."

Leaping from a foot inside the free-throw line, Jake delivered a behind-the-back pass to a not-quite-ready-but-wide-open Doug underneath the basket. Doug shot the ball hard off the backboard, sending it ricocheting off the front of the rim and into the crowd of defenders.

"3 – 2..."

Reacting faster than a cobra strike, Jake crashed the board right into the middle of the much-taller El Capitan defense. His fingertips brushed the errant ball, tipping it toward the rim. His body was sandwiched by two EC guys, their momentum knocking him hard to the wood floor.

The final horn sounded, and a suspenseful hush fell over the crowd as they waited for the ball's decision. From the ground, Jake breathlessly watched it dance around the rim. Finally, unaware of the significance of its next move, it dropped nonchalantly through the net.

The gym exploded. Random articles of clothing flew into the air. Strangers embraced indiscriminately. The bleachers bled out onto the court, and the tide of bodies swept Jake up. Before he knew it, he was floating above the masses on someone's shoulders.

After handshakes with the opposing squad, hugs from half of the student body, interviews with the local media, and an emotional team meeting where the coach told every guy on the team that he was like a son to him, Jake was finally alone in the Pacific High boys' locker room an hour later. His legs ached from playing all thirty-two minutes, his shoulder throbbed under a bag of ice from his crash landing, and a bump pulsated on the back of his head. And he felt just a little empty. After all, this was it—his days as a high school basketball star were over. With a tinge of sadness, he heaved his body off the bench, hoisted his Louisville duffle bag over the glacier on his shoulder, and slowly made his way down the long row of benches toward the door. His fingers traced the coolness of the lockers, and he took one last wistful look around. Finally, he emerged into the brisk Southern California spring night.

Scattered chattering clusters of basketball fans still remained. Jake discreetly scanned the small crowd of people looking for two specific faces but, as usual, his parents weren't there. He had become so accustomed to their lack of interest that he didn't usually even look anymore; but tonight was different. It was the last game of his high school career. His mom and dad had been on some business trip, but they had promised to be back in time. Nevertheless, Jake had already learned what a promise was worth from them. At some point during his freshman year, he just stopped inviting them to games. It was easier not to care. *Forget them*, he thought. At least Amy would be waiting for him.

As he turned toward the parking lot, something caught his attention about a guy chatting with one of Jake's teammates. Wearing an El Capitan hat and Pacific T-shirt, the guy looked strangely familiar. He held the hand of a cute little boy, who was giving everyone passing by a free high-five. The kid's dark complexion and tight curls didn't resemble the man at all, but they still looked related. Jake puzzled over how he knew him.

He couldn't be a scout—there was no way he'd be talking to Danny Rivers, the worst player on the team. *Maybe the man is Danny's supplier,* Jake chuckled. He wouldn't put it past Danny. Even though Jake really didn't know him that well, everyone knew about his habit. Rather than hanging out with the other jocks, Danny preferred the stealthy company of the stairwell potheads. *To each his own,* Jake figured and kept walking.

Danny didn't seem too interested in the conversation and was just leaving as Jake passed by.

"Good season, Taylor," Danny muttered.

"Yeah, good game, man," Jake replied automatically.

"I didn't play," Danny chuckled.

"Oh, yeah. Well, you know what I mean." Jake slowed his stride to allow Danny to walk by in front of him. Even though they were walking toward the same parking lot, Jake wanted to avoid a longer conversation.

Jake glanced back to the mystery man, who was now whispering in the little boy's ear. Jake racked his brain trying to figure out why the guy looked so familiar.

The man finally made eye contact. "Nice game, Jake!" He strolled over, hands in his pockets. The kid ran ahead to give Jake an enthusiastic high-five.

"Do I know you?" Jake asked, scrutinizing the guy's face.

"Roger's funeral."

"Oh." The memory of that miserable day flooded back. It felt like a toxin. But it was too late to run away, so Jake glanced around to see who was in earshot. "You're that priest."

The man chuckled as if Jake had told a joke. "You're that point guard," he countered. "My friends call me Chris." He extended his hand, adding, "And this is my son Caleb."

"Hey, Caleb." Jake smiled at the boy and shook Chris' hand. Caleb grabbed his dad's leg and shyly waved back.

"What's with the hat?" Jake scowled a little at Chris's EC ball cap.

Chris smiled and took the hat off. "I know guys on both teams." Under his breath he added, "Your last shot cost me $20."

"Seriously?" Not the words Jake expected from the mouth of a priest.

"No, I'm just playin'. It would have been a good gamble, though."

Jake nodded, not exactly sure how to take this guy. *Isn't gambling a sin? Are priests allowed to make jokes about stuff like that?*

"Sorry, man. My wife says I crack too many jokes." Chris pulled out a card from his wallet and offered it to Jake. "Anyway, I just wanted to introduce myself."

"I-I don't know, I'm not really religious." Jake hesitated.

Chris smiled back. "Neither am I."

What is that supposed to mean? Jake wondered and awkwardly laughed, stuffing the card into his pocket. As he floundered for a polite exit, Amy appeared out of nowhere.

"I've been looking everywhere for you," she chided playfully. She was still wearing her cheerleading makeup, but she'd changed into a silky tank-top that mesmerized Jake. He couldn't help but let his eyes roam over her flowing curves, down her tiny denim skirt that left her long, slender legs bare. She was wearing her little black high heels, which Jake loved; they made her almost as tall as him, and he loved it when she draped her arms around his neck and looked him straight in the eyes with that gaze that told him she was so into him.

She enveloped him in her warm arms, tenderly kissing his lips—and completely ignoring Chris and Caleb.

"Did Doug thank you yet for bailing him out?" She pulled back slightly, her soft finger lightly tracing the contours of his face.

Jake suddenly remembered that Chris and his son were still standing a few feet away. Hyper-aware of Amy's arms draped around his neck, Jake turned her body to face them. "Amy, this is Chris."

Chris extended his hand to shake, but Amy kept her arms tightly wrapped around Jake and just smiled. Jake wasn't an expert in non-verbals, but he was pretty sure Amy had just told them that they could leave now.

Chris appeared to get the message, picking up his son and placing him on his shoulders.

"Everybody's waiting for us," Amy added, urging Jake with her eyes to come.

"Well, it was nice meeting you." Jake politely offered his hand to Chris while slowly turning his body and full attention back to Amy.

Chris took his hand and held it firmly. "I know what you're going through," Chris said softly. "If you ever want to talk—"

Jake patted his pocket to signify that he had the number and gave a half-smile. Chris finally wrapped his arms around his son's ankles and walked off.

Amy pulled her body even closer to Jake. "Who was that?" she asked, a little too loudly.

"Just some guy." He looked back one last time at Chris walking away, then turned to Amy and swung her delicate body around until they both got dizzy.

IT WAS NEVER A QUESTION of *if* there was a party Saturday night—it was *where*. Some parties were bigger than others, but two things remained constant: loud music and lots of alcohol. Inevitably, some student would announce to a couple of friends that his parents would be out of town for the weekend, and before you knew it, the place was packed with teenagers. Invitations weren't necessary; everyone just understood who was welcome and who was not.

It was always easy to find the hosts: They were usually the ones running around telling people to keep the music down, begging slobs to clean up after their own mess, and pretty much not enjoying themselves. Hosting one of these parties was a big responsibility, but it also could bring great rewards. For the lucky ones who managed to get through the evening without too much damage, the prestigious reputation was well worth it.

Tonight's party was at some sophomore named Emily's house. Or was she a junior? And was her name even Emily? It didn't matter. Saturday night was Party Night, and this weekend there was a big basketball win to celebrate. This always meant

more people and more booze. Cars were parked everywhere, legally and illegally, filling the cul-de-sac and surrounding streets of the upper-class suburban neighborhood. Hopefully none of the neighbors would need to get out.

Jake and Amy parked at the end of the next street and could hear the music pounding from the party house as soon as they stepped out of Jake's truck. Jake honestly wouldn't have minded going home to his empty house and just watching *SportsCenter* (with Amy, of course). The ache in his legs had seeped through his whole body, and he knew it would only get worse. But as the star of last night's game, his absence from the party would not be tolerated. So Jake inhaled the cool air and stretched his neck, pumping himself up to join in on the action.

He took Amy's hand and started walking, but she resisted, tugging him toward her as she leaned against the tailgate. He turned to face her, a curious grin playing at the corners of his lips. *Maybe this won't be so bad.*

She cocked her head and smiled, toying with the zipper of his jacket. Her fingers dropped to his beltline and lightly rubbed the bare skin underneath his shirt. He shivered and pulled her into a bear hug, loving that she knew just what he needed.

Jake still had to pinch himself every once in a while to make sure Amy wasn't just a dream. She could have her choice of any guy on campus, yet for some reason she chose Jake, and she'd remained faithful to him for three years. Before they became a couple—toward the end of freshman year—Amy unabashedly described herself as a boyfriend-shopper. She had never gone for more than a week or two without falling in love with the next guy in line. But with Jake, she told people she had finally found a guy "worth buying." Jake didn't know he'd been for sale, but he sure didn't mind being bagged. Sometimes guys teased him that he was whipped, but he knew that any of them would jump onto Amy Briggs' leash at the first opportunity. And Jake loved being the guy she really wanted. It was almost as big a boost as basketball.

"You were amazing tonight," Amy admired. "Did you hear me cheering for you?" She squeezed his biceps and added in a whisper, "You were so hot out there." Her breath tickled Jake's ear.

"Yeah, you looked great, too," he responded, choosing the words he knew would make her happy. He bent to kiss her neck, inhaling the sweet scent of her hair, and wrapped his hands around her tiny waist.

Amy playfully pushed him away. "You weren't really looking at me during the game, were you?"

Here was a test that would affect the rest of the evening. "I was! I swear!" Jake lied. Then he thought of a good one: "Why do you think the game was so close? I couldn't focus."

Amy giggled, wrapping her arm around Jake's waist and pushing herself away from the truck. Jake draped his arm around her shoulder and pulled her closer. They walked the empty sidewalk, bumping hips goofily as if they were tied together in a drunken three-legged race. In a second, he'd have to put on his cool face, but for the moment, he would enjoy their silly side.

Amy was sexier than chocolate, but she was also more fun. His favorite times with her were away from the rest of their friends, when they could be a little crazy—like chasing seagulls down the beach at low tide, or seeing who could swing the highest at the park behind her house, or watching the Spanish TV channel on mute and creating their own dialogue (and then wrestling over the remote until neither of them cared anymore what channel they landed on).

Turning the corner into view of their peers, they smoothed their gait and glided toward the thumping house. Discarded cups and empty beer bottles littered the neighbors' driveways and lawns as the party spilled into the cul-de-sac, and Jake and Amy were hailed by a chorus of the semi-cool kids relegated to the outer limits of the action. Teens with half-filled plastic cups of beer greeted Jake with unintelligible words of affirmation as he passed. Garbled shouts celebrated his fierce play, praising his sweet shot, glamorizing his heroic fall, and pumping him full of the recognition he craved. Some of the guys roved Amy's barely clad body with their eyes, boosting Jake's strut even more. His hand gripped her shoulder, silently but firmly reminding them all that Amy was his. His brief conversation with that Chris-guy had left him unsettled; it was good to be back in stride.

At the front door, self-appointed bouncers Matt and Tony welcomed them. "Reporters finally done with you?" Matt joked, knocking knuckles with Jake.

"Those guys at ESPN just won't leave me alone," Jake kidded back, but he continued to push through the crowd. Amy tugged Jake's arm toward the dance floor but he shook his hand free and let her go off on her own while he searched for the keg. He had to loosen up a bit.

Doug elbowed his way through with a couple of beers held high. "The party has arrived!" Doug slurred loudly, apparently well into his party-night routine. Jake grabbed one of the red plastic cups and downed it in a few gulps.

Doug raised his cup and shouted over the fray, "Can I get your attention everyone?" The music stayed loud, but Doug was louder. "Last night, yours-truly bricked a last-second shot that really was a lot harder than it looked." He ignored the chuckles. "Anyways, our main-man Jake here saved my...saved the day." He paused, then swung his cup higher. "To Jake—who always has my back!"

The masses raised their cups in unison and shouted back "To Jake!" They swallowed reverently, then went right back to whatever they were doing.

Doug belched and leaned heavily on Jake's shoulder, pulling an orange flyer out of his back pocket. "Check this out, Taylor." He waved it in front of Jake's face.

Across the top of the flyer, big letters announced "Wizard Wars Party" with the location and date the same as their party. In a scribbly font at the bottom, the caption "Costumes Mandatory" was underlined several times.

Jake was confused. "Wizard Wars?"

Doug's drink sprayed from his mouth as he laughed. "It's some game geeks play. I gave this to a loser at school. He swore he'd come."

Jake shook his head. "You're crazy, man." He crumpled the paper and let it fall to the floor, heading to the kitchen for a refill.

A few more refills later, Jake and Doug still sat perched on the kitchen counter next to the keg. As Doug yapped incoherently, the realization wandered across Jake's mind that he'd lost track of Amy. He scanned the hordes just in case someone else had her on the dance floor.

Noticing Jake's wandering eyes, Doug chimed in, "Lots of beautiful honeys here tonight." One of the ladies meandered by, brushing Jake's knee and giving him the eye over her tanned shoulder. Doug whistled, "Ay senorita!"

Their eyes followed her to the next room, which was packed with writhing bodies. In the middle of it all was Amy. Her skimpy top had somehow adjusted to reveal even more of her toned abs, and her belly-button jewel twinkled among the pulsing arms and legs. Jake jumped off the counter. It was time to reclaim his prize.

"You are one lucky man, Taylor," Doug drawled a little too loudly into Jake's ear.

Jake chugged the rest of his beer and sloppily shoved the side of his friend's head. "Go get your own, dude."

As Jake crossed the room, he missed Doug's mumbled reply: "But she's the one everyone wants."

Jake nudged through the crowd and winked at Amy as he approached. She drew him in like a magnet, and finally they meshed together as one. Unfortunately, Jake's ability to dazzle on the basketball court did not translate into coordination on the dance floor; but Amy's natural rhythm more than made up for it. He slid his hands around her waist and swayed along with her. What the basketball court was to him, the dance floor was to her. It was as if she were in another time and place as she moved her body in perfect rhythm to the music.

"Hold me," she whispered in Jake's ear.

Of course, he didn't refuse, though he felt a little lightheaded. She turned her back toward him and latched her soft arms around his head. He encircled her as the feverish music pulsed. All the troubles of the world were melting away.

Jake had no idea how long he'd been there, but all of a sudden he tuned in to Doug's familiar voice calling once again for everyone's attention.

"Check out this fruitcake!" Doug cackled over the crowd. In the doorway, Doug posed next to a young black-haired stranger dressed in a full wizard costume—starry robe, pointed hat, magic wand, and all. His dark eyes pierced Jake's from under his purple hood. He held a trembling orange paper, as if for proof that he belonged.

"Hey, hey, what level are you?" Doug prodded, eliciting laughs from the rest of the party. "You gonna cast a spell on me?"

The guy just stood there, frozen. His eyes glistened and his lip quivered, but his feet seemed glued in place.

Normally Jake would have been standing right next to Doug sharing in the prank, but not tonight. Tonight, Jake found himself ticked off. He was irritated at Doug. He was fed-up with the room full of drunks who had nothing better to do than laugh at this kid who just wanted to fit in. Even more than that, Jake was angry with himself. As upset as he was, he found himself doing absolutely nothing. *Why can't you just leave him alone?* Jake screamed in his head, but his voice locked up in his throat. He just kept staring at the poor kid. *Why are you still standing there?*

Even though the kid was the center of everyone's attention, Jake could swear the kid's eyes were fixed solely on him. His gaze bore through Jake until he had to flinch and look away. Jake knew those eyes; they were just like Roger's. Their horrible confrontation weeks earlier snapped back into Jake's head as if it had never left, and he winced as it replayed again and again. He narrowed his eyes in anguish and let his head drop.

The group had one more laugh as the boy finally turned away with a stifled sob, and Doug slammed the front door behind him. Jake jerked his head up and stared at the door, briefly considering running after him. He needed to prove he was different from the rest of these idiots, that not everybody was so cruel, that he...

Amy's hands crawled under his shirt as the music pounded unabated by the visitor. All other thoughts vanished at the touch of her fingers running along the elastic of his boxers and her warm breath whispering in his ear. She grabbed his hand and led him through the throng of bodies toward the staircase. She had his full attention, and he quickly surrendered to the opportunity at hand. At the bottom of the steps they passed Doug and Matt, who leered and gave Jake a knowing nod.

Halfway up, the staircase turned, and Jake paused momentarily on the landing, grabbing the railing to balance himself. He scanned the hordes partying mindlessly below. *Is this all there is?* his conscience questioned. But Amy kept tugging, and his troubled brain kept pushing, so he left the overlook and followed his girlfriend's invitation down the hall.

6

"IT'S THE PO-PO!" Matt yelled, startled out of his lethargy by the red and blue lights flashing through the front window. A heavy pounding on the door sent the students rushing the exits, knocking over everything and everyone in their way. Matt took one last gulp from his cup before tossing it aside and joining the chaos headed out the back doors.

Three cops busted through the front door and tried to block the exodus. Five more outside mopped up the students who thought they'd escaped. Students who attempted to drive their way out of trouble were caught by squad cars blocking the road, and many of those escaping on foot were impeded by their own lack of sobriety.

Upstairs, Amy scrambled to put her clothes back on. Jake had passed out as soon as they were done and was only now rising into semi-consciousness. Still naked under the covers, he groaned and put a pillow over his head. It was already throbbing, and the muffled sirens and screams didn't help. Amy ripped the pillow out of his grip and cursed under her breath. Jake's eyes tried to follow her as she scurried around the room picking up their clothes, but it just added to his headache, so he gave up.

"Do you hear the police? Get dressed!" Amy warned, throwing Jake's jeans at his head.

Jake laughed and threw them back at her. "One more time!" he pleaded.

Amy angrily threw the pants back, harder this time. "I'm not kidding! Let's go!"

"You know you want me..." Jake drawled with a sluggish smile.

Amy stomped over, glaring at him. Grabbing his hand, she tried to pull him out of bed, but Jake ripped his hand away, causing her to lose her balance and fall into the dresser.

Jake giggled. "Oops."

"What is your problem?" she snapped.

Jake winked. "You're stressing me out."

She picked up his jeans for one last try, and his keys dropped out onto the floor. "Screw it!" she muttered and bent over to pick them up.

Jake still couldn't understand the urgency and was distracted by the view down her top. "Baby, c'mon," he grinned, reaching out to her.

Amy stormed to the door. "If you want to get caught and lose your scholarship, be my guest." She peeked out into the hall and quietly slipped away.

Jake lay there while he came to his senses. When the reality of his situation hit, he spent a few seconds shouting obscenities into his pillow before sitting up. He was far from sober, and as he looked for his clothes he pictured the cops parading him downstairs totally naked. For a second, he actually considered letting them do it. *That'd give them a show.* He sputtered a laugh at the thought and scooped up his jeans from where Amy had dropped them.

After much exertion, Jake stumbled toward the door, his shirt inside out, shoes untied, and jeans half-tucked into his socks. He peered through a crack in the bedroom door down the staircase. *Ugh!* Standing guard at the front door were two policemen talking with the homeowners, who stood with arms crossed in the entryway. Jake knocked his head against the wall and cursed.

"We told her she could have a few friends over," the mother cried, taking in the junk heap that her home had become.

"Are you sure you caught 'em all?" the dad growled.

One of the policemen glanced up the stairs. "We're doing a full sweep of the house right now—almost done."

Jake cursed to himself again and silently closed the bedroom door. On the other side of the room was a sliding-glass door that opened to a small balcony. Jake stepped out into the dark and gazed over the railing. It was about a ten-foot jump to the cement patio below in the backyard. He crawled over the side and hung on like an awkward octopus, trying to coordinate his landing. Finally, he just jumped, hitting the ground hard and rolling onto his back. He choked back a groan, clutching his ankle.

A light switched on in the bedroom above. Jake forced himself to his feet and limped into the darkness of the backyard. At the side of the house, the wooden gate leading to the front was locked. *Just my luck*, he whined to himself, but movement on the other side caught his attention, and he peeped through a crack in the slats.

Lined up on the curb at the end of the long driveway, under the watchful eyes of a handful of cops, sat dozens of his classmates. He looked for Amy or Doug or Matt, but they were nowhere in sight. He groped through the pitch-black along the fence until he felt a cinder-block wall. With much pain and little grace, Jake lugged his 195 pounds of stiff, drunk muscle over the wall head-first, falling with an aching thud on the other side. *It could be worse,* he chided himself, sneaking through the neighbor's yard and staggering away.

He re-emerged onto the sidewalk four houses down and one street over from the party. He slowly crept back along the path he and Amy had playfully walked together just hours earlier. But when he got to the spot where he'd parked his truck, all he found was empty pavement. Even with all the alcohol in his system, Jake knew he was in the right spot.

"Amy!" he groaned and dropped to the curb. A police car drove by, and he ducked down into a shadow.

What happened to tonight? Just the night before, he had been carried off the basketball court as a game-winning hero, and now here he was, wasted, sitting on some curb, dodging the police, and stranded with no ride home.

Jake pulled out his cell phone. Amy was the last person he wanted to talk to, but who else could he call?

He tried Doug. He heard the ring, and then, "Hola! Doug here..."

"Doug, where are you? I'm still at the party..."

"Gotcha!" the voice mail interrupted.

Jake punched the End button and almost chucked his phone across the street—that stupid recording had fooled him at least a dozen times before.

Jake whipped through a list of names.

"Matthew, where the hell are you? Come pick me up!...Ha! Your grandma calls you Matthew..."

"Tony! Where are you, man? Don't leave me hanging."

Jake stood up and started pacing.

"Hector-hector-bo-bector. Banana-fana-fo-fector..."

"Bobby-boy! Hey! This is Jake. Sober up and pick me up."

"Deon-tae. Dude, where's your car? Ha! Call me...or text me...or help me..."

His voice sunk in misery.

"Jimbo!"

"Damian..."

"Joe?"

Each call ended the same—straight to voice mail.

"Aarrrrggghhh!" he finally exploded. Either all his friends' cells had been confiscated on their way to lock-up, or they were all sleeping soundly in the comfort of their own beds. At this point, he hoped for the first one.

Jake banged his phone against his head and slumped down again on the cold cement curb. He debated attempting the long walk home, but his ankle was starting to swell from the jump. *Why did I drink so much?* Shaking his head in disgust, Jake stared down at the ground between his knees. There in the gutter lay the business card from that priest guy, Chris. It must have fallen out of his pocket with his cell phone.

Jake picked up the card and tried to get his eyes to focus on the print: *Chris Vaughn, New Song Community Church, Youth Pastor.* A cell number was listed underneath the title. Jake was about to flick it away, but something stopped him. His fingers rubbed the letters back and forth, and he read the name over and over. Finally, he opened his cell one more time.

"What the hell," he mumbled.

CHRIS AND CARI snuggled on their ugly maroon garage-sale couch. Wedged between them was Caleb, fast asleep in his Spiderman pajamas, Alfredo the monkey tucked under his arm. Cari's eyes were moist as she sat engrossed in *The Sound of Music* while Chris ran his fingers through his wife's tangled curls and watched his son's chest rise and fall with every precious breath. He'd assumed one of the perks of having a son would be renting more action/adventure movies, but so far, this had not been the case. Tonight's classic was the flip-side of a tough deal—Cari had approved of the boys going to the basketball game if, and only if, she got to pick the movie. Their premarital counselor had never warned him of the perils of a deal like that.

Still, if he was truly honest, he was enjoying the movie, and as the Von Trapp children reunited with the smiling Julie Andrews, something wet rolled down his cheek.

"Urgh! I hate chick flicks," he muttered, wiping at his eyes.

"Your secret's safe with me..." Cari whispered, adding with an elbow jab, "...girlie boy."

Chris waved his hand in front of his face and blinked rapidly. "No, seriously, I think some kind of bug flew in my eye."

She nodded knowingly and nestled her head in the crook of his neck.

They both jumped when Chris' cell phone rang, and Cari paused the DVD so Chris wouldn't miss anything.

"Who's calling at 11:30?" she complained, gently scratching her husband's back with her fingernails.

"Hello?" After a moment, a long sigh escaped Chris' throat. "I'll be right there," he conceded and hung up.

Cari sat up as Chris stuffed the phone into his pocket and threw his EC hat back on. "Where are you going?" she asked.

"Another drunk kid," he sighed again. "Guess I shouldn't have gotten the car detailed." Although the call was unexpected, these kinds of late-night outings weren't really foreign territory.

Chris grabbed his jacket and headed for the door. As he reached for the knob, he sensed he was being watched. He turned around to see Caleb standing in his bare feet clutching his little jacket from the coat closet just like his daddy.

"Where are you going, Daddy?" he asked, half-asleep and rubbing his eyes.

Chris hoisted his son in the air and carried him down the hall to his room. "Daddy's got to go help a friend."

"Can I come?" Caleb's arms draped around his dad's neck.

"I'll tell you what, big man. You go to sleep now, and we'll go to Costco for lunch tomorrow."

Caleb's eyes lit up. "Samples!"

Chris nodded and smiled. If his son were always so easily pleased, this parenting thing would be a piece of cake. He carried the boy over to his race-car bed and gently slipped him underneath the comforter, brushing untamed curls off his forehead and kissing him.

"G'night, Daddy," Caleb murmured, folding his hands across his chest and shutting his eyes tight the moment his head hit the pillow.

Chris paused in the doorway, thanking God for Caleb as he always did when the boy was safe in bed. Then he trekked back into the living room, where his wife was folding their blankets and carrying the popcorn bowl back into the kitchen. He intercepted her, spun her into a pirouette, and dipped her dramatically, leaning over to kiss her goodbye and grab one last handful of popcorn.

Sill hanging in mid-air, Cari looked deep into his eyes. "Honey, I'm proud of you."

He kissed her again. "Life of a youth pastor," he shrugged. But he knew he didn't have to explain it to her. He pulled her up and sent her into another twirl, then winked. "What a ride!"

Eight years earlier, Chris had used the same line when he dropped to one knee in the middle of Knott's Berry Farm. They were still woozy from the jolting wooden roller coaster, Ghost Rider. He'd told her that, while he could not promise that they'd ever be rich or famous—or that he would even always have a full head of hair—if she'd only say "yes," he would promise that at the end of every day they'd be able to look at each other and say, "What a ride!" He had definitely delivered on that one, and those three words had become their mantra, evoking happy memories of their wonderfully crazy life together.

Cari swatted Chris' backside on his way out. But before Chris could make it out the door, Caleb reappeared, Alfredo the monkey in tow.

"Caleb, I told you we'd hang out in the morning." Chris adopted the sternest air he could, squatting down to look his son in the eye.

"Good moe-ning!" Caleb smiled mischievously.

Chris did everything he could to stifle a chuckle as he silently pointed back to Caleb's bedroom. Caleb hung his head and moped back down the hall, dragging Alfredo behind him.

JAKE FELT LIKE he'd been sitting on that cold curb for hours, but it had really been only seventeen minutes when a greenish Toyota Corolla pulled up alongside him. In the flickering streetlight, Jake jumped to his feet, but the effects of too much alcohol and standing up too abruptly caused him to lose his balance, and he nearly fell a few feet short of the door. Too drunk to get embarrassed, Jake regained his equilibrium and stumbled into shotgun, greeted by a surprising whiff of orange and pine.

"Thanks," Jake said in a voice that sounded a little too much like Bullwinkle.

"A few too many?" Chris probed.

Jake laughed too loud, and a belch slipped out.

"Whew!" Chris waved his hand in front of his face. "What's up with Louisville?" he asked, pointing to Jake's red shirt.

"Basketball for the Cardinals, I'm playing—tweet tweet." Jake giggled, then he groaned because it hurt his head.

Silence filled the car like cotton balls, and the street lights

whooshed by in a blur. Jake pressed his forehead to the cool window and closed his eyes. Passing on the obligatory small talk was okay with him.

Then Chris shattered the quiet. "I'm curious...why did you call me?"

With great effort, Jake lifted his head—it now felt like a bowling ball on his neck—and turned to Chris. "Friends ditched me; parents would freak out." He pronounced the words carefully, waving his hands like an orator.

Chris nodded. "What about your girlfriend—Amy, wasn't it?"

As if on cue, Jake's phone rang, and Amy's face appeared on the caller ID.

"Speak of the devil," he snickered, rejecting the call. Turning back to Chris, he shrugged. "She took my truck. Take a right at the light."

Chris turned the corner into Jake's neighborhood and let out a chuckling sigh. "Not your best night, huh?"

"I'll drink to that!" Then, remembering that he was talking to a minister, he stuttered, "I mean, yeah."

Chris started to pull the car over to the curb. Jake was confused. "This ain't my house."

"I know."

Jake squinted out the window through his headache at what was once Roger's mailbox. His heart began to pound, and he started gasping for air, but couldn't seem to get enough. He stared at the dark house beside him, the particularly bleak and judging second-floor window staring back.

Chris turned the car's engine off. "Tell me about you and Roger."

Jake was caught off-guard, and his reflexes pushed back. "What do you care?"

Chris absorbed Jake's pointed response with a ragged exhale. "I just can't get him out of my mind." His fingers danced nervously on the steering wheel, and his eyes stared blindly into the swallowing darkness. "Roger came to my youth group once. The Sunday before—" His voice echoed in the car. "It must have been a last-ditch effort. And yeah, I talked to him—I shook his hand and moved on to the next kid." He beat his palm on the steering wheel. "There he was, going through hell and hoping that church or God might be the answer—" His voice broke, and he could only muster a whisper. "It didn't work. We...I...missed him. We let him down."

Already softened by the beer, Jake found himself disarmed and his burdened heart released by Chris' confession. "There was a kid at the party tonight," he blurted out. "They didn't let him in because he wasn't—he wasn't cool enough." He paused as the dam in his heart cracked even more. "Can you believe how messed up that is? He wasn't cool enough?"

The weight Jake had been carrying for weeks melted and flowed from his soul. He couldn't stop now, and he didn't try. "The other guys didn't want Roger around, so I ditched him. They'd mess with him, and I didn't say anything. It was every day. I'd see him walking to school or in the halls—I didn't even say hi. I was...too cool." Jake's voice finally collapsed, his eyes fixated on Roger's lonely bedroom window.

They sat together in silence for several seconds. Then Chris quietly added, "I know what you mean. We have to own how we treated him."

Jake turned to face Chris. "I was his only friend. And I—" He interrupted himself, half-hoping Chris would absolve him of his sins, or at least give him some spiritual words of advice to make him feel better.

Chris did neither. "So we're both living with regrets." He shrugged, turning the ignition. The car pulled forward. The street snaked around before them, and they drove deeper into the neighborhood as the homes became increasingly lavish. "Which one is yours?"

"Around the corner. 1535. On the left," Jake answered weakly, exhausted all of a sudden. But he couldn't help asking one more question. "What did you mean when you said you weren't religious?"

Chris smiled as he pulled up to Jake's house, the biggest one on the street. "I'm not religious because that's not what it's about."

"But aren't you like...a priest?" Jake persisted.

Chris chuckled. "Come by tomorrow morning and see for yourself."

"I don't know, man," Jake retreated, speaking under his breath. There was no way he was going to church tomorrow.

"Not really your thing?"

Jake just shrugged.

Chris raised one eyebrow. "Well, neither is leaving my family on a Saturday night to pick up a drunk kid."

"Touché," Jake smiled. He deserved that.

"The service times and map are on the back of my card." Chris shook hands for their second goodbye of the evening, and Jake stumbled out of the car.

"Thanks again, man," Jake said, waving a little.

"Anytime. See ya tomorrow," Chris winked, and the car grunted down the street into the darkness.

Jake couldn't help shaking his head at the guy's persistence. He limped quietly up his driveway, staggered into his room, flopped onto his bed still dressed, and was nearly asleep when his cell phone rang. He groaned and fumbled in his pocket to turn off the annoying song Amy had selected for her incoming calls. He would need to download a new one in the morning.

Four times later, Jake acknowledged she wasn't giving up, but he was—at least for the night. He pelted the phone against the wall with enough force to stop the stupid song from ringing in his tired ears. Within seconds, he was sound asleep.

UNLIKE THE AVERAGE TEENAGE GUY, Jake was incapable of sleeping in. His buddies would brag about waking up at one or two or even five in the afternoon after a late-night party, but Jake could never stay in bed past nine. This especially stunk after big parties because, while others could sleep their hangovers away, Jake got to experience the last few hours of his fully awake. *Why did I drink so much?* he always asked himself as he stumbled to the bathroom with a migraine crushing his skull. The only remedy that ever worked was a lot of aspirin and a resolution to continue with his normal routine, despite his misery.

This routine always included grabbing the local newspaper from the driveway and reading every detail from the sports page. Jake was pretty sure he'd never even glanced at the other sections unless there was a natural disaster or something.

Jake peeled the sports section out of the paper, tossed the rest of it on the kitchen table, and poured his normal bowl of Honey Nut Cheerios. Of course, the story that first caught his attention was the full-page spread on the cover that featured him getting clobbered by two El Capitan players as the ball crawled over the rim for the winning shot. The title underneath captured the moment like a Polaroid: "Taking One for the Team."

Jake's mind sped through the eternity that had occurred since Friday night, and he shook his head. He scooped a spoonful of cereal and glanced at the contents of his pockets, now littered on the counter from the night before. He lamented his missing keys in the pile of his wallet, gum wrappers, lint, and a business card.

Jake picked up the card and spun it around his fingers, trying to decide whether to take it seriously. The conversation from last night echoed through his throbbing head, and he couldn't shake the feeling that maybe this Chris guy could help him get rid of those annoying Roger-thoughts that wouldn't stop. *It can't hurt,* he finally conceded, and flipped the card over to see the map on the back. Underneath it, Chris had handwritten:

The microwave clock read 10:27. Jake sighed indecisively and stabbed his spoon into the cereal bowl.

Just then, the front door opened and his parents trampled in. As usual, they were arguing. Jake stuffed the card into his back pocket and stared into his breakfast.

His mom walked into the kitchen looking weary from their red-eye. Still, she was beautiful. Jake got most of his good looks from his mother; at age forty-five, she still made heads turn, although Jake was pretty sure his dad had stopped noticing.

"Good morning, sunshine," Pam Taylor greeted him on her way toward the coffee pot.

Jake glanced up. "How was your trip?"

"Sorry we missed your game," she replied. "I tried to get us back in time, but Dad had so much work that he missed his flight. He landed the big beach condo account."

"I see you were the last-second hero again." Jake's father entered the kitchen at his normal volume: loud. He slapped his own copy of the newspaper next to Jake's.

His dad had aged well, too, and his good looks paired with his natural charisma had led him down a very successful path. With over fifty people working for him in three Southern California offices, Glen Taylor was already a millionaire several times over. The high-rolling lifestyle suited him well. The combined price of the Rolex on his wrist and the briefcase at his side probably could have clothed a small village, and then there were the countless suits, dress shirts, and ties hanging in his closet. He was a member of the local country club, cigar club, and flying club, and had recently talked about buying a boat and joining the yacht club. He got invited to prestigious parties and events, had friends in high places, and pretty much could have anything he wanted. He was a self-made man living the American Dream, and it seemed to Jake that he was riding it for all it was worth.

The only problem was he worked all the time, and he never really seemed to enjoy his accomplishments. Jake and his mom certainly did, but they had repeatedly assured him they would settle for a much simpler lifestyle if it meant he'd be home more often. Jake had given up on that dream years ago, but judging from so many of his parents' arguments, it appeared that his mom had not.

While many parts of his dad frustrated Jake to no end, he always found himself striving to impress him. Or at least that's what the shrink had said that one time they went for "family counseling" back in junior high. Sometimes Jake felt like a fly going back for more honey, even though he kept getting stuck in it.

"Oh, Dad, it was perfect." Jake stood up and reenacted his game-winning shot. "When that ball came off the rim, it was crazy! I just knew where it was going. And just as I was tipping

the ball, these guys totally hacked me, and I hit the ground hard, and then—"

His dad slapped him on the back. "You've got a lot going for you, Jake. Don't be stupid with this kamikaze ball."

Jake froze. *Would it have been so hard to say "nice shot"?*

"Do you know how easy it would be for you to lose your scholarship? Not like you'd get in with your grades. You've gotta be careful, son."

Jake sighed. This was his old man's favorite subject, and Jake sensed he was in for another sermon. But then, just as abruptly as he had walked in, his dad looked at his watch, slapped Jake lightly on the cheek, and headed toward the front door.

"I'm late. I'll call."

Pam barely managed to hand him a freshly toasted bagel and a clean tie. She was always trying to keep the peace. But Jake knew the truth: When his parents thought they were alone, they were anything but peaceful.

"You're working on a Sunday? You just got home!" Jake yelled after him, partly for his dad to hear, but mostly just to yell.

Dad called back, always with the last word, "Someone's gotta pay the bills, kid."

Jake turned back to his mushy bowl of Cheerios, milk splashing on the table as he whisked it angrily with his spoon.

"What your father means is we're proud of you."

Jake looked up at his mom, who was wearing her smile like a fake ID. "Yeah," Jake grumbled. "I really felt that when he came to that *one* game!"

"It's been real busy at the office, Jake."

"Mom, quit defending him."

"He just—"

"He just doesn't get it. This isn't his life. It's mine."

It was obvious his mom wanted to say something, but she didn't. As usual, she took no one's side; she just picked up his unfinished bowl of cereal and took it to the dishwasher. Pam was a neat freak in the worst way. She seemed physically unable to leave something out of place, and her favorite companions were a bottle of Windex and a roll of paper towels. The shrink had called it a "coping mechanism."

Oh well. Jake wasn't in the mood for soggy Cheerios anyway. He grabbed his wallet and stomped to the door.

"Where are you going?" his mom called after him irritably.

"I'm going to church!"

Slamming the front door made Jake feel better for a second, but the empty driveway stirred him up again. He'd forgotten that Amy still had his truck. His hangover rushed back with a vengeance, and he glared at the sky, the street, the whole world.

Maybe the walk would do him good.

10

JAKE HAD DRIVEN BY the old warehouse a million times but had never given it a second glance until this morning. Now he was standing in the parking lot, staring at the large red sign that said "New Song Community Church." This looked nothing like the old church he used to visit with his grandma on Christmas Eve. *Aren't churches supposed to have a steeple and stained glass?* Jake looked down at the T-shirt, jeans, and flip-flops he'd thrown on in his hung-over stupor. Was he supposed to be wearing a suit or something?

He started to have second thoughts about walking in, but before he knew what was happening, an old bald guy strangely resembling a bowling pin grabbed his hand and began pumping his arm like the lever on a slot machine. If the guy wasn't careful, remnants from last night's carousing and this morning's cereal might be the jackpot.

"Hey! I'm Marv. Welcome to New Song! I'm so glad you made it. Come on in!" the guy gushed. Had he been waiting for Jake? Who was he? He could have been a greeter at Wal-Mart if he exchanged his outrageous Hawaiian print shirt for a blue vest.

And then the bowling pin hugged Jake! Jake tried not to cringe. He wasn't sure he knew exactly what a cult was, but this sure felt like one. Unable to escape, Jake let the happy guy lead him toward the entrance of the church. They walked together through the front doors and across the nearly vacant lobby. Another smiling man, this one with a shock of red hair, gave him a brochure, a pen, and a smile that beamed with weirdness.

Jake peeked in another door that led to a big auditorium. A man whose voice reminded him of his dad's deep baritone stood talking on stage in front of rows of chairs filled with listeners—some young, some old, some dressed-up, some not. He started to step inside, when a hand grabbed his elbow and spun him around.

"Jake Taylor? What are you doing here?" It was pothead Danny Rivers. He sounded almost accusing. Jake wasn't sure which one of them looked more surprised.

"What do you mean?"

Danny leaned in with a smirk. "Well, it's not like you're, you know, the church type."

"Uhhh, I'm just looking for Chris," Jake whispered back. It wasn't like Danny was exactly the church type, either.

"Vaughn? He's back here."

Danny led Jake back through the lobby, where a stoop-shouldered gray-haired woman tottered up to them. She grabbed both of Danny's hands like he was her long-lost grandson.

"Tell your father I just love his preaching. I can see it in your eyes—you are going to be just like him." The woman gave Danny a wobbly pat on the cheek and shuffled back into the service.

"Your dad's the priest?" Jake marveled.

"Yeah, something like that." Danny frowned.

"How did I not know this?"

Danny shrugged as they turned the corner back to the youth area. "It's not like it's something I'm proud of."

They passed a donut and coffee table, where Danny grabbed two old-fashioned glazed and ignored the jar requesting a fifty-cent donation. They walked toward a hallway where a peppy Filipina was grabbing a handful of pens from a welcome table littered with leftover nametag stickers and markers.

"Jake, right?" she asked as she quickly set the pens down to scribble him a tag. She was cute, but definitely a little weird: Her rainbow-striped tank-top was paired with a camouflage skirt and army boots, and her multi-colored bangle bracelets reached all the way up to her skinny elbow.

"Yeah," Jake responded, realizing that he was still wearing sunglasses. He took them off and casually placed them in his back pocket, hoping his eyes wouldn't give away his late night. The bright fluorescent lights pierced his lingering headache, and he tried to conceal a grimace. Apparently his long walk in the fresh air hadn't done as much good as he'd hoped.

The girl stuck out her hand. "I'm Andrea; welcome to Souled Out. Here's a nametag." She smiled warmly.

Jake took the sticker adorned with his quickly scrawled name and embellished with a smiley face. He let his fingers play with its stickiness. He hadn't needed one of these things in a long time. And he wasn't sure he wanted everyone to know his name today.

"Didn't know it was Rainbow Bright day," Danny scorned as he turned to walk into the youth room.

Quicker than a hummingbird, Andrea grabbed Danny's hand and gave him the biggest, sweetest puppy-dog eyes. "Ohhhh, you didn't get my call? Don't worry, you can borrow this." She slid one of her three dozen colorful bracelets onto his wrist and gave him a wink.

Danny ripped his hand away and kept walking.

"Thanks." Jake waved his nametag to signal he was good to go.

"I'm so glad you're here." Andrea smiled genuinely. Her whole face lit up with an inviting warmth. Jake was used to being greeted wherever he went, but not with this same geniality. He could feel his tentativeness slowly eroding.

"That girl freaks me out," Danny muttered, his mouth stuffed with one last bite of donut. He threw his new bracelet into a garbage can next to the door and directed Jake to an old couch in the back of the room. The room was bigger than it looked from the doorway, extending forward to a wide stage where Chris stood talking, a wireless mic strapped to his cheek. In front of him sat rows and rows of high school kids, some in chairs, some on the floor, and some sprawled on ugly, stained couches that lined the back wall.

"Where's your nametag?" Jake whispered to Danny.

"Everybody knows me here," he growled back.

On Danny's approach, students sitting on the furthest couch took their cue and scooted apart to make room; one slid off to sit on the floor. Jake sat down next to Danny and slipped his nametag into his back pocket. A few girls in the back row smiled over their shoulders and silently mouthed, "Hi Jake," then turned around giggling. A guy sitting next to one of them put his arm snugly around her and pulled her closer with a grunt.

Up in front of the room, Chris seemed to be incredibly passionate about whatever he was talking about. He was definitely dressed up nicer than the night before, but his jeans and polo shirt were a far cry from the suit and weird collar-thing Jake had seen priests wear in the movies. Jake leaned back into the worn couch and did his best to listen in on the end of Chris' message.

"So in closing, let me ask you guys, what would you do for $20? Would you French kiss a dog?" Groans echoed from around the room. "How about this—would you take your mom to the prom?"

Some kid in the front turned to his neighbor, speaking loud enough for everyone to hear. "I'd take your mom—she's hot." The room burst out laughing as the student raised his hands feigning innocence.

Chris walked over to the guy and knocked knuckles with him. "Thanks, Billy," he winked, then whispered loudly, "but she's way out of your league." He turned back to the whole group. "We would do a lot of crazy stuff for $20. But what would you do for a penny? Kiss your dog? Take your mom to the prom?"

The whole group looked to Billy, who said nothing.

"What's crazy is that we treat people the same way. Some are worth our time and some we just pass right by—like they're worthless."

At this, Jake leaned forward, surprised at his own interest.

"See, in this story we just talked about, this guy gets jumped, and two people walk right past and won't help him out. How many times do we do that? We just give a head nod and keep walking. Why don't we help? Why don't *I* help? Sometimes I just don't know what to say, or I don't want to get involved." Chris sat down on a stool that was next to him and looked silently at the group. Jake could have sworn Chris was looking straight at him.

"I recently conducted Roger Dawson's funeral." Chris pulled a framed copy of Roger's senior portrait off his music-stand podium. Without saying a word, he stood up, walked across the room, and hung the picture on a nail next to the door. In a much softer voice, he continued from the back of the room. "You may not have known that he came to our group the Sunday before he..." Chris pinched his eyes for a moment to regain his composure.

Those thoughts Jake had been trying to stuff down all week swelled as if on cue, and he shifted in his seat, hoping nobody noticed.

"It's easy to cast blame. But last week, Roger looked at his life and said, 'I'm not worth it.' Whatever he had hoped to find here, he obviously didn't." Chris' voice had faded to almost inaudible, but suddenly he erupted. "Do we get this?! The consequences are huge if we miss it."

Jake's head jerked back, filled with images of that terrible day in Senior Hall.

Roger stands in front of him. The gun in Roger's hand trembles, yet it dares anyone to challenge him.

"You don't have to do this, man."

Roger looks Jake straight in the eyes and mouths those four words...those four awful words. He raises the gun to his chin.

CRACK!

Drums shattered the memory, and Jake's eyes sprang open. Perspiration beaded along his forehead, and the hair on the back of his neck stood stiff. Chris had finished, and magically a student band had appeared on stage. Everyone around Jake stood up and began clapping with the music. He noticed Andrea, the techni-colored nametag girl, was on stage singing passionately into a mic next to another girl Jake recognized from the pot crew. He thought her name was Kelsi, and he was pretty sure he had seen her wasted at the party last night. Yet here she was this morning, hands up in the air and eyes closed, singing fervently for all to see. Jake awkwardly attempted to clap like everyone else but felt like a seal at the circus. After enduring a couple minutes, he made a beeline for the door.

He had made it halfway through the lobby, dodging the smiling bowling pin guy and the redhead arranging the coffee table, when he heard a familiar voice call his name. Jake reluctantly turned to face Chris, who was hustling around the corner to catch him.

"You made it!" Chris smiled breathlessly.

With nothing else to do, Jake shook Chris' extended hand.

"You okay after last night?" Chris asked.

While Jake appreciated the help from the night before, he begrudged the fact that Chris now had the upper hand. "Sorry I was late," he stammered.

"Hey, I'm just stoked you're here!"

Stoked? Jake hadn't heard that word since at least middle school. "Um, I liked your speech," he said.

"Thanks, I appreciate that."

From behind Chris, Danny's dad walked up and interrupted their awkward conversation.

"Chris, I need to talk to you for a sec." He sounded urgent.

"Yeah, yeah, but first you need to meet Jake. It's his first time here. Jake, this is Mark Rivers, our senior pastor."

Looking annoyed, Mark gave Jake a half-smile and a weak handshake. Jake took a stab at breaking the ice. "Yeah, I know your son, Danny. I'm on the basketball team with him."

"That's nice. Chris, a word?" Mark pulled him away, leaving Jake standing there alone.

Jake shifted his weight. Could he just leave? That didn't seem quite right. He watched the dialogue between the two men from across the lobby. The way Chris stood and listened reminded Jake of himself when his dad was on a roll lecturing him. *What could Chris have done wrong?* Before he could observe too much, Chris was back, smiling but obviously a little rattled.

"Sorry about that...Girlfriend still got your truck?"

Jake nodded with a wry grin.

"I'll tell you what. Give me ten minutes and I'll give you a ride." Chris patted him on the shoulder, then quickly retreated in time to meet the mass of students exiting the youth room.

"It's high-five Sunday, guys! Slap me some skin! Joey! Sierra! Mike! Ronnie! Max! Ryana! How's it hangin' Larry-boy?"

Jake just stood and watched all this. This place was weird, but something about it was oddly appealing.

The ten minutes was really more like twenty, but eventually the crowds dissipated, and Chris was finally ready to go. Out of nowhere, Chris' curly headed son bounded up and attacked his dad.

"Roarrrrr! I'm a polar bear!" Caleb announced as Chris swung him up and around in a circle.

"I thought you were a grizzly bear," Chris reminded him.

"I am a grizzly bear!"

"Well, Mr. Bear, do you remember Jake?"

"Roarrrr!"

"How old are you, Caleb?" Jake asked the only question he could think of.

"Three!" Caleb shouted, holding up four wobbly fingers.

Chris folded Caleb's pinky finger down. "The boy's good at sports, not so much at math."

Jake smiled.

"Is he coming to lunch?" Caleb pointed at Jake.

"What do you say, man? A quick detour on the way home? It's on me."

Jake had nothing else planned for this afternoon, but this was a little strange. *Oh well, why not? It's free food.* "Uh, okay."

Caleb started squirming in his father's arms and reaching away from him. Jake followed his gaze and saw a pretty African-American woman walking up.

That explains the kid's looks, Jake thought.

Cari grabbed Jake's hand in a firm shake. "You must be Jake. Chris told me you might be here. Did I overhear you were joining us for lunch?"

"I think so."

"Well, I apologize in advance," she grinned.

What does that mean? Jake puzzled as they walked out to the car together.

11

CALEB STOOD UPRIGHT in the shopping cart, clinging to the sides for balance as Chris pushed him down the aisles of Costco. Cari shook her head watching her boys play another round of their favorite supermarket game. The rules were simple: Shake, turn, and twist the cart in any way needed to get Caleb to fall. So far, there had been no serious injuries, so Chris happily continued the rodeo with no interruptions from Mom. Cari and Jake flanked either side of the cart, each with a hot dog in one hand and a soda in the other.

Chris sprinted ahead, zigzagging through the oncoming traffic, jerking the cart back and forth until Caleb nearly spilled out onto the cement floor. Cari gasped, but Caleb stood firm and squealed with laughter. A middle-aged woman with a cartful of groceries gave Chris a nasty look as she passed, but Caleb kept pleading for more. So without warning, Chris spun the cart around 180 degrees and joined back up with Cari and Jake. Caleb remained upright and grinned in satisfaction.

"I'm tellin' you, this is the best deal in town!" Chris exclaimed for the seventh time. "And we haven't even gotten to the best part yet!" He nudged Jake with his elbow.

Jake marveled at his situation. His family would never have even considered eating lunch in a warehouse store. On the rare occasions the Taylor family did go out to eat together, it was always at the country club or a fancy restaurant that required Jake to dress up. They certainly never had *fun* on these outings—there were only the forced conversations about the weather or work or school, and then inevitably his dad would see someone he knew and go talk with them while Jake and his mom watched their food get cold. If Jake was really lucky, he might get to enjoy another of his father's famous lectures on the importance of hard work. But now, Jake was honestly kind of enjoying himself, in a very unusual, slightly out-of-his-comfort-zone kind of way. As he tried to walk and talk holding the cheap hot dog drenched with ketchup and onions, he couldn't help wondering how things would be different if his family exchanged their expensive dinners for ones like this.

Caleb's gleeful squeal interrupted Jake's thoughts. "Daddy! Faster!" Caleb pointed forward, gripping the sides of the cart even tighter.

Chris jolted forward, finally throwing Caleb backward in the cart. "That's one point for Daddy!" Chris bragged to his three-year-old.

"Chris!" Cari scolded.

Chris cocked his head with innocence. "That was fun, huh?" He reached in the cart and gently pulled Caleb upright.

"Do it again!" Caleb shrieked, laughing.

"Do what?" Chris feigned ignorance.

Just as Caleb started to answer, Chris lunged the cart forward again. Caleb lost his balance and fell on his belly.

"Two points!" Chris cried again.

Cari looked at Jake and shook her head. "Men," she sighed.

From his sprawled position in the cart, Caleb looked up and exclaimed. "Samples!" He scrambled to his hands and knees.

"Now this is what I'm talkin' about!" Chris grinned to Jake over his shoulder.

The Vaughn men made a beeline to a table, where a sixty-year-old server with a name tag that read "Beatrice" was slicing up French bread pizzas.

"I told you this was going to be a great day," Chris rejoiced as Jake and Cari caught up.

Back on his feet again, Caleb spun around in the cart and gave his dad a high-five. "I'm a race car driver!" Caleb announced to the grandmotherly pizza-lady. Caleb was just too cute to resist, so she gave them each an extra slice. Caleb attacked her with a surprise hug, and she beamed. Chris grabbed yet another slice.

Jake watched the whole thing from a few feet back, head lowered a bit and fists stuffed into his pockets. He couldn't decide if he felt uncomfortable or jealous.

"They're shameless!" Cari smiled, grabbing Jake's elbow and tugging him closer. She gave him a wink. "So this is the time where I go looking for laundry detergent. Can you try not to let my boys make fools of themselves too much?"

"You're leaving me alone with them?" Jake only half-joked.

"I'm leaving you *in charge*." With that, she turned the corner down the next aisle.

Nine sample tables later, the boys' pace and enthusiasm had waned a little. Chris gave Jake a turn pushing the cart, to Caleb's delight, and the kid promptly drew Jake into a conversation that was only barely intelligible. Jake thought it might have something to do with playing soccer with Chris, but it didn't matter—as long as Jake dropped an enthusiastic "Oh!" or "Really?" every few seconds, Caleb contentedly kept the conversation going on his own. Jake had never spent much time with little kids, but Caleb was a blast.

At the frozen fish aisle, Caleb turned his babble to another sample-lady, and Chris leaned toward Jake. "Can I ask you something?" he asked.

"Shoot."

"Why do you think he did it?"

Startled at the question, Jake's lungs seemed to collapse, and he hunched over the cart handle. In spite of the chilly conditions in the freezer section, his hands started to sweat.

"I think we're both asking ourselves that same thing," Chris offered.

Jake looked around at the nameless faces all around him in the aisles, pushing their carts along, choosing items from the shelves, living their lives with blank indifference. His mind struggled for a response, the pain simmering in his chest. He blurted out, "If Roger could just kill himself like that, what does that say about life?"

Chris nodded. "I know. Things like this kinda make you think."

Jake frowned. This wasn't the response he anticipated from a minister. *Isn't he supposed to have the answers?*

They continued to stroll down the aisle, Caleb rambling off his new list of friends by memory. Jake walked in silence, waiting for Chris to fill the void. At the next sample table, Caleb grabbed a little cup of ravioli and presented it to Jake like a birthday gift. Jake took the cup without a response, so Caleb contentedly dug into his own, burrowing his nose and tongue in the sauce.

"What do you want out of life, Jake?" Chris suddenly asked.

A year ago, Jake would have responded without hesitating. But now... "I don't know," Jake admitted. "I've spent my whole life trying to be a sports star. For what? What's the point? My dad's successful, but my parents hate each other. They're not happy." Jake stared straight ahead as people passed them in every direction. He finally muttered, "At least Roger's not hurting anymore."

Chris stopped the cart and faced Jake. "Maybe life is more than that."

Jake chuckled sarcastically, knowing where this was headed. "Oh, like what? God?" he quipped.

"That's something you need to figure out," Chris answered, unabashed. And then a smile crept onto his face as his eyes locked in on something behind Jake. Jake turned around to see Cari approaching them from the right. Chris grabbed his shoulder. "Remind me to give you something in the car."

Cari walked up carrying her box of laundry detergent, as well as a new pink skirt. Caleb turned to her and reached out over the side of the cart, covered in tomato sauce. "Oh my gosh, Chris!" she cried.

Chris glanced at his messy son, then smiled at his wife and gave her a wink. "Cute skirt!"

Back in the car, everyone laughed as the radio blared. "Okay, okay, my turn," Chris shouted, sounding the horn to get their attention.

"This should be interesting," Cari smiled, flipping through the stations. She finally landed on an oldies' program. Jake could almost see Elvis gyrating as "Hound Dog" bounced from the speakers, and he had to laugh.

Cari nodded and pointed at Chris. Chris cleared his throat and crooned, *"You ain't nothing but a hound dog, cryin' all the time. You ain't nothing but a hound dog, cryin' all the time..."*

Jake imagined Chris with black duck-tailed hair, swinging his hips in a white leisure suit cut to his navel. Cari leaned over and abruptly pushed the power button, leaving only Chris' voice to continue, *"Wellllllll, you ain't never caught a rabbit and you ain't no friend o'mine!"*

Caleb put his hands over his ears and wailed, "Daddy, stop!"

"Don't tell me that wasn't amazing!" Chris cried. Jake and Cari groaned, and Chris hung his head, pretending to be hurt.

The car neared his house, and Jake sighed with contentment. He couldn't remember the last time he had laughed so much. He gave Caleb a final high-five and unfastened his seatbelt.

But just as Jake reached for the door handle, Chris said, "Looks like you got company." He nodded toward Jake's drive-

way. Five feet away stood Amy, leaning against Jake's truck, now freshly washed and waxed. Her arms were folded across her stomach, and her mouth was turned down in a half-pout, half-snarl. Her eyes shot fireballs. Chris waved to her, but she didn't respond.

"Do you think she saw me?" Jake covered his face with his hand and slumped down in his seat.

Chris smiled. "Good luck out there."

Cari turned around in her seat and looked Jake in the eye. "Look, I don't know anything that's going on, or who did what, or whatever. But us girls, we just want to be listened to." She reached over the seat and squeezed his arm. Jake nodded and slowly climbed out of the car.

"Can he babysit me?" Caleb asked, waving his pudgy hand at Jake.

"Jake?" Chris called out. Jake looked back into the car as Chris pulled out his own pocket Bible and handed it to him, along with a CD. "Take these."

"What are they?"

"Just check 'em out."

Jake took the gifts and slipped them into his back pocket. He shut the car door and turned to slowly walk the gauntlet toward Amy.

He measured each step, giving his brain an extra second or two to calculate a strategy. Jake knew from experience that his first words were critical to the outcome of the argument; his opening words had splatted like water balloons on pavement too many times before, but he convinced himself that today, he wasn't going to blow it. As his feet reached the truck, his eyes lifted off the ground, and he sat down on the bumper next to Amy.

12

"**HEY.**" Jake tried to smile. Amy remained a statue, cold and unflinching. Strike one.

Jake stared straight ahead, evaluating his options. He decided to let her make the next move.

The seconds of heavy silence ticked by, like he'd pulled the pin on a grenade. Still, Amy didn't budge. Jake started to fidget. Out of the corner of his eye, he tried to read her body language, but he only got distracted by her tight blue tank-top with those lacy straps and her little white daisy-dukes on those long, golden-brown legs. Jake shook his head, battling to stay focused, when he had a realization: Amy always seemed to dress like this when they were in a fight. It couldn't be a coincidence. *Women never fight fair!* With effort, he put up his guard and looked away.

"Oh my gosh, Jake! Where have you been?" Amy finally exploded, getting up from the tailgate to face him directly.

The little diamond pendant hanging around her neck winked at him, drawing his gaze. Again he fought back and concentrated on the neighbor's house over her shoulder.

"I don't even want to talk to you," she fumed, crossing her arms. "I've called you like a bazillion times, and you don't even have the decency to...to call back." Her voice quivered, and she dropped her arms to her sides, her slender fingers hanging inches from Jake's knee.

Jake breathed in deeply through his nose. It was his turn again, and as much as he abhorred the thought of plunging deeper into the drama, he decided against faking an apology. He gripped the edge of the tailgate and glared at Amy. "I'm sorry—did I miss the part where you apologized for stealing my truck?"

"You've got to be kidding me!" Amy sputtered. "You were acting like a complete idiot. Do you realize what you've put me through?" She re-crossed her arms, and her left spaghetti strap fell off her shoulder.

Jake waited for her to fix the strap, but her arms didn't move, and he was riveted by that little piece of lace. Again his mind wandered. He attempted to refocus his attention, but even staring eye to eye, Jake had no response. Looking away showed his weakness, so he tried to piece back together what had happened last night while staying strong and defiant. Everything seemed so foggy all of a sudden. What exactly had he said and done? He'd never thought about it from her perspective. It had seemed like any other party night, but maybe there was more to it.

"Say something!" Amy impatiently stepped closer, leaning over with her hands on his knees and her face right in his.

He kept his gaze at eye-level. If she got any closer, they would be kissing. *Is that what she wants?* Jake startled himself with the realization that he didn't really want to kiss her.

"I went to church today," Jake replied, hoping the change in topic might release some of the tension. It didn't. But it caught Amy by surprise. She removed her hands from his knees and straightened her back so that she was now a full six inches taller than the seated Jake.

"Yeah?"

"Yeah."

"Well, my dad used to do the church thing, and then he left us," Amy scoffed.

Jake had never known Amy's dad; he had left long before they ever met. In their three years of dating, she had only brought him up a handful of times. From what Jake could deduce, her dad simply decided he didn't want to be the head of a family anymore. One day Amy had the normal mom and dad, and the next it was only Mom. Her dad had sent a birthday card each year; Amy kept them in the bottom drawer of her desk, all unopened. One time Jake had joked about opening the envelopes just to see if there was any cash inside—Amy hadn't spoken to him for an entire day after that. Now she was comparing Jake to this man he knew she despised. Strike two.

"Amy, I'm not your dad," Jake countered and stood up from the tailgate so he was face to face with her.

"Well, what's going on, Jake?" she shot back. "You don't go to church. And who's that guy I keep seeing you with? You're scaring me!" She turned her back to Jake and combed her fingers through her hair.

Part of Jake wanted to just reach out and grab her waist and enfold her in a reassuring hug. Instead he fought back. "What do you want me to do? Say I'm sorry? OK, I'm *sorry* for you stealing my truck!" His own aggressive tone surprised him, but seriously, what did she expect? He sank back down on his tailgate, causing the whole truck to creak noisily. Amy spun around, causing her other spaghetti strap to slip down. *Focus on her face*, Jake coached himself.

"I'm sorry? I'm sorry! You don't talk to me for almost an entire day, and that's all you got?" Amy was now screeching. A tiny tear formed in the corner of her right eye and rolled down her cheek. She hastily brushed it away.

Jake was used to the raised voice, but not to the tears. Amy had no problem expressing herself, but she just didn't cry very often, and never because of him. What was going on here? *How did I let this happen?*

Jake tenderly took hold of her hands and interlocked his fingers with hers. He pulled her closer until their knees were touching. "Amy, maybe this isn't the best time. I've just got a lot on my mind right now," he whispered, trying to soothe her.

Amy retreated from Jake's grasp. "What? About us? Is that it—you make love to me Saturday nights and then confess on Sundays? Is that the new plan?"

Strike three.

"Amy, you don't know what you're talking about," Jake sighed. He placed his hands delicately on her hips, stroking the sides of her stomach with his thumbs.

"At least I talk!" Amy double-chopped Jake's grip and turned her back once again.

Jake breathed in sharply. *Maybe she's right. Maybe talking about it would help. Maybe she could actually help me sort this out.* He hadn't wanted to admit the raging in his mind over Roger's death, but why not? His recent conversations with Chris had already started the dominoes falling, so Jake decided to tip a few more. He took another deep breath, willing Amy to understand. "You know that kid who killed himself?"

"Yeah, so?" Amy didn't turn around. Her tone and pose still oozed irritation.

"I knew him."

Amy looked back suspiciously, as if trying to decipher whether Jake was actually sharing his heart or just trying to change the subject. "It's sad," she responded vacantly, "but seriously, it's not like he—"

"Mattered?" Jake jumped in.

Amy turned around. "No. I was going to say, it's not like he was your friend."

"We were *best* friends," Jake corrected, his heart starting to beat faster. It struck him that it was easier to talk about this stuff with Chris. *Why is this so difficult?*

Amy didn't look like she was buying it. "Jake, we've been going out for three years. I never even met him."

"We grew up together. His house is just around the corner." Jake's voice cracked as he pointed down the street. It suddenly occurred to him that his friendship with Roger had ended the very moment his and Amy's had begun. Maybe that was why he struggled to share with her: Her beautiful face reminded him of his choice that night his freshman year. What if he had chosen differently? Would he still be with Amy? Would Roger be alive? But Amy didn't need to help him answer those questions. He had made the choice alone, and now he would bear the blame alone.

Amy broke into Jake's self-interrogation. "So your former friend almost kills people, and *you* feel bad?" Her voice was quieter now. "Get over it. It's not your fault."

Jake shook his head. "Then whose fault is it?" He wiped his sweaty palms on his pants and stood back up from the tailgate to pace.

"Nobody. His. The parents. I don't know." Amy shrugged. Her irritation was melting into concern, and she grabbed his arm to stop his pacing, turning his body toward hers. She placed her hands on his biceps and added softly, "Jake, it wasn't your job to watch over him." She slid her arms around him and whispered coyly, "You can watch over me."

Normally, this would have sent Jake's heart racing, but at this moment it had little effect. He withdrew and focused his attention on a single crack in the driveway. Maybe she could just pass the blame onto someone else, but he couldn't. The anger about last night had subsided, but Jake was more bothered than ever. "I've just got a lot to think about," he muttered.

Amy slipped her hands into Jake's back pockets and pulled him even closer to her. Her straps still hung helplessly on her arms, allowing her tank-top to shift further and further down. "I know what you're thinking about," Amy smiled at him, pouting her lips.

This was her one look that Jake could decipher with certainty, and yet here he was, disinterested. Earlier that day, he had been talking to Chris about the existence of God, and it just didn't feel right to now escape his plaguing questions by

going upstairs with his girlfriend. Even so, Jake wasn't one to say no, especially when she was saying yes. But really, what did that say about him?

Suddenly, Jake was aware of Chris's gifts resting in his pocket right next to Amy's fingers. He let her hold him for a few awkward moments, then pulled back.

"Do you think there's a God?"

"What?" Amy removed her arms from around his waist and fixed her spaghetti straps as if they'd just fallen. "You're acting so weird," she groaned, resting her hands on the top of her head.

They stood there in the driveway, looking anywhere except at each other. This wasn't exactly where Jake had envisioned the conversation going, but she was the one who had complained about him not talking. Silence settled like soot between them, neither making the next move. Finally, Jake closed the tailgate on his truck. "Come on, I'll drive you home." He instinctively reached in his pocket for his keys, but Amy still had them. He weakly smiled. "Can I have my keys?"

"No," Amy shot back, pulling his Louisville Cardinals keychain out of her back pocket and throwing them at him anyway. Wordlessly, she climbed into the passenger side of the truck. Her door-slam sent a clear message: This fight was not over.

Jake sighed. His attempts to douse the fire had only made it worse; but what could he expect when he couldn't even extinguish the inferno raging inside him?

Well, at least I've got my truck back.

THEY DROVE TO AMY'S HOUSE in complete silence. Jake wasn't sure which was worse, the fire or the ice. Amy remained squished against the far side of the truck's bench seat, her eyes fixed on the road ahead. In the stillness, Jake couldn't help noticing the sparkling windshield and forest-pine scent wafting through the cab, the polished dashboard and controls, and the vacuumed carpets. He knew this was Amy's way of making up to him and that a simple "thank you" from him would work wonders, but stubbornness took over, and he sulked in silence, firmly planting his hands at ten and two on the steering wheel.

They finally reached her house, and Amy flung her door open and jumped out before the truck fully came to a stop. As her door swung back, Amy delivered her first and last words of the ride: "You're welcome!" The door slammed shut before Jake had a chance to respond. She marched into her humble house without looking back.

"Thanks," Jake grunted, pounding his fists on the steering wheel.

✚ ✚ ✚

Two and a half hours later, Jake lay on his bed staring at the ceiling. He'd tried to do homework for almost an hour but couldn't focus on English or Econ. This wasn't the first time he'd been distracted from doing homework in his bedroom; his twenty-seven-inch flat screen, surround-sound stereo, and three different video gaming systems were just a few of the ways his parents spoiled him, and Jake was sure his GPA would be higher if *Madden 360* had never been invented. But on this early Sunday evening, his two-thousand-dollar entertainment system held no appeal. Sprawled on his back on his queen-sized bed, Jake's eyes just wandered around his room, his mind racing like Dale Earnhardt, Jr.

Everything on Jake's bedroom walls screamed Louisville Cardinals. His fascination for this college two-thirds of the way across the country began when his mom bought Jake a Louisville basketball T-shirt for his seventh birthday, a year the Cardinals made it to the Final Four. She thought her son would look good in red; she had no idea that it would become his favorite piece of clothing.

Louisville became a fixation, and over time that fixation became an obsession, probably fueled at least in part by Jake's father's disapproval. "What ties do we have with Kentucky?" Glen Taylor had often questioned irritably. He'd say it was ridiculous to be such a fanatic when there were plenty of respectable teams closer to home. But each year during March Madness, Jake always picked the same team to go all the way. Eleven years later, it was well-deserved destiny when he was offered the full-ride scholarship to Louisville.

His eyes finally fell on his mahogany nightstand, where the pocket Bible and CD from Chris rested in front of a framed candid of Jake giving Amy a piggyback ride last summer. They were both smiling widely in the shot; they looked so blissful. Jake's gut wrenched. Why did Amy have to make such a big deal of things? Why couldn't she just hear him out? He thumped his head against his pillow and glanced again at Chris' stuff. He leaned over to pick it up. He'd never seen a Bible that small.

The one on his parents' bookshelf was much thicker—and much dustier, for that matter. Jake flipped through the feathery pages and scanned the camouflage cover. Was it legal for Bibles to be anything other than black? And did people really even read these things? He was pretty sure the one on their shelf hadn't been opened in years; maybe when his grandma was still alive—she had been a very religious person. Jake rested the Bible on his chest and grabbed the CD. The royalblue face was splashed with graphic water droplets, and white letters titled it *Devo2Go. Sounds like some kind of sports drink,* Jake mused. At the bottom of the sleeve were simple instructions to download its contents onto an MP3 player. Intrigued, Jake went to his computer and pulled up his iTunes account. Within minutes, he was back to his comfortable position on his bed, headphones in place. Ready or not, Jake pressed play.

"Thanks for checking out *Devo2Go,*" Chris' familiar voice spoke into Jake's ears. "This is Day One of our 'Life's Questions' series. Since you're listening, I'm going to presume you're at least interested in God...You know, God gets a bad rap these days. There's all this crap going on all over the world, and we wonder why He doesn't do something. Why doesn't He stop it? But do you think maybe God wants to ask us the same question? The cool thing is, God is not afraid of or offended by our questions. In fact, He welcomes them. Turn in your Bible to Luke 9:18-20."

Jake lifted the camouflage Bible from his chest, unsure of where to go. He wondered if it had a Table of Contents. Just as he opened the front cover, Chris' voice directed him: "If you're using the *Soldier* Bible, turn to page 922."

Jake turned and noticed that his heartbeat had picked up speed, just like it did when he used to pull out the *Penthouse* magazines from underneath his mattress, the ones he'd found in his dad's desk drawer. He wasn't sure which one would require more explaining if his parents happened to barge into the room. He got up and locked his bedroom door, just in case.

When he located what seemed to be the right verse, he read silently along with Chris.

"One time when Jesus was off praying by himself, his disciples nearby, he asked them, 'What are the crowds saying about me, about who I am?' They said, 'John the Baptizer. Others say Elijah. Still others say that one of the prophets from long ago has come back.' He then asked, 'And you—what are you saying about me? Who am I?' Peter answered, 'The Messiah of God.' Jesus then warned them to keep it quiet. They were to tell no one what Peter had said."

Jake paused his iPod and reread the verses one more time, unsure of what to think. *Am I missing something?* Still clueless after skimming it another time, Jake pressed Play again.

"Today's Life Question is simple: Who do *you* say Jesus is?" Chris' voice continued. "It's the most important question you'll ever have to answer, and you'll have to decide for yourself. Think about it, and we'll talk more tomorrow."

The track ended, and Jake stopped his iPod, looking up at the ceiling, hands crossed behind his head. How was it that he had come so far in his life without ever thinking about these things?

A knock on his door interrupted his concentration. "Jake? I made you dinner so you can eat while you're studying," his mom's muffled voice echoed through the door, and the doorknob clicked.

"Just a minute!" Jake jumped, stuffing his Bible—of all places—under his mattress. He got up and opened the door, where his mom stood holding a large bowl of macaroni and cheese, one of his favorites.

"Why was the door locked?" His mom looked a little hurt. She handed him the steaming bowl and a cold can of soda.

"I didn't even realize it was. Guess it's just a habit." Jake feigned nonchalance.

"How's the studying coming along?"

"Just about finished."

The next morning, Jake walked briskly through the parking lot of Pacific High with a smile on his face. The sun mimicked his cheer, having already fought through the marine layer that normally blanketed the school for the first few hours on spring days. It was already seventy degrees and fair, and Jake inhaled the warmth deep into his soul.

He'd left home early to stop by 2Spoons Coffee to pick up Amy's favorite morning drink. He'd tossed and turned all night rehashing the previous thirty-six hours, and he knew he could have handled things a little better. Jake confidently carried Amy's grande-double-shot-espresso-mocha-latte-with-lots-of-whipped-cream toward their lockers. This recipe had gotten him out of a bind before, so how could it go wrong on a glorious day like today? Besides, Amy could never stay mad at Jake for very long once he turned on the charm.

Jake turned the corner around the gym, greeting everyone with an Orbit smile. While Senior Hall was where Pacific's brightest and most beautiful hung out, under the stairwell was the normal pot smoking group that Jake had intentionally ignored throughout the basketball season. Jake shot a glance at the eclectic group taking a few last puffs before the morning bell. Seven students huddled together while one stood guard looking for passing security.

Out of the darkness, a familiar voice called out to Jake as he passed. "Season's over. No more drug tests."

It was Danny Rivers. Had it just been yesterday that they spoke in the church lobby? Now they were socializing in a cloud of marijuana. Jake chuckled at the irony.

"What's up?" Jake smiled with a touch of disdain. He was on a mission to make things right with Amy, but struck by the incongruity of the situation, he paused.

Danny offered a hit, apparently oblivious to the paradox.

Jake declined but cautiously approached the group, stopping a few feet away to maintain his separation. He listened, incredulous, to the conversation.

"This week is gonna be hell," complained Kelsi, taking a hit of her own.

Jake looked at the beret, camouflage capris, and army boots she sported—a rebel of her own making, in sharp contrast

with the nice-girl image she portrayed on stage yesterday. He wondered if the two worlds were difficult to balance. As Jake watched, it became obvious that she was the leader of the group—the huddle listened to her diatribe like a choir focusing on their conductor.

"Mr. Bee is such an A-hole. It's like he doesn't want us to have a life," Kelsi blabbered, pausing to glare at Jake and curtly ask him, "What?"

"Uh, nothing," Jake answered, turning his attention to Danny to avoid her stare. "Long time no see."

Danny didn't even turn to respond, seeming to pretend not to hear. Unfazed, Jake took another step toward Danny and the others. He had never had a problem with the group before— but this morning was different. *They go to church. Danny's dad is the pastor. Shouldn't they be different?* Jake couldn't balance this with his recent conversations with Chris. Was this the real side of religion?

"Does the good preacher know about this?" Jake half-smiled and raised an eyebrow.

"He has no clue," Danny smirked with an edge Jake had not anticipated. "Anyways, smoking weed's not in the Bible."

"I guess you would know," Jake scoffed.

"Besides, who cares?" Danny retorted.

"What about God?" Jake shot back. The impulse surprised him, but he wanted to know.

"You believe that crap?" Danny snapped, and the entire group of smokers laughed.

Jake looked at Danny, surprised. "You don't?"

"I believe what I believe," Danny declared confidently.

The kid standing guard coughed a mumble under his breath, "Security."

Danny and the rest of the group quickly dropped their joints, stomped them out, scooped up the pieces and stuffed them in their pockets. Kelsi and another guy pulled out bottles of cologne and sprayed them into the air. Jake took a few steps away to disassociate himself from them. Backing away, he bumped right into a frowning Clyde Will.

"What's going on here?" Clyde's voice challenged more than questioned.

Jake's heart skipped a beat, knowing what this must look like. His mind ran through a list of horrifying consequences if he got suspended for drugs, all the more horrendous because this time, he was innocent.

An apparently unruffled Kelsi spoke up cheerfully. "Sorry, Mr. Will. We were just having a prayer group before school. The hallway is too noisy." She switched back into her nice-girl guise like a pro.

Clyde scowled and waved his hand in front of his face. His eyes rested on Jake, but he spoke to the others. "I think a few of you might have put on too many *puffs* of cologne this morning."

Kelsi boldly stepped even closer to Mr. Will. "These guys got really bad B.O.," she whispered, wrinkling her nose and eyebrows.

Clyde looked them over one last time, lingering again on Jake. "Go to class," he finally ordered.

"Good call. We want to be early," Kelsi smugly agreed as she led the group of saints away from the stairwell.

Jake followed her, but Clyde grabbed his shoulder and held him back. Jake smiled, trying to hide his fear and agitation, but his stomach plunged.

"Didn't know you were the praying type, Jake," Clyde grilled as the group disappeared.

"Isn't everybody?" Jake squirmed.

"Just be careful who you *pray* with," Clyde warned and released Jake on his way.

By the time Jake got to his locker, the bell was about to ring. Amy was waiting there, two coffees already in hand. The sour scowl on her face awakened Jake to the realization that his

detour had taken much longer than he could afford, and his hopeful morning was flushing rapidly down the drain. The hot drink that had scorched his hand earlier was now tepid, and the fluffy whipped cream had melted into nothing more than a thick film. Jake's confidence dissipated like the morning fog, and the dread of impending failure slowed his previously buoyant steps.

"Where have you been?" Amy spun away from Jake toward her open locker, blind to the pictures of the couple in happier times plastered on the inside walls.

"Uh, I got this for you." Jake offered her the coffee.

"Hello, I have one." Amy waved an identical cup in his face.

"I just thought—"

Amy grabbed Jake's gift and took a sip. "Mmmm, lukewarm coffee. My favorite." She dropped it into a nearby trash can as if it were an old sock, then sniffed suspiciously. "Do I smell pot?"

"No! It's not mine," Jake stammered. He screwed up his face in a pleading grimace.

Amy just laughed and slammed her locker shut. "Sure, church boy," she scoffed and walked away toward class.

Jake growled a sigh. He clenched his fists and collapsed against his locker, his head bouncing heavily against the cold, rattling steel. The day had started with such promise. He tossed his coffee in the trash can and shuffled off to class.

14

SECOND SEMESTER of senior year only really mattered to two types of people: those battling to be valedictorian (which Jake definitely was not) or those trying to make up for three and a half years of screwing around (not Jake's deal either). Most everyone else skated by in a state of indifference. Some liked to call it senioritis; Jake called it cruise control.

After Jake's flop of a morning, the assonance in line seven of some Shakespearean sonnet and the symmetry to the y-axis of some function held zero relevance. Sitting at his desk, Jake mentally checked out, trying instead to calculate how to pick up the pieces of his life. Lunch was the only subject that held any appeal, but even that had its own problems: He'd have to face Amy again. By the end of fourth period, he still hadn't landed on an acceptable Amy-strategy.

Finally the lunch bell rang, and Jake dragged himself past the long cafeteria lines toward his usual hangout. The pleasant sunny morning had become uncomfortably hot, and Jake grumbled to himself as he walked past the lunch tables. In his four years at Pacific, he'd not eaten one meal there. It

wasn't like the lunch area was specifically set aside for the uncool, but it was just where they all seemed to flock. Jake's friends much preferred the grassy hill on the far side of the open quad, their elevated spot an unintentional but constant reminder of their respective social position.

As he headed toward the hill, Jake unexpectedly spotted Andrea, the rainbow girl from church, at a table just a few feet away. He'd never noticed her sitting there before—but then again, why would he? Her long brown hair fell in a French braid down her back, accented by bright red hoop earrings that Jake was confident he could've fit his hand through. She sat with two other girls who had similar taste.

Jake quickly turned his head to avoid a hello. It's not like one quick introduction at church meant he had to acknowledge her at school, right?

"Jake!" Andrea yelled in the same cheery voice from the day before.

Jake pretended to be surprised to see her. "Hey! Andrea, right?"

"Yeah, yeah. Good memory," Andrea beamed, standing up from the table. "How's it going?"

Jake moved closer to her so they wouldn't have to talk so loudly. "It's all good," he lied. He hadn't seen them yesterday inside the church, but now in the sunlight he noticed a few cute freckles dusting her nose and cheeks.

Andrea stepped even closer and crossed her arms. "Jake, does anybody ever ask you how you're really doing?"

Jake's heart skipped. *Does she know something? Did Chris blab to the whole group about the stuff I'm dealing with?*

"What do you mean?" Jake answered guardedly.

"It's just, I was watching you walk across the quad, and it didn't look like everything was 'all good.'" Andrea held up her bag of chips. "Frito?"

Jake grabbed a chip with no interest in eating it. He fiddled with it in his hand, then blurted, "Today's just not going how I thought it would go." He wasn't sure why he said it—maybe it was something in her face—but it felt good to unload.

Andrea nodded her head like she understood and finished off the bag of Fritos. "It was cool to see you at Souled Out," she said.

Jake looked around. People walked by in a steady stream, but it didn't seem like any of them noticed the odd couple sharing a bag of chips. "Yeah, it was kinda cool," Jake answered sincerely.

"Are you coming tomorrow night?"

"Tomorrow?" Jake repeated, confused.

Andrea laughed to herself, crumpling up the empty chip bag and hooking a finger onto one of her gigantic earrings. "Chris didn't tell you?" she grinned. "Tuesdays are youth group. It's at 7:00 at the church."

"You go to church twice a week?" Jake was staggered.

"Oh my gosh, I'm scaring you, huh?" Andrea playfully punched his shoulder. She was a good six inches shorter than he was, so it was more like an uppercut. Jake smiled, enjoying her playful charm.

Suddenly, Andrea covered her heart with her hand and gushed, "I'm sorry! Natalie and Carla, this is Jake." She motioned to the two girls sitting at the table behind them, watching their conversation like a tennis match. Both sported braces and an obvious crush on the senior basketball star in their midst.

Jake didn't really feel like making any more friends, but he greeted them anyway. "Hi." He waved absently, hoping this would be the end of their interaction. His path to making up with Amy had already been derailed once today, and he really wanted to get back on track. Time was ticking away.

The girls waved back in unison, goofy grins plastered across their faces. A piece of lettuce from Carla's sandwich was wedged into her braces.

Jake's smile weakened, and he sought a polite escape. He dropped the Frito still rattling in his palm and wiped his hands against his shorts uneasily.

During this whole encounter, Jake hadn't noticed Amy and Doug standing fifteen yards away. They had been walking by just as Andrea offered Jake her chips. When she touched Jake, Amy had stormed away, and Doug had started toward Jake and Andrea.

Suddenly, Doug's six-foot-six frame cast a large shadow that swallowed Andrea and startled Jake. Andrea warmly smiled at him over Jake's shoulder and looked to Jake to make the introduction. Jake dropped his head and cringed. This was why he had tried to avoid this encounter in the first place. He shuffled his feet as the tension built.

"Jake, what are you doing?" Doug said, almost accusingly.

"Doug!" Jake tried to play cool, knocking knuckles with his friend like they met with strange girls all the time. He pointed at his new company. "This is Andrea, Natalie and—"

"Carla," Andrea chimed in, still smiling.

Natalie and Carla redirected their grinning gaze to Doug, their matching braces glinting in the sunlight. Doug barely glanced their way with a look of disgust. The girls got the message and retreated to the remainders of their brown bag lunches.

"Am I missing something?" Doug demanded.

Andrea apparently hadn't noticed that she was no longer a part of the conversation and boldly patted Doug's elbow. "Jake and I were just talking about Sou—"

"Social Studies," Jake quickly finished. The moment it slipped out, he wished he could take it back as he watched Andrea's face. Her smile remained, but her eyes were all-too-reminiscent of Roger's when Jake had ditched him for Amy that night. Could he never escape?

Doug slapped Jake on the back. "Whatever. Let's get out of here."

Jake glanced at Andrea apologetically, but she had turned away. With a sigh, Jake turned to follow Doug back to their usual lunch spot. Doug waited for him to catch up, then threw his arm around Jake's shoulder.

"Bro, what are you doing with those chicks?"

Jake ignored him.

THIS IS TOTALLY STUPID, Jake thought to himself. He slumped in the seat and doodled with his finger on the car window. Pros and cons had battled in his head for the past hour and a half as he sat behind the wheel of his truck in the darkness. One hand gripped the door handle, the other held the key still resting in the ignition. *Why am I afraid of going in?* Then he thought, *Why am I here in the first place?*

Students trickled out of the church in groups and singles, each in their own worlds. There was Andrea, hugging a couple of the other students on her way toward a shiny new Lexus. Jake was sure she hadn't missed him at youth group after his stunt at lunch yesterday. Danny and Kelsi walked out hand-in-hand. *It figures,* Jake snorted. The couple paid no attention to most of the people they passed. A number of other students squawked and flirted and tossed a football until they either got picked up by their parents or drove away in their own cars. But they all seemed oblivious to the lone truck sitting in the far back corner of the lot.

Jake watched enviously the ease with which they were all able to fit into this church thing. They didn't stress about what

others would think, they didn't struggle with what to believe, and they sure weren't carrying their friend's suicide on their shoulders. Was there any hope for him?

Jake sighed. The past ninety minutes of internal debate left all his arguments a moot point now that the service was over. Jake scolded himself for waiting so long to leave. Now he'd have to wait until the last dozen or so students had gone to avoid their questions and stares. *Oh well, what was another fifteen minutes?*

One by one, the parking lot emptied of students and cars until only one was left, one which Jake knew all too well after last weekend. The lights inside the church finally went out, and Chris walked wearily to the car, tossing his bag in the front seat. He got in and started his engine, but instead of heading out toward the street, he drove directly over to Jake's truck, as if they had agreed on the rendezvous. Chris pulled up alongside and rolled down his window. Jake did the same.

"So she gave you your truck back," Chris called over his engine.

Jake nervously chuckled, a little embarrassed that he'd been found out.

"How long have you been out here?" Chris asked.

"The whole time," Jake admitted. There was no point trying to play it cool here—not now, not with Chris.

Chris turned off the engine, got out of his car, and walked over to Jake's open passenger-side window. He rested his arms on the window frame and peered in. "Why didn't you come in?"

"I don't know." Jake ran his hand nervously through his hair. His fingers ached; he hadn't realized how tightly he had been clutching the steering wheel. "I'm just not sure."

Chris opened the passenger door and took a seat next to Jake. "Not sure about what?"

That was precisely the question he had spent the past hour and a half asking himself. Maybe saying it out loud would help. "So...I believe that you believe," Jake began. "But why are there so many fakers in there?" He paused for a moment, then added quickly, "I mean, I'm not calling your group fake. I just think—"

Jake stopped midsentence as Chris started to laugh. Jake looked at him, puzzled.

"Jake, I know there are fakers in the group; in fact I probably know of more than you." Chris nodded in agreement. "But you know what? So does God."

Jake didn't see how that made it any better.

Chris smiled sadly. "I don't know; I guess there are always going to be people who are willing to settle." He gazed into the empty parking lot for a few heavy moments before turning back to Jake. "But you know, that's not what it's about, Jake. It's about you. What are *you* going to do?"

A chilly breeze swept across Jake's sweat-beaded forehead as he digested Chris' words. Jake knew all kinds of people who took the easy way in life, but his full scholarship was evidence enough to him that he wasn't one of them. He had fought back so many times against his dad's accusations of slacking off; now he wondered if he had been struggling in the wrong direction. He couldn't deny the voice inside him longing to know if there was something more to the life he was currently living.

"So let's say that I...I don't want to settle," Jake said carefully. "Is it worth it?"

Chris' fingers drummed on the dashboard reflectively. "Jake, I've asked myself a lot of the same questions you are. At some point, we've all got to ask ourselves, 'What's my life going to be about?' Pleasure and success is great, but it's exhausting. We end up constantly chasing after it, because none of it ever lasts. We get drunk time after time and sleep with as many women as we can, trying to convince everyone that we're the greatest thing they've ever seen, trying to make ourselves happy—and we always end up at the same place: totally alone." Chris kept his gaze fixed on Jake.

Jake broke eye contact and gripped the steering wheel again, turning to his reflection in the driver's side mirror. He couldn't find the confident face of the guy that had everything

going for him. Instead, staring back relentlessly were eyes full of fear and uncertainty.

"I'm happy enough," Jake responded, his voice pockmarked with trepidation. He wasn't even convincing himself.

"Well, it wasn't enough for me, Jake." Chris shrugged. "I finally had to look honestly at my life and ask the question, 'Is there something more?' Look, I'm telling you, if you are willing—I mean really, truly willing—to search hard, and to ignore everything that friends might say or whatever might happen, I'm telling you, Jake, you're going to find that He's more than worth it."

The church parking lot lights went out, leaving them in complete darkness. Jake glanced at the outline of Chris in the light of the moon. His head hurt; his mind had never swam so hard or so deep. Did Chris even fully understand the risk he was asking him to take?

"And if nothing happens?" Jake questioned, hoping Chris could promise some sort of money-back guarantee.

Even in the shadows, Chris' grin was unmistakable. He opened the door of the truck and set one foot out. "Well, I don't know how it's going to happen or when it's going to happen, but Jake, give it some time. One thing I've learned about God is He won't leave you hangin'." He stepped out of the truck and stood up, then turned back to Jake and leaned against the inside of the open door.

Jake coughed uneasily; he'd never heard someone talk about God in such a personal way. He glanced at the clock on the radio; it was a few minutes past ten.

"It's late, man." Chris reached toward Jake with both hands and shook Jake's hand with his right while patting him on the back with his left. "Next time, let's meet in my office. There's more light there," he joked. He stood back up and shut the door between them.

Jake turned his key to start the car. What had he just agreed to? While he was intrigued by what Chris said, he couldn't just drop everything and become a Jesus freak. He yelled out the window just as Chris was getting into his car. "Hey! I'm not just gonna become some Christian!"

Chris looked back at Jake and laughed. "Good! I wouldn't want you to!" he shouted as he pulled his door shut.

✚ ✚ ✚

A few hours later, Jake lay in bed, wide-awake in the darkness, his mind assessing the past three weeks of his life. He identified at least a dozen times over the past few years when he had consciously walked by Roger without saying a word. *What could I have done differently?* His mind kept returning to that awful day, standing just inches away from his childhood best friend holding a gun. His attempt to talk Roger down had been pathetic at best, his last-second words of comfort worthless. Jake rehearsed different words that might have met with more success, but no matter what he said, each scene ended in the same way: Roger raising the gun to his chin, staring directly at Jake as the blast rang out.

Jake threw off his covers and sprang to his desk. The glow of his laptop filled the dark room as he cracked it open and typed in his password. The arrow on the screen glided toward the Internet icon, and up popped his homepage: ESPN. But the sports scores that Jake usually followed with devotion remained unread. Instead, he typed two words into the search engine that he'd never thought much about before: *teen suicide.*

He'd had no reason to pay attention to the subject in freshman health class, but now he could think of nothing else. He simply had to find out what he could have—or should have—done to help Roger. He clicked Search and leaned over the keyboard as the list populated on the screen in front of him.

16

"I FORGIVE YOU!" Amy engulfed Jake in her arms as he approached her in the Pacific High hallway. She kissed him long and hard while carefully holding two steaming coffee cups in her hands behind his head.

Startled, Jake wondered what had prompted this. His first thought was to automatically respond, "I forgive you, too!" but his need for reconciliation was easily outweighed by his need for justice. Jake could stick anything out until victory—he did so often on the court. But even he knew that this reverse of fortune had less to do with him and everything to do with Amy. She hated it when people were upset with her. Before this, they had never fought for longer than a day or two, and never with such intensity. Typically he and Amy exchanged at least two dozen texts a day, but there had been none since the silent drive home three days ago. While Jake was yet to offer an apology—and had no intention of doing so—he knew Amy was reaching out in her own way.

Jake finally pulled his face away from Amy, his arms still fully wrapped around her slender body. "Nice way to be forgiven," Jake smiled, reaching in for one more quick peck. "I've been missing my mocha espressos."

Amy handed him his cup with the flirty little grin that always drove Jake crazy. If making up was this easy, why did he ever let the fights drag on? The whole fight seemed so silly now.

"I called you last night," Amy whispered, holding his hand and rubbing it tenderly with her thumb.

Jake knew—she had called him seven times. He'd finally turned his phone off completely while waiting in the church parking lot. As much as he longed to tell her about his conversation with Chris, he wasn't sure she would understand, and frankly he wasn't ready to go there again.

"My cell phone's busted," Jake lied, hoping Amy would simply let it go. Before she could question him any more, Jake turned to Doug, Matt, and Tony, who had been standing by letting the couple make up. In their loaded lettermen jackets, their egos seemed to fill Senior Hall and touch everyone passing by. They targeted a group of the girls' volleyball team, all wearing shorts that clearly showed off their well-toned glutes. The girls never turned their heads, but whispered and giggled to each other.

"Now that's what I'm talking about!" Matt exclaimed, lightly banging his head on a nearby locker as his eyes followed the tall blonde beauties.

Doug reached out to them longingly, as if caressing a ripe fruit. At the end of the hallway, the girls finally looked back and smiled at their admirers. The boys cheered and raised their fingers like telephones as they mouthed, "Call me!"

Jake sighed and shook his head. He could usually join the others in their daily appreciation of the "scenery," especially when Amy wasn't around. Today, however, she definitely was, and Jake felt her arms tighten around his waist as the guys whooped and hollered.

"She wasn't even looking at you, man." Doug playfully shoved Matt as the girls turned the corner.

"Whatever, dude. We had a soul-to-soul connection," Matt crooned.

Doug turned and placed his arms on the shoulders of Jake and Amy, forming a group hug. "Bro, biggest party of the year Saturday," he announced as if he were standing ten feet away, not ten inches.

They're all the biggest party of the year, Jake mused to himself.

Matt and Tony joined the other side of the huddle and shouted in unison, "Beer pong championships!"

For some, beer pong was merely an excuse to consume large quantities of beer; for others, it was a serious sport that just happened to involve alcohol. Jake's past interest in the activity fell somewhere in the middle. As the name suggested, the game was sort of a combination of drinking and ping-pong. But while the simple task of throwing a ball in a cup seemed easy at first, it became more and more difficult with each passing drink. Jake had seen a few guys pass out before the game was even over. To be great at beer pong, a person needed accuracy and the ability to hold his liquor. Both came easy to Jake.

But after last night's talk with Chris, the last thing Jake wanted to do was get publicly wasted. It didn't even sound fun. He figured this new life he was exploring with Chris would at some point collide with the old one, but he'd hoped he could experiment with the church-thing alongside his normal routine until he figured everything out. Now that plan didn't seem possible. As much as he wished he could get Chris' words out of his head, he was unable to. It's not like he owed him anything, but strangely, he didn't want to let him down.

As Jake struggled with this, his friends kept squawking. "You're the reigning champ, man. You got the belt," Doug proclaimed to all who passed by.

Jake draped his arm around his buddy's neck and spoke in his ear. "I don't know if I can make it," he whispered, trying to sound casual.

Doug spun around to face Jake as the late bell rang. "What?" Amy, Matt, and Tony stood looking at Jake in silence, waiting for the punch line.

"I said, I don't know if I'm going to be able to make it," Jake repeated softly.

Doug laughed and lightly slapped Jake on the cheek. "Whatever. Taylor never misses a party." Doug smirked at the rest of the group. "Can you believe this guy? Not going to the party! Hell would have to freeze over first." They all sniggered and slapped Jake's back as they headed to their classes.

Jake attempted to laugh along with them, but inside he felt totally lost. He'd assumed there would be a little push-back with his God-experiment, but he never imagined he'd have a tough time just getting people to take him seriously. *Well, it is what it is,* Jake thought. He decided to take more time to think this whole thing through before making any socially paralyzing decisions.

Clyde turned the corner and motioned to the crowd to hurry it up. Amy held tightly to Jake's arm as they headed off. "Can we just pretend the last couple days never happened?" Amy whispered in Jake's ear, resting her head on his shoulder.

Jake nodded out of habit, not agreement. *If she only knew what she was asking.*

17

IT HAD ONLY BEEN seven days since the last party, but it seemed like another lifetime. Jake had tried to distract Amy into a romantic walk on the beach or a date at the movies that night, but she would not relent and was getting annoyed. He even thought about faking an illness, but for how many weekends could he keep using that one? At some point he would need to just shoot straight, but tonight it seemed like more than he could do. He was the reigning Pacific High Beer Pong Champion, and he was expected at this party. What would people think if he and Amy were a no-show? Lately, Jake couldn't care less about the latest drama and gossip, but he knew the party mattered to Amy.

The party had been going strong for two hours by the time Jake and Amy finally made their entrance. Jake had done his best to get lost on the way, but he could only make so many wrong turns before Amy started getting really irritated. He'd also considered sneaking out when no one was looking, but that plan didn't solve the problem of Amy. So he finally decided he'd have to stay sober—a feat he had yet to accomplish at a weekend party.

They strolled hand-in-hand through the house that was far too elegant for this crazy of a party. Huge, abstract paintings hung over an enormous grand piano, which had been transformed into a collection site for half-empty beer cans. Teens swayed and danced underneath a crystal chandelier on the pristine white carpet. Jake and Amy nodded their usual hellos as they scanned the room for their friends.

An unmistakable booming voice bounced off the creamy taupe walls. Doug Moore swaggered into the room, carrying two open beers and wearing a black tuxedo T-shirt he reserved for special occasions, with a matching hat that said something in Japanese. He intercepted Jake and Amy in front of the piano and bestowed a beer on each of them as if he was knighting them. Jake took a microscopic sip and placed it next to the dozens of unfinished cans on the edge of the piano's lid.

"Taylor. Garage. Now!" Doug belched out.

Amy laughed in delight and latched onto Jake's arm, pulling him toward the garage door. "Let's get it on!" she cheered, raising her already half-empty can in the air with her free hand.

Only a week ago, Jake would have been soaking all this in with elation. All eyes were on him, his classmates admiring and expectant, the thrill of victory certain. This is what he lived for—or so he thought. But tonight, it all felt so empty, so meaningless.

He let Amy lead him, desperate for an escape, his drunk classmates cheering him on. The crowd parted as he moved through it, as if he was Moses leading the masses through the Red Sea. But rather than anticipating freedom on the other side, Jake dreaded the looming sinkhole that threatened to swallow him whole. The music blared so loud that it rattled the paintings on the walls, but Jake only heard the quickening beat of his own heart pounding in his ears. He smiled to the fans as his same-old cocky self, but inside, Jake was quaking.

The teeming crowd marched through the backyard landscaping, packed with even more drunk teens. They raised their cans in salute as Jake, Doug, and Amy paraded past them toward the back of the property, around the far end of the pool, underneath an arch covered in ivy and white lights, and up to their destination. Before Jake could even see the garage, he could hear the familiar chant bellowing from within: "Jake! Jake! Jake! Jake!"

Jake thought about the first time he'd played this game: He and Doug were just messing around in his backyard after hearing about the sport from an older friend. Now it had morphed into a gigantic school-wide spectacle. Matt had created this ridiculous belt with beer cans and bottle caps super-glued all around it, which Jake had won at the inaugural event last year. Since then, he had dominated every challenger he'd faced en route to tonight's rematch.

For the first time in his life, Jake longed to be just another face in the crowd. He peeled his sweat-drenched hand out of Amy's grasp and wiped it on the front of his shirt. Doug held open the garage door as Jake entered.

The garage lay in utter disarray. Spilled drinks, discarded cans, crushed chips, and displaced power tools mingled together on the floor under the careless feet of at least fifty teenagers, crammed three-deep along every wall. The brisk spring night outdoors transformed into a humid, smelly sauna on the other side of the garage door. Amy squeezed close to Jake, her skin sticking uncomfortably to his.

Matt emerged from the mob and made his way to the center. Standing a good six inches above everyone else, he raised his giant hands in the air to silence the crowd, while a Fisher-Price microphone attached to fishing line descended from the rafters above his head. One of the volleyball girls from the day before, in a strapless dress that was barely hanging on, joined Matt on his right, holding a dry-erase board to keep score.

"The moment we've all been waiting for!" The Mouth roared like he was announcing Wrestle Mania 43. "Today we have the clash of the titaaaaaaannnnnnns. This is going to be a fair fight; you all know the rules. Let's get ready to beeeeeeeer poooooooooong!"

The room exploded into cheering as another dozen students pushed their way in to see the action first-hand. Jake

was led to one side of the ping-pong table where a ping-pong ball sat in a red tumbler waiting for him to make the first toss. Across the table stood football jock Tommy Rhoades, who looked like he may have already downed a few too many.

Jake was pretty sure Tommy could crack his skull open in a fist-fight, but in this game, Jake could conduct the beat down. Football players always talked a big game, but Jake had a natural consistency and an uncanny ability to hold his beer. He'd probably inherited it from his father. His mom got tipsy after a glass of wine with dinner, but he'd seen his dad nurse an entire twelve-pack while still engaging in a relatively sophisticated conversation about politics.

The mob started up the "Jake! Jake! Jake!" chant again. Massaging the ball in one hand, Jake took one last look around the room. *What am I doing here?* He watched Amy parade the trophy belt around the room, reminding everyone that her boyfriend was the champ. Her midriff-baring halter and short skirt left little of her body to the imagination, and Jake watched with disgust as the guys leered over her. Amy trotted over to Jake and posed next to him, then passionately kissed him on the mouth. The crowd howled with approval. What could he do?

Jake dipped the ping-pong ball in his cup, cocked his arm, and swished a perfect shot into his opponent's cup across the table. Game on. Tommy chugged down the full red cup of Budweiser, belched insolently, and proceeded to nail a shot right back at Jake.

The bitter, lukewarm liquid tasted sour in Jake's mouth, and he grimaced before gulping it. He usually could down the cupful in one swallow. *What is happening to me?* The momentum of the crowd carried him forward into another shot, then another. The game continued back and forth, each shot taking longer to line up, each swish growing further apart. The crowd cheered and groaned and drank from their own cups and bottles as more and more people packed into the inferno. By the time the score reached 5-3, Jake was running on autopilot, but just wasn't having as much fun as he remembered.

He needed some fresh air, but every breath was suffocated by the stench of reeking sweat and stale beer.

Two shots later, Jake was on the verge of victory and was dominating in terms of sobriety. Tommy looked terrible—his cheeks and nose flushed, his eyes glassy, his stance unsteady. With one hand on the table for balance and the other gripping the ball, Tommy suddenly spun around spewing in the direction of a nearby trash can. Of course, only the final chunks got that far; most of the filth landed on a couple guys who were themselves too wasted to get out of the way. The crowd laughed hysterically.

Jake stared at the remaining three cups he was supposed to force Tommy to drink so that he could claim the victor's title. He backed away and scanned the delirious bodies of his peers, still doubled-up in laughter. He glanced over at Amy, looking so fragile underneath her minimal layer of clothing, and he spotted Doug and Matt, each busily groping their own volleyball girls.

And then, at the back of the muggy garage, Jake saw her— or not so much her, but what she was wearing. Kelsi, the church-worship/pothead-gang leader, held two beer bottles above her head, displaying for all to see a "Jesus is my homeboy" T-shirt with a cartoon picture of Jesus. The face stared right at Jake.

Jake burned with anger at the hypocrisy of it, but then he thought, *So what does that make me?* Immediately Chris' words from the other night flashed to the forefront of his brain: "Look, I'm telling you, if you are willing—I mean really, truly willing—to search hard, and to ignore everything that friends might say or whatever might happen, I'm telling you, Jake, you're going to find that He's more than worth it."

Is this worth it?

Tommy regrouped, and the crowd cheered at his comeback. His next shot flew a good two feet from the nearest cup, and Jake was handed the ball for his turn. But inside Jake's head, the cheering uproar faded into a deafening silence behind the

whirling questions. He breathed deeply, rattling the ball in his hand, trying to answer them. *What's the point of all this?*

He was only three successful shots away from victory. *Is this all there is?*

His so-called friends pressed all around him, living vicariously through his every action. *So why do I feel so alone?*

With one last glance at Amy and the cheering crowd, Jake dropped the ball into his own cup and walked toward the exit. Doug stopped him at the doorway. The crowd quieted down, confused. "What's going on? You're killing that guy!" Doug fumed for all to hear. They stood waiting to hear Jake's response.

"I...just can't do this anymore," Jake mumbled.

Doug waved his hand sloppily in front of Jake's face. "Hello? Jake, are you there? What's wrong with you?" He belched, and a whiff of alcohol blew right into Jake's nose. To Doug's right, Amy stood with arms crossed, also waiting for the reply.

Jake shook his head and pushed past Doug into the cool backyard. The fresh air was a welcome relief to his parched lungs, but the sharp temperature shift chilled the sweat on his body. He turned around, beginning to shiver, and threw up his arms in surrender. "I'm done with this!"

"What the HELL?!" Doug exploded, throwing his beer to the concrete. It sprayed everywhere.

Jake looked apologetically at Amy, then walked resolutely away. He could hear the insults and speculations rumbling behind him, but there was nothing he could do about that now. He kept marching back to his truck, somewhat astonished at his own boldness. *What did I just do?* he marveled.

His truck, parked illegally at the front of the driveway, stuck out several feet into the street. Jake pulled his keys out of his pocket and, with great focus, shoved the correct one into the door. He pulled it open and collapsed into the driver's seat, knowing he shouldn't drive, but how could he stay there? *Why is all of this bugging me now?* Carefully aligning the key with the ignition, Jake prepared to turn the engine over when a loud pounding on the passenger window startled him, and he dropped his keys on the floor. Amy was staring right at him, her face pressed to the cold glass.

"What do you think you're doing?" she yelled.

Jake stretched his uncooperative body to open the passenger-side door. *This truck has turned into drama central,* he mused, as he watched Amy slide in, her high heels nearly tripping her on the floorboard.

"I asked you a question," she insisted.

Jake fumbled for a reasonable explanation for his erratic behavior, but his brain was covered in clouds. There was no point hiding the truth any longer, especially from Amy. "I left because..." he faltered.

"Because...?" Amy tried to help him finish.

Jake finally gave up. "Because I want to give Jesus a fair shot," he muttered, embarrassed.

Amy laughed, spraying a mouthful of beer she had just sipped all over the dashboard and front window. "Sorry," she snorted, wiping off a few drops with her hand.

Jake ignored the mess. "I just kind of need to do this," he said, delicately taking the can out of Amy's hand and placing it in the cup holder. He hoped it would help her listen.

"So you're a Christian?!" Amy questioned with a look of disgust Jake had rarely seen from her. Another teenage couple staggered by, prompting both Jake and Amy to remain silent until they passed. The flickering streetlight cast shadows on Amy's face, betraying her confusion.

"No. I'm just checking stuff out," Jake corrected as he felt for his dropped keys along the dark floor.

Amy shook her head. "Don't you think you're rushing into this?" She reached over to Jake's side of the cab and fished up his keys in one swoop.

Jake agreed—he probably was rushing into it—but what was he supposed to do? Let life just keep pushing him along the brink of meaninglessness? Plus, he badly needed answers.

"No. Maybe. I just...know I need to do this." Jake translated his thoughts.

"Can't you check it out but still be the same Jake?" Amy's voice had softened, and she tenderly placed the keys in his open palm, allowing her hand to remain in his for an extra moment.

Jake wished it was that easy, but that's what he had tried to do tonight, and it had definitely not worked. He pulled his hand away and looked straight ahead. "What?" he frowned. "The same Jake who can put a ping-pong ball in a keg cup? What is that? I'm not sure I even like that Jake."

Amy grabbed his chin and turned it to face her. "But that's the Jake I fell in love with! That's the Jake I am following to Louisville. That's the Jake I want to spend the rest of my life with!"

Jake looked helplessly back at her, desperate but determined. She let go of his chin and scooted away from him to the opposite side of the bench seat. "I know what's going on." She crossed her arms. "This is still about your 'friend.'"

Her three-dimensional silhouette blinked with the broken street light. Jake rested his back against his door to face her. "Maybe it is. I don't know," he responded softly.

Amy bent forward and rested her hands on his knees. "It wasn't your fault, Jake," she insisted. "You didn't pull the trigger!"

The guilt Jake had been carrying around the past few weeks broke through, and he banged his fist hard against the steering wheel. "Why do people gotta keep saying that? You don't listen anymore! I know I didn't kill him! I know I didn't tell him to bring a gun to school. I know I didn't do anything!"

Amy looked at Jake in the darkness, then tenderly reached over and rubbed his knee. "None of us did," she whispered.

"That's my point!" Jake jerked his head to look out his window, turning away from Amy and the flickering light. "Why didn't I?" Muffled rock music blared outside, and a shrill cheer went up from the house's backyard.

"Jake," Amy whispered.

He didn't move, lost in thought, his gaze fixed on a lighted fountain in front of a house halfway down the street. Amy opened her door and stumbled to the ground. Kicking off her high heels, she reeled around the front of the truck and opened Jake's door. She rested one hand on the metal frame and rubbed his back with the other.

"Jake, you're the captain of the basketball team. You're getting ready to graduate. You have a girlfriend...You're busy."

"He saved my life," Jake said bluntly, without looking at her.

"Excuse me?"

Jake breathed deeply and looked into his lap. "When we were in sixth grade. He pushed me out of the way of a car and took the hit himself." Each word felt like a confession to treason. *What kind of jerk turns his back on someone who saved his life?* What would Amy think of him now? In their three-year relationship, he had never felt more vulnerable, and he gripped the steering wheel to brace himself.

"Is that what this is about?" Amy retorted casually, as if what he had just copped to wasn't really that big a deal.

"What?" Now Jake was confused. *Did she even hear what I just said?*

"He saved your life. So, like, you owed him or something?" Amy asked.

The dark clouds rolled back into Jake's mind as he attempted to make sense of Amy's response. *Did she miss the part where I told her Roger SAVED my LIFE?* What was wrong with her? "What if I hadn't ignored him?" Jake defended himself. "Could I have saved him?"

"Look, Jake, I know this is tough, but you've got to let it go. There is nothing you can do to bring him back." She slid her arm around his shoulders and rested her forehead against his. "I'm sorry you feel this way, but I think you're overreacting."

"Overreacting?" Jake erupted, pulling away to look her in the eyes. "Did you hear anything I just said? He's dead, Amy, and I could have done something about it!"

"Don't try to turn this on me, Jake. If it's so important to you, then why am I just hearing about it right now? We've dated for over three years!" Her irritation melted into worry, and she dropped her head. "I feel like I don't even know you anymore."

Jake had to admit he wasn't sure how well he knew himself lately. What could he say? That's what he was trying to figure out. He went for broke: "You want to go to church with me sometime?"

Amy jerked her head up and stared at Jake. "Seriously?!"

AN HOUR LATER, Jake ambled into his bedroom, unsure of everything. Jake had attempted to explain his conversation with Chris to Amy, but the more he shared, the more she just stared blankly at him. Amy had a 4.2 GPA and all honors classes, but she looked at him like he was speaking gibberish, and just raised her eyebrows and smirked. She repeatedly said she wasn't mad at him, but he could see it in her eyes: She felt betrayed, and it made Jake feel even worse.

He flopped on his bed, still smelling of alcohol and Amy's perfume. She'd told him she'd find a ride with someone else because she wasn't ready to go home. And as he'd watched her walk back toward the party without him, he could almost feel their lives slowly ripping apart.

Too awake to sleep, but his mind a little too drunk to concentrate, Jake got up from the bed and sat down at his computer. He surfed the Internet, not looking for anything in particular. With no new sports scores to interest him, he signed into his MySpace page. He moved the cursor to the Search box, typing in a name like he had done a million times before. But he typed a different name than usual: *Roger Dawson.*

That now-familiar pounding of his heart started up again as he clicked Search. He stared feverishly at the screen, which cast a pale, eerie glow on his hands. Jake wondered who his childhood friend had become while he wasn't looking, and how he had gotten to the place where suicide was his only option.

A list of seven "Roger Dawsons" popped up on the screen. Jake read them aloud under his breath as he scrolled slowly down the page. Then, the third one from the bottom stopped him cold: The accompanying face was unmistakable. Roger stared back at Jake from the icon, his eyes lasers boring deep into Jake's soul. The hair on Jake's arms immediately stood up straight, and his heels began to tap against the floor. A cold sweat beaded on his forehead and down his back.

Jake double-clicked on Roger's picture and waited nervously for the page to open, desperately hoping it wasn't set to Private. Even safe in the confines of his own bedroom, Jake felt like he was sneaking through Roger's house. Jake glanced over his shoulder and around the room, just to confirm he was completely alone. He checked the time at his bedside clock; it was 1:04. He stared at the clock for what seemed like forever, waiting for the numbers to move to 1:05, but they would not budge. His heart thumped against the walls of his chest, raging to be free from its agonizing cage of guilt.

The screen turned black, and Roger's page opened. At first glance, there was nothing overly sinister about the page, but that was just the problem: There was *nothing*. Like a yearbook without any signatures, the page was virtually devoid of human interaction.

Jake clicked on Roger's pictures and found three. One was of Roger with his little sister Rudie at some formal event. They both appeared to be happy enough. *What happened?* In the next photo, Roger was sullenly flipping burgers on a barbecue. In the last one, he was glaring at the camera from a couch. Jake tried to remember Roger's face from the countless times they had passed as strangers in the hall, but his memory was blank. How many times had those hurt-filled eyes stared at him, pleading with him for help, and he had walked blindly on by? Jake groaned, banging his head on the edge of his desk.

He clicked on Roger's profile, wondering what he'd find.

Roger's Details	
Status:	Call me anytime
Here for:	Friends
Orientation:	Straight as a board
Hometown:	O-side
Body type:	Sizzling
Ethnicity:	I'm a brotha
Religion:	Searching
Zodiac Sign:	Taurus
Best Friends:	
Children:	I'm only 17!
Education:	Senior in High School
Occupation:	Artist

As he read down the column, Jake smiled at the glimpses of Roger's old, clever charm leaking onto the screen. But it was cut short by the one empty box, a void that even Roger's humor couldn't find a way to fill. The space swallowed Jake's breath as he contemplated the weight of it. *If Roger had found a name to put in that box, would he be alive today?* Jake wished more than anything that he could go back in time and get a second chance, an opportunity to do the things that would have put his name in that empty box.

With hands now trembling, Jake clicked back to the comments to see what other classmates had to say. After such a tragic event, there was sure to be a myriad of notes from mournful classmates. Even if they didn't know him, he had walked their halls and sat in their classes. If nothing else, didn't they at least have something *nasty* to say about the school shooter? Jake scrolled down to the bottom of the page. There was nothing.

Jake glanced at Roger's list of friends. Even though Jake didn't spend a lot of time on MySpace, he had hundreds of acquaintances. In Roger's box, there were only three. A photo of one of them, "Jonny Boy," looked familiar, but Jake couldn't figure out why. The other two were girls that Jake was pretty sure he'd never seen before.

Underneath his nearly empty Friend box, Roger had uploaded some of his artwork. One in particular grabbed Jake in a chokehold. It was a picture of an anguished man reaching up in desperation as his body sunk into the concrete sidewalk below.

What did it mean? *Was that how Roger felt?* Jake could only imagine how much that represented Roger's existence, and nobody had lent a helping hand to pull him out. Jake continued to scroll down past several other disturbing drawings, all with themes of despair or crushing hopelessness.

With one last surge, Jake scanned back to the top of the page to see if Roger had posted any blogs. The most recent entry was dated February 17, the day before the shooting. Jake's head started throbbing. *Is this what I think it is?* No one had visited the site in the past three weeks, and Jake realized he would be the first person to read his former best friend's suicide note.

His stomach started lurching, and he stumbled to the bathroom, hoping his mom wouldn't hear and come check on him. Tears mixed with vomit in the toilet bowl. Afterward, Jake just lay there on the bathroom floor, paralyzed and drowning in his own anguish. He wasn't sure he ever wanted to get up. Was there any way to just move on with his life and pretend like none of this ever happened?

After about ten minutes, Jake took several deep breaths and reluctantly returned to his room. Through blurred vision, he focused on the screen and began to read Roger's last words.

Roger's Blog

Last Updated:

2/17

Send Message
Instant Message
Email to a Friend
Subscribe

Date: 2/17   **Current mood:**

I feel so alone, like I'm the only person in the world who feels this way, and it doesn't even matter. It's not important.

Maybe because I'm not important.

I'm screaming out, doing everything I can do to be heard, yet even silence is louder than my screams.

What can I do to be heard, other than

   tear down this world,

      break apart my life,

DIE?

Sometimes I wonder whether or not I'm becoming more alive or dying. Sometimes I wonder if there is any difference.

Desperation is worse than frustration.

   Is living worse than dying?

      Is screaming worse than my crying?

If I break apart this world around me, maybe people will start to understand. I just want somebody to think I'm not crazy, somebody to understand and to listen to me and not get angry that I'm not content, because I'm not.

I'm not happy.

I feel like I'm trapped in a life that doesn't want me, in a world where I'm so completely different. I can't ever fit in or be understood. I can scream as loud as I want, but the screams will always fade away because no one really knows how to listen.

Maybe this will show them.

The gunshot of that fateful day echoed in Jake's mind as he read the last line over and over in his head. Guilt-ridden questions begged for answers: *Who is "them"?* Was it the entire school, or was it referring to a particular group—or a particular person? *Why did Roger choose Senior Hall of all places to make his last stand?* He surely must have known it was where Jake hung out before school. *Was it a coincidence that I was standing closest to Roger when he raised the gun to his head?* Or was the whole thing a blatant message to his friend-turned-jock who was to blame? Just the thought sent chills throughout Jake's whole body. He reached over and yanked his comforter off the bed, wrapping it around his shivering back. Jake imagined the intense anguish it took to write this. *Why couldn't someone have reached out before it was too late?*

Jake pounded his fist on the desk and growled, "Damn it, man! Why didn't you tell me?" But Jake knew very well why Roger hadn't come to him. Years earlier, Jake had made it as clear as glass that they were no longer friends. How many times had Roger tried to approach him? How many times had Jake been too cool to notice? Jake stared at the lonely picture of Roger at the top of the page, then stared at his own faint reflection in the computer screen.

"I'm sorry, Roger," he whispered, tears streaming down his cheeks.

He clicked back to Roger's three friends again, jotting down their names on a pad of paper: Cara Mervin, Sarah Sooners, and Jonny Garcia. He was sure he'd seen the last guy, but he couldn't place the face, and his mind was already overloaded with questions. The transition from being drunk to hung-over was shifting into a major headache. He slumped into bed, committing to keep his eyes open for "Jonny Boy" at school next week. If Jake could find him, maybe he could get some more answers.

19

TWO WEEKS LATER, Jake and Amy strolled hand-in-hand into the New Song Church front lobby. While Jake was obviously excited to have Amy with him, there was also a certain nervousness that accompanied her presence. Her phone call yesterday afternoon saying she would go had nearly knocked him off the kitchen stool. But she had made one thing clear: She would agree to come once, and after that she was promising nothing. As they turned the corner toward the youth room, Jake's palms were drenched with sweat. He knew a lot was riding on the next hour.

Another cause for his discomfort was Amy's apparel. Compared to the party two weeks ago, she was modestly dressed, but as they walked through the lobby, Jake was painfully aware of how much skin she was exposing. Her thigh-length skirt could have been shorter, but she had paired it with five-inch heels. And while her pink top covered most of her, it was sheer enough to grab any guy's eye. Jake knew New Song was casual enough, but he would rather not draw any extra attention. When he picked her up, he had debated asking her to throw on a sweater (because it might be cold), but the 80-degree morn-

ing squelched that idea, and he knew that one wrong remark could negate the whole deal. So he kept his mouth shut and just hoped people would keep their eyes up.

Jake had also tried to explain to Amy that fashionably late did not have the same effect here. But Amy was accustomed to making an entrance, so the two of them arrived a good twenty minutes into the service. Jake sighed in frustration, but he had to admit that he had yet to arrive on time on his own. As they approached, Chris' voice echoed warmly down the hallway, followed by a chorus of laughter.

They opened the brown double-doors into the back of the room, and Jake instinctively dropped Amy's hand. The musty smell of the old youth room greeted them, and Amy covered her face. It had rained the day before, and apparently there were leaks in the roof.

They walked past the portrait of Roger hanging inside the doorway, and Jake felt the twinge of remorse he was growing so accustomed to. Amy didn't even seem to notice the picture and instead scanned the room for familiar faces. The room was mostly full, like the week before, but they found two seats in the back row. Jake spotted Andrea in the front, sitting next to the kid who liked moms. Out of the corner of his eye, he saw Danny and Kelsi slouched comfortably on the back couch, more absorbed in each other than anything around them. No one seemed to notice Jake and Amy, which was okay with Jake.

The more Amy looked around, the more she appeared self-conscious. She pulled the top of her blouse up toward her neck, fixing the cleavage problem, but now it showed a little tummy. She gave the blouse another little tug down, pulling it right back to where it had been before. She crossed her arms over her chest and drew closer to Jake. "I think I'm underdressed," she whispered in his ear.

Jake had never seen Amy so fidgety about her appearance before. It was as if she had shown up in the wrong costume to the wrong party. "Don't worry, you're fine," he assured her without even glancing in her direction as he guided them to a couple of empty seats. Chris and another student were pulling a table covered by a red sheet onto the stage, while Chris rambled on about some trip to Mexico coming up.

Amy clutched her boyfriend's arm, scooting her body over to the edge of her seat, almost joining Jake on his chair. She tucked her feet under her chair and subtly tugged down on her skirt. She checked her watch for the fifth time and sighed loudly.

"You look beautiful," Jake tried to comfort her, afraid this morning was like a semi headed the wrong way on a one-way street. Telling her she was beautiful had gotten him out of so many sticky situations in the past, but it was having no effect now. He leaned forward, trying to figure out what the heck Chris was so excited about.

Chris pulled four chairs onto the stage. "Okay, okay. I'm gonna need four volunteers," he announced, pacing back and forth across the stage. He stopped in the middle and did one last sweep of the room, smiling briefly when his eyes met Jake's. "This game will test your manhood, your determination, and just your sheer insanity." Chris pointed to four eager freshman boys with hands frantically waving. "Matt, Arona, CJ, Mudge." As he called their names, Chris directed each to a different seat behind the cloaked table.

Turning to watch the volunteers, several students suddenly noticed Jake and Amy. One girl nudged her friend, and they rolled their eyes and giggled after scanning Amy's outfit. Another whispered with a sneer to the girl sitting next to her. A couple guys let their eyes rove shamelessly, until they caught Jake staring them down. Amy shifted slightly, her eyes locked on the action ahead, and her body tensed still further.

On stage, two of the boys beat their chests wildly, eliciting a roar from the group. Jake sat back, relieved to let someone else take the spotlight and hoping Amy wouldn't check out yet.

Chris continued. "This is a race to see who can chug—a can of soda, that is—the fastest."

He whipped off the red sheet draped over the table, revealing four cans of soda. Jake laughed to himself: They were going to have a chugging competition at church! Maybe Amy would

get more comfortable now. The competitors, along with most of the room, groaned in underwhelmed disappointment. Apparently this was a feeble challenge compared to the normal stunts Chris liked to pull.

Chris continued unfazed, growling into the microphone. "On your marks! Get set! Oh no! I forgot one of the rules."

The four boys sat frozen with their sodas only inches from their mouths.

"I'm going to need each of you guys to take one of your socks off and place it over the can," Chris laughed, clapping his hands.

As expected, the crowd erupted—many gasped, others cheered, and a few shook their heads in disgust. Jake hollered support from the back row as the boys cloaked their cans with grimy socks.

Amy's response could not have been more opposite. She rolled her eyes and looked nauseous, as if someone had asked her to drink through a dirty sock. Jake laughed and placed his hand protectively over her eyes. He wrapped his other arm around her shoulders. She seemed to relax a little, and Jake's smile widened.

With the competitors back in position, their faces slightly less eager, Chris started the countdown again. "On your marks! Get set! Oh, wait!" Chris raised his pointer finger in the air, grinning broadly as he looked around the room to increase the tension. "I forgot to tell you the last rule," he whispered.

A stunned silence blanketed the room as Chris turned to his four white-faced volunteers. Chris dropped the last rule like a rock: "Pass your can one person to the left!" he shouted into the mic. Gasps, cheers, and uncontrollable laughter greeted the boys as they reluctantly exchanged cans like dirty diapers.

"Go!" Chris yelled before they had the chance to think too long. Music from the movie *Rocky* began to play perfectly on cue. The smallest of the four volunteers pinched his nose and tore into his soda, sucking the lukewarm carbonation through the dingy threads of his neighbor's sock. Not to be outdone, the other three began gulping down the nastiness with abandon, to the squeals of the audience. Their heads stretched back like pelicans, their necks flowing with soda suds and their throats pulsing up and down, up and down.

In the front row, Andrea turned away in disgust and spotted Jake and Amy. She jumped up and approached them, smiling from ear to ear. "You made it!" Andrea greeted them both, giving Jake a firm side-hug.

"Andrea, this is Amy," Jake responded awkwardly. He tried to not look overly enthusiastic.

On Andrea's wrist was a whole new collection of bracelets that discordantly complemented her bright tie-dyed T-shirt. Andrea reached out her jingling hand to Amy, who responded with a half-smile and weak hand.

"I'm really glad both of you could join us," Andrea beamed.

Amy put her arm around Jake possessively and scowled, "I told my boyfriend I'd check it out."

"That's cool." Andrea smiled awkwardly, her peppy personality somewhat dimmed.

The sound of aluminum slamming against the table broke the tension, and they all turned quickly to see Chris raise the little guy's hand in victory. The others dropped their cans as awareness of their futile efforts sank in. A clean-up crew quickly stepped in to remove the table and chairs, and before long the stage was back to normal, ready for the student-led band to take their place. The drummer went straight to work on his kick-drum, sending out a beat that got the audience on its feet.

"Oh my gosh, I gotta go...I'm so glad you're here." Andrea smiled, her eyes locking on Jake one last time before she turned to hurry on stage. Amy grabbed her arm before she could get away and whispered in her ear. Jake couldn't hear what was said, but Andrea's smile quickly drooped and her eyes rimmed with tears. She nodded uneasily and rushed onto the stage, despite looking a bit shaken.

"What did you say to her?" Jake snapped.

"Nice to meet you," Amy smirked, grabbing Jake's hand and pulling it up to her mouth to kiss it. He pulled his hand away and stood up with the rest of the room as the band rocked out to some upbeat song. Out of the corner of his eye, he noticed Danny slip out, probably for his donut fix or who knows what else.

Everyone clapped their hands with the beat, which Jake found a little weird, but he joined in, if for no other reason than to show Amy that he was really serious about this thing. He glanced back at her, still seated with her arms crossed over her chest, insolently staring at the chair in front of her. Jake felt the muscles in his neck and back tighten in irritation, but he focused on the lyrics on the screen above the band, trying not to let Amy's silent tantrum affect him. He read the words everyone was singing:

"Send me, but not without your power, Lord,
Teach me, 'cuz I can't do this on my own.
Use me in any way you want to use me.
Send me, don't let me leave without your power."

Jake wasn't sure he knew what they meant, but they sounded okay. He was intrigued by this habit the church kids had of closing their eyes and lifting up their arms while they sang. Not everyone did it, but Andrea sure did with gusto. It seemed peculiar, but then again, it really wasn't much different than some of the concerts he'd been to. And Andrea looked so peaceful and happy while she belted the words into the mic. Kelsi did the raised-hand thing too, but it looked like more of an act coming from her.

All at once, Amy stood up from her seat, her transparent top rubbing against Jake's arm. She leaned over and spoke into his ear, "That girl on the right is a pothead." She nodded toward Kelsi and smiled for the first time that morning. Amy seemed pleased with herself.

Jake thought about Kelsi from two weeks ago, completely wasted and flaunting Jesus as her "homeboy." *How does she live with herself? Does Chris know about her double life? How many more of the students here are just pretending?* But even with all his questions, Jake knew Chris' faith was the real deal, and he was pretty sure the same was true with Andrea. And besides, who was he to judge? The last thing he wanted to do was give Amy another reason to criticize. He decided not to affirm or deny anything; he just shrugged his shoulders and stayed focused on his clap.

Danny Rivers strolled back in, propelled by the firm hand of his dad, Pastor Mark. Danny clearly would rather be anywhere but here. Jake couldn't help feeling a little sorry for the guy—what must it be like to be the pastor's kid? Jake's relationship with his own father was hard enough, but at least his dad gave him space. Maybe Danny's "extracurricular activities" were his way of maintaining some form of control over his life, sort of like why Jake chose Louisville.

Jake discreetly watched Pastor Mark, trying to get a read on him. The pastor scanned the room, appearing to count the number of students in attendance. His smile wasn't really much more than a slight upturning of the mouth. And it transformed quickly into a frown the moment he saw Amy. Jake instinctively averted his eyes, but in his peripheral vision, he saw the pastor shake his head in obvious disapproval.

Danny's eyes also lingered on Amy, but definitely not in disapproval. Pastor Mark caught his son in the middle of his gaze and gave him an elbow to the stomach. Far from remorseful, Danny winked at his dad and sauntered along the back wall until he plopped himself on the grubby couch. Jake secretly wished the couch would swallow him whole.

Jake put his arm around Amy's shoulders. Her eyes focused ahead, mesmerized by something on stage. He followed her line of sight to the plastic drum-shield a few feet to the right of Andrea and Kelsi. In its reflection, Pastor Mark's crossed arms and condemning stare could not have been more crystal-clear.

Amy turned to Jake with a pained look. She had had enough. "This is weird. Let's get out of here," she demanded.

As much as Jake wanted to protect her, he still wasn't quite ready to bail—they hadn't made it to the good part yet. Chris was just about to give his speech, and Amy would finally un-

derstand why he wanted to try this whole God-experiment. "What?" Jake pretended he didn't hear.

Amy grabbed her purse and took a step toward the door, but Jake grabbed her arm. She spun around and faced him, her lower lip now trembling.

"Are you going to drive me home?" she quivered.

He could barely hear her broken whisper over the drums. "Not yet," he shouted, trying to infuse compassion over the band. He knew that if Amy left now, she would never come back.

"Fine!" Amy yanked her arm away and stomped toward the exit. Jake looked up at the ceiling in exasperation, then surveyed the room to see if anyone was watching. Everyone seemed focused ahead. He slipped out of the room and jogged around the corner after Amy.

She was already halfway through the lobby. The bright mid-morning sun poured in through the glass doors so he could only see her brisk silhouette. Fortunately, the service was still in session, so the area was vacant. "Wait...Amy!" Jake called out, sprinting after her. He finally caught her arm near the front door.

She turned to face him, her eyes moist. "Why can't you just take me home?" she begged in a tone mixed with frailty and frustration. She dried her eyes with the back of her wrist.

"No," Jake answered gently. He moved in closer and took both of her hands in his.

"No?" Amy pulled her hands loose and took a step toward the doorway.

"Come on, we just got here," Jake reasoned, taking a step with her. "What's really going on here?"

"I'm not going to let them judge me," Amy snapped, her hand flipping forcefully in the direction of the youth room. A tear escaped and raced down her cheek.

"Who? Nobody's judging you," Jake objected. Even as the words left his mouth, he knew they weren't true.

Amy pointed again to the youth room and shook her head vehemently. "It's either me or them, Jake."

Jake shook his head in disbelief. How could she threaten him like that? He was still trying to figure this whole thing out himself. And he didn't want to choose "them" anyway—it was God he was interested in. She hadn't even given it a full chance! Jake tried to smile and placed his arm tenderly on hers. "Please give it another try. I really want you to meet Chris."

Amy shook her head and looked around the empty room. "Jake," she whispered almost too softly for Jake to hear. "There's something I need to talk to you about." Her voice was weak, and she bit her lip and looked away, brushing at the flood of tears that now threatened to spill.

Jake stepped toward her, slipping his hands around her waist. "What is it?" He cocked his head to look in her eyes.

"I don't feel comfortable telling you here," she answered.

"Can't it wait till after the service?"

Amy shook her head. "I can't."

He dropped his hands from her waist. "Yeah, I'm not falling for that," he scoffed.

She looked at him coldly. "Never mind." Her tone was one Jake had never heard before. She sounded frustrated, fearful, tired, and defeated all at the same time. She reached in and kissed Jake on the cheek, her lips pausing above his skin. She waited a moment, as if mustering up all her strength. "Goodbye, Jake," she whispered.

She turned slowly to leave, head hung low and shoulders slouched. Jake knew the right thing to do was to go after her, but he was so tired of chasing her. *She'll be back*, he reasoned. Still, as he stood there watching her walk away, it felt different—serious, like a part of him was being cut away.

"Amy?" Jake called out feebly.

She kept walking.

20

JAKE JUST STOOD THERE, watching Amy walk away from him and out the church doors, a fading mirage in the glare from the morning sun on the glass. The lobby grew quiet, except for the muffled voice rumbling from inside the auditorium doors. Jake's thoughts whirled, and he couldn't do anything but look around the room, trying to regain a sense of what just happened. He found himself retreating slowly toward the youth room again, away from Amy. A few short weeks ago, it was the strange unknown, but this morning it harkened to him, a safe haven in the midst of his hurricane.

Jake paused at the entrance, the enormity of Amy's exit suddenly hitting him hard. He grabbed a seat on the carpet and leaned against the back wall. A torrent of thoughts besieged his mind: Had he just made the biggest mistake of his life? Was he taking his guilt over Roger out on Amy? Was it too late to run after her?

Chris' voice melded with his thoughts. "...They did a survey to find the places people least like to be. Some of the top responses were the DMV, the dentist, and the principal's office. But you want to know what number one was? Church..."

How would Amy get home? Who would she call? Jake worried. She didn't really have any close girlfriends; she'd neglected those relationships over the years to spend more time with him. Her mom was always too busy, and most of the guys would be too interested in sleep this time of the morning to go out of their way...except Doug.

Doug. Jake suddenly cringed. Doug was his best friend, but Jake couldn't trust him. Jake envisioned Amy pouring her heart out to Doug, making Jake out to be the villain. Of course, Doug would take full advantage of that, especially after their fiasco a few weeks ago. Jake could just picture Doug gently holding Amy as she cried, whispering comforting words in her ear. But Jake knew Doug well: There would be only one thing he'd want to give her, and it wouldn't be heartfelt compassion. Jake clenched his teeth and pressed the back of his head against the wall.

Chris' voice broke in. "...boring, judgmental, hypocritical. We can sometimes be the exact opposite of what the Bible teaches." Chris shook his head, stood up from his stool on the front of the stage, and stared at the audience with passion in his eyes. "That's not how it's supposed to be! This is supposed to be a place where you don't have to pretend like you've got it all together or you've got no problems, where you can be who you really are and not feel judged..."

Jake sat upright and shifted his weight. Once again, it felt like Chris was speaking directly to him, as if he knew his thoughts. Jake wiped his damp palms on his jeans as he listened closer.

"That's not how it was for me, though," Chris continued, lowering his voice to almost a whisper. "I remember my first time at church. I was seventeen years old. My dad was in the military, and we'd just moved for the seventh time in six years. I had given up on the hope of ever making friends: What was the point? We'd just move again. Then out of nowhere, my dad informs us that in our new city, we would be going to church. I told my dad he was wacked...then he whacked me with the back of his hand.

"So I went. For three months, I attended every week. And I felt like a leper. In all my time there, nobody once ever sat next to me or remembered my name or included me in their group..."

Jake pictured Amy sitting there uncomfortably only a few minutes ago, plenty of people looking, but almost no one saying hi.

"Years later, I met Jesus for real from my college roommate. I found out that Jesus went out of His way to hang with the outcasts, the forgotten, the lonely, the rejected. He did everything my church did not. And I swore that if I ever attended a church again, I would make sure we did the exact opposite. So here we are. I know we're not perfect; in fact, I know that we've probably hurt many people along the way. If that's you, I want to say I'm sorry. I'm sorry we haven't shown the real Jesus to you..."

Jake's heart was beating fast again. *Why did Amy have to leave? If she would have heard Chris, she might have just given them a second chance!* Hearing Chris' story made Jake admire him even more. He had experienced so much in his life, but he decided to do something about it. Chris had something that Jake knew he was missing—and he wanted it.

Chris sat back down on the stool. He looked over at the back wall and locked eyes with Jake, as if he'd known he was there all along. "So that's my story, but what about yours?" he asked the group. "We've all been judged. We've all been mistreated. But I want you to take thirty seconds of silence and answer this question: Who have *you* judged, and what are *you* going to do about it?"

Seventy teenage heads bowed in unison, and Jake followed suit. Closing his eyes, he reflected on Chris' challenge. It was easy to point fingers, but he knew there was at least one pointing right back at him. But all he could think about in that moment was Amy. She'd used that exact same word: *judged.* *Could I have done something differently? Did I judge her? What did she mean when she said "goodbye"?*

Then another tormenting flood rushed over Jake. *What about Roger?* Jake had absolutely judged him. That night after the game his freshman year, he had judged him as not cool enough. And he had done it over and over again a hundred times since. What had Roger ever done to him? Yet, what could Jake do about it? *Roger's dead. And it's my fault.*

Accusations pelted Jake's conscience like fireballs, searing his heart. *I deserve to lose Amy. I deserve to lose it all.* He sought to block out the whispers, until he realized they were coming from outside his head.

Crowding into his distressed thoughts, Jake started hearing whispers all around him from different parts of the room. His eyes popped open. There was Chris, still sitting on stage with his eyes closed, taking his own challenge. But around the room, at least a third of the students were casually chatting with their neighbors during this supposedly "silent reflection." Frowning, Jake started to listen in.

"Did you watch the game? I can't stand Jackson!" A kid with shaggy hair that he recognized from school grumbled to an unfamiliar face in the back row.

"Oh my gosh! She won't stop texting me," another kid complained with his cell phone open, typing in a response.

There was no way THIS was what Chris had hoped for. *How can he just sit there on the stage and be mocked like this? What's wrong with these people? Didn't they hear what Chris just said? Am I the only one in the room taking him seriously?*

"He is SO hot!" A brunette girl with freckles snickered much too loudly to her friend seated in the row behind her.

"Are you kidding me?! Gross!" another girl with blonde hair and pimples interrupted.

Jake looked to Chris to stop the nonsense, but his head remained bowed, his chest heaving. On the couch on the other side of the room, Jake watched a small, plastic baggy pass from Danny to Kelsi. She stuffed it in her back pocket and stealthily handed some green bills back. *Is this really happening?*

"Did you see what she was wearing?" a girl laughed to her friends, sitting near where Jake and Amy had been earlier.

A rage seethed inside of Jake that he usually only felt on the basketball court. His blood began to boil, and his eyes darted about the room, glaring at the group of hypocrites. *This is not right, in church or anywhere.* The pounding of his heart grew louder, but not loud enough to drown out the voices. His head felt like it would explode. Cursing under his breath, Jake struggled to contain his rising emotions—his instincts warned him not to make a scene. He looked around the room one more time. *Doesn't anybody care?*

21

"DAMN IT!" Jake yelled out, jumping to his feet.

Seventy startled heads whipped around to stare at him in the back of the room. A deafening silence instantly replaced the undertone of giggling and gossip. Chris finally opened his eyes, seeming as astonished as anyone. Jake narrowed his eyes, shook his head, and pointed accusingly at the group. "Did anyone even hear what he just said?"

The room remained silent. On the couch, Danny sat smirking, more engaged than Jake had ever seen him. At the front of the room, even Chris stood speechless.

Jake quickly began to regret the outburst. He could storm the basketball court any day, where his talent kept the action predictable and his attitude cool and confident. But he was in completely uncharted territory right now, and the idea of just walking out and never looking back crossed his mind. But his feet stayed still, and his mouth kept moving.

"I'm new to this whole church thing, so stop me if I'm sinning or something," he started quietly. "But how the hell are you going to change anything if you can't even get it right

here?" The more the words flowed out, the more passionate he became. "Chris' speech was so true, and like five seconds later you pretend like it never happened."

Jake stopped a second to regroup, then he just kept going. "My girlfriend came today, and left...because she felt *judged*. And nobody even noticed." A few heads lowered at this. Jake turned around and faced Roger's picture. "Roger walked onto our campus and started shooting." Jake walked over and slapped the wall next to the portrait as the students squirmed. "I knew Roger. He wasn't crazy! Has anyone even stopped to ask why? I mean, how did he get to the point where his only option was shooting himself?" Tears stung Jake's eyes, but he ignored them. He noticed two guys from the earlier game, now sitting in the front row without socks. "There are people killing themselves, and you're drinking soda through a sock?"

Chris shifted his weight uncomfortably and crossed his arms. Jake didn't mean for it to be a slam on him, but he was past the point for apologies.

"I mean what's the point of all THIS..." Jake waved his arms emphatically, "...if it doesn't change you? What are you all doing here?"

Jake paused, suddenly exhausted and out of words, but all eyes were still fixated on him. Each passing second felt like an hour while Jake stood motionless, quite sure this would be the last time he'd step foot in this church, or any other for that matter. With nothing left to say or do, he shrugged his shoulders and started toward the door.

Chris' voice didn't let him get any further. "What do you think we should do, Jake?" His voice was remarkably calm, without a trace of anger. Jake had just ruined his service, yet Chris was asking him for advice?

The problem was, Jake had absolutely no idea. After all, who was he to tell them what to do? He was just trying to figure all this out himself. "I don't know," Jake mumbled.

Danny muffled a laugh, but he was met with a flood of scowls from all over the room. Andrea slowly stood up from her front-row seat and faced Jake, addressing the crowd in a soft but hopeful voice. "We could, like, hang out together at school," she volunteered.

The room full of students still did not respond. "Loser!" coughed a female voice from the back. Kelsi sat beside Danny, trying to conceal a grin.

Chris turned his head and shook it in disgust in their direction. Unfazed, they merely averted their eyes.

"That's a great idea!" Jake spoke up again, propelled by Andrea's enthusiasm. "We should all eat lunch together."

Andrea's face beamed. Students started murmuring, and a buzz began to spread. "I'll be there..." Billy responded from the second row, then added with a smile, "...if your mom's coming." Many laughed at the welcome comic relief, and the tension began to dissipate.

"Dude," Jake winked back. "You don't even know her!"

The room erupted as small conversations broke out everywhere, debriefing the crazy last few minutes and chattering about the new lunch plans. Another couple of girls approached Jake and hugged him; one even apologized for not reaching out to Amy. Chris got caught up in a conversation across the room, but when Jake locked eyes with him, he smiled and nodded.

Jake couldn't help but smile a little. *What just happened?* he marveled to himself.

AN HOUR LATER, Jake turned his truck down his driveway. He was little shaken up. *What in the world was I thinking?* It was a big-enough deal just to show up at church, but it looked like he just traded his girlfriend for those people. And if that wasn't enough, now he was going to announce to the whole school that he was one of them—at least, that's what it would look like if he ditched his friends to eat lunch with the church group. And he hadn't just promised to eat lunch with them—he actually came up with the idea! The longer he thought about it, the sicker he felt, which could be an excellent excuse for not showing up the next day. But what would that say about him? He'd just condemned the group for their lack of commitment, and here he was, scheming how to flake out!

He fought his urge to call Amy and tell her what had happened. Maybe it was stubbornness, or maybe it was fear, but whatever it was, his phone stayed safely tucked away in his back pocket. He rolled to a stop, flicked his hair out of his eyes, and pushed himself out of his truck. Maybe an escape with *Madden* would soothe his soul.

Opening the heavy front door, Jake could hear his dad's television tuned to the Lakers game in his office. When his dad wasn't working, he spent his Sundays locked inside his office nursing a six-pack of beer and watching sports. His mom's car wasn't parked in the driveway; she was probably out shopping, a habit she'd picked up to avoid her husband's cranky disposition when his team wasn't winning.

"Kobe Bryant steals the inbound pass and steps back for an uncontested three from downtown..." the announcer squawked as Jake quietly slipped past his dad's office door, avoiding the creaky spots on the floor boards that he'd memorized over the years. The aroma of Budweiser wafted from the office, stinging Jake's nose. While the tangy scent usually whetted his cravings, today it made his head ache. Jake crept halfway up the staircase, thinking he was home free.

"Jake?" Glen Taylor's voice suddenly echoed up the stairs.

Jake knew that tone: His dad had a bone to pick with him. As graduation neared, his dad's speeches had grown more and more frequent. Jake paused only five steps from the top, contemplating his options. He could easily pretend he'd never heard his dad calling, but it would only result in a much longer conversation later. Jake reluctantly retraced his steps and peeped his head into the office door.

Glen Taylor wore his vintage Magic Johnson jersey that he'd kept since the eighties and was already four cans into his six-pack routine. The stench from the alcohol was more intense inside the room, and Jake waved his hand in front of his face to clear the air. Jake was pretty sure his dad knew about his drinking, but they never talked about it. During his sophomore year, Jake had grabbed one of his dad's beers from the fridge while watching a game together, which had prompted a whole lecture series about responsible drinking.

Besides the beer cans and a large bag of pretzels, the office was immaculate. A long row of real-estate books filled the top shelf above a large mahogany desk. The requisite family portrait perched next to a few trophies and plaques on the lower shelf. A 55-inch flat-screen was uncovered from a cabinet on the adjacent wall—it was only brought out during non-business hours. A multi-colored Tiffany lamp stood tall in the corner. And that was it. There were no files strewn about or scratch paper with phone numbers. Everything about Glen Taylor's life was organized. As a result, Jake had learned to keep his room pretty clean, but it never did meet his dad's expectations. In his dad's personal religion, cleanliness was really *higher* than godliness.

"Hey Dad, what's the score?"

"Lakers are up twenty-three." Jake's dad replied with a slight slur and leaned back in his chair to get the last few drops out of the can.

"Awesome! Well, I'm going to go get my homework done," Jake lied, trying to avoid the ever-popular homework speech.

"You want to watch the game?" Glen nudged the bag of pretzels in Jake's direction. "I think there are a few Cokes left in the fridge."

As much as his dad could be a jerk, Jake always found himself agreeing to the infrequent invitations to spend time together. "Sure," Jake shrugged and plopped down in a chair. He reached over and grabbed a handful of pretzels, making sure not to make a mess on the expensive rug.

Glen pressed Mute on his remote and turned his attention from the game to face his son. Jake knew that the Mute button was never a good thing. They would not be watching the game: this was a setup. Jake begrudgingly turned to face his dad, slowly munching down on a pretzel as he awaited the lecture.

"Your mom said you went to church again?" Glen said, seeming calm.

Jake nonchalantly nodded his head, not really sure what his dad was getting at. He leaned back in the leather chair, accidently dropping a pretzel in his lap. His dad didn't seem to notice.

"That's twice this week, isn't it?" his dad probed, still calm, but making it sound more like an accusation.

Jake wasn't fooled by his dad's leading questions, but he really didn't want to get into it. Not now. If he couldn't explain the thoughts going through his head lately to Amy, there was no way he'd even attempt it with his dad. Everything was black and white with Glen Taylor. The slightest hint that Jake was pursuing a relationship with God would get him the label of a religious fanatic, and that was the last thing Jake needed.

Jake picked up the dropped pretzel from his lap and popped it in his mouth. "The other time was youth group," he clarified. He was pretty sure the man had not set foot in a church once in the past few decades, maybe not even since his wedding.

Glen leaned back in his chair, arms folded behind his head. With one eye on the muted Lakers and the other on his son, he was trying to appear casual, but Jake had learned long ago that this was never the case. His dad had a deep-seated opinion about every little detail of his life. How much time was he spending on homework? Was he eating right? Where did he buy gas and how much did he pay? What kind of haircut did he get?

"Son, I've got nothing against a little religion, but are you sure you have time for this?"

"Time?" Jake couldn't believe his ears. Was the king of misplaced priorities lecturing him on how he used *his* time? Jake popped another handful of pretzels into his mouth to stifle any inappropriate retorts.

Glen grabbed Budweiser number five and took a healthy chug. "It's your senior year," he drawled, as if Jake didn't know. "Louisville could still take your scholarship away if your grades are bad. Are you hitting the books?" He set the can on the desk and again leaned backward in his chair with his hands behind his head.

The scent of his dad's new beer mixed with the salty residue in his mouth, and all of a sudden Jake felt thirsty. He glanced at the final can sitting peacefully on the edge of the desk, and it tempted him. It was almost as if it all was part of his dad's plan. But Jake snapped himself out of his momentary lapse and tried to look casually at his father.

"Of course, Dad." Jake placed his hands on the arm-rests, hoping this was the end of it.

"Don't slack off, son," Glen warned. His pulled his arms from behind his head and rested his elbows on the desk. He leaned toward Jake so that their eyes locked. "You got to work hard to be successful. This is what separates the good from the great." He glanced around the room, as if to imply that his fancy home office and flat-screen demonstrated his point.

The intensity in his eyes made Jake momentarily ignore the nasty stench of beer-breath. "You got your whole life ahead of you, son. Don't screw it all up." Glen kept his eyes on Jake for an added second, and then leaned back in his chair again and turned the volume back up. Jake had apparently served his purpose, and his dad could go back to the game having done his fatherly duty.

Jake had heard this don't-screw-it-all-up speech at least once a week since junior high, and he hated it. Who did his dad think he was? He shook his head and laughed inside, ready to retreat to the safety of his bedroom.

"Don't worry, Dad, I'm not going to disappoint you." He gave his dad two thumbs-up. Glen faintly nodded in acknowledgement with both eyes glued to the flat-screen.

The announcer screamed in excitement, "The Kings are on an 11-0 run and with 2:03 to play, it's anybody's game." Glen leaned forward, finishing off Budweiser number five. He instinctively reached for number six as Jake backed out of the room.

"Good talk," Jake mumbled as he headed back up the stairs.

23

LATELY FOR CHRIS, Sundays had felt like they were blurring into insignificant monotony, like passing telephone poles along an empty highway on a Midwest road trip. This week on Saturday morning, Chris begged God to liven things up with something unexpected—and He'd done that all right. "That's just how God is—you never know what He is going to do next," Chris explained to anybody who would listen.

Cari had heard the retelling of the story the most. She'd missed that service, taking her once-a-month turn helping out in the church nursery. But by Monday morning, she could describe it as if she'd been right there. Cari had been Chris' sounding board all through their marriage, for the good and the bad. Recently, it had been more ranting and complaining about the state of the church and the apathy of his students than excitement. Chris would sometimes apologize for dumping so much junk on her, but he was just never good at keeping things in. Cari knew his biggest secrets and occasionally reminded him that she had enough dirt on him to bury a corpse.

Just the week before, they had stayed up together until one in the morning, debating whether Chris was still called to

youth ministry. As he entered his thirties, the students seemed to get younger and younger, and his patience was growing shorter and shorter. But yesterday morning was different. No matter how hard he tried, he couldn't stop retelling Cari every detail of the service: how the new kid had stood up and called out his youth group right to their faces; how Chris had, right at that moment, prayed that God would somehow grab their hearts and minds; how over a dozen students had actually agreed to eat lunch together at school. "It's just like in the book of Acts!" Chris had burst out loud at three in the morning, waking Cari from her cherished sleep. She tried to sound annoyed, but Chris caught her smiling as she whispered, "I kind of miss the telephone poles," and faded back to sleep.

Chris was still singing as he entered the church offices for an unscheduled meeting with Mark. He thought maybe Mark had heard the good news and wanted to congratulate him or, even better, ask for advice. He sauntered past Mark's secretary, Ruth, who had worked for Mark since he'd started over a decade ago.

Chris held out his fist to the sixty-year-old assistant. "Give me a pound, Ruth," he kidded as she knocked knuckles and gave him a wink.

He strolled cheerfully into Mark's large corner office, where his boss greeted him from behind a massive oak desk. Mark's office resembled a library more than a place of work. Three of the four walls were covered with hundreds of books that Mark had picked up over his last twenty-five years in full-time ministry. Chris had often borrowed some of them and appreciated the freedom to treat the library as his own.

"Come in. Have a seat," the graying pastor greeted him with an unmistakable edge.

"Everything okay?" Chris inquired, sitting in the padded black leather chair that always made him feel like he was in a counseling session. He didn't think it was intentional, but the chair was slightly shorter than Mark's and always left Chris feeling like he was a step down. He straightened his back posture to make up some of the difference.

Mark leaned forward. "Tell me about yesterday."

So Mark did hear about yesterday. Chris eagerly broke into a fresh recap, an unstoppable smile spreading across his face. "It was amazing. I've never seen anything like it. This new student—"

"Jacob Taylor?" Mark interrupted, staring back blankly. Chris' smile was apparently not contagious.

Unabashed, Chris continued, telling the story the only way he knew how. "Yeah, Jake. He just—"

Mark interrupted again. "My son informed me that this Jake stood up in the middle of the service and was cursing at everybody." He leaned back in his chair and stroked his prickly goatee.

"What?!" Chris reacted. *How could anyone ever describe it like that?* He had completely missed the point. Chris scooted forward in his seat and insisted, "No. I mean, that wasn't the—"

"So he didn't curse?" Mark asked, his dark blue eyes staring down at Chris from his elevated perch.

Chris exhaled sharply. He and Mark had not always seen eye to eye, but this was outrageous. He began to stand up, but caught himself, praying it was just a misunderstanding. "I don't know, he might have used an inappropriate word or two, but that's not—"

Mark had interrupted all of Chris' other sentences, so he almost expected it this time. "So you're saying students can jump up and curse all they want, and it's okay?" Mark put his elbows on the desk in front of him and waited.

A few choice words came to mind that Chris knew would make Jake's outburst seem frivolous, but he bit his tongue. If he could handle his three-year-old's behavior, surely he could cope with this. He leaned on his right arm and savored a long inhale to ensure he wouldn't say something he'd regret.

"No, of course not," Chris conceded, "but it was his second time here. He doesn't know any better." *I can't believe I'm making excuses for Jake's behavior,* Chris thought. They should be

taking notes about what this kid had pulled off. Besides, Chris was certain he'd heard Danny spout off much worse more than once. Of course, that kind of rebuttal would only raise the stakes, and right now Chris just wanted to get out of the conversation without losing his cool.

"Which is why I wanted to meet." Mark flashed his first smile of the morning. Chris had seen that very same smile dispersed to thousands of people in the church over the years. It *seemed* so genuine. "I'm not upset," Mark reassured. "But our church is not doing well financially, and the last thing we need is families leaving."

Chris tried to nod like he understood, but inside he was shaking his head vehemently. He slouched back in his chair. Clearly, sitting up straight was not going to bring Chris to Mark's "level" today.

Mark continued, "I'm sure this Jake is a passionate kid. I love that. But could you inform him that while this kind of behavior might be normal in the locker room, it's not okay at church?" The pastor leaned back and folded his arms across his chest, indicating that he was done with the conversation.

Chris didn't mean to be a punk, but he couldn't help himself. He chuckled a little too loudly and placed his fingers on the edge of the oak desk. "You know, maybe we shouldn't let any kids come who aren't perfect."

Mark's furrowed his eyebrows and pursed his lips, but did not dignify the comment with a response. Chris dejectedly pulled himself up from the leather chair and glared into the eyes of his boss. "Have a nice day," he growled, knowing his was ruined.

THE SUNNY BLUE SKY that normally blasted through the fog by noon time over Pacific High hid its face Monday. Dark grey clouds hung pregnant and ready to burst all over the beachside school. Jake wouldn't have minded. A drenched quad would mean no meeting place for the church lunch group that Jake had been dreading from the moment he walked on campus. But the clouds stubbornly held tight, not even giving up a few drops.

The lunch bell rang, and students flowed out of their classes like streams of lava finding paths of least resistance. Jake let himself be swept away in the melee, his turbulent feelings mirroring the troubled storm clouds overhead.

He'd already experienced a taste of what was to come. During the ten-minute break between second and third periods, he'd informed Doug that he would not be at their normal lunch spot. His hopes of Doug accepting the news without a second thought had flopped miserably. After several minutes of prodding, Jake finally admitted to his lunch plans in the quad and even invited Doug to join them. But Doug went ballistic. If his outraged response was any indication of what was to come, then Jake knew he had a long day ahead of him.

Adding salt to the wound, Doug had also jeered at what an idiot he was for breaking up with Amy. *As if he cared.* Jake knew he should have called her last night. But they had dated long enough for him to know that, in a few days, things would blow over. Besides, he was in no state of mind to listen to her yell at him. *Why not let her cool off a little?* he figured.

Jake turned the corner around the B-Wing and caught his first glimpse of the lunch spot. Pacific High was laid out like an outdoor amphitheatre. The gym and athletic fields were at the north end of campus; the administration offices were to the east. Senior Hall connected them to the educational buildings fanning out to the south and west. At the center was a circular walkway that wound around the entire school.

Inside this loop, the quad was broken in two. On the north end was a grassy area that sloped down to an outdoor stage. This hill was where Jake's friends usually spent their half-hour of freedom each day. On the south end was the cafeteria and concrete lunch area, where Jake had spotted Andrea the week before.

After Jake's fiery challenge to the kids at church yesterday, several of them had decided (at Andrea's suggestion) on the perfect lunch spot: right smack in the middle of the quad. While it had seemed like a good idea at the time, Jake was now questioning his sanity. Routine was so nice—like a comfortable pair of boxers. So why did he suddenly need to mix things up so much?

A few pimple-faced freshman boys meandered by him, laughing about something they'd seen on television the night before. The boy closest to Jake held a Styrofoam lunch tray that smelled like imitation lasagna. Jake watched them walk toward the picnic tables, seemingly without a care in the world, and he longed to exchange places with them. How convenient it would be not to worry about what people think or about upholding your reputation!

As the human stream propelled him forward, Jake considered the possibility of fleeing lunch altogether and finding a hideout in his truck. A little solitude didn't sound so bad right now, considering the options. But that probably wouldn't be so great either. He kept succumbing to his suddenly sensitive (and somewhat annoying) conscience. He couldn't just lead a tirade in front of the whole youth group and then not show up.

As he nervously shuffled his feet toward the spot, a ray of hope filled his mind. Scanning his eyes around a twenty-foot radius, he didn't see a single face that he recognized from the morning before. *What if nobody shows?* Then he'd be off the hook!

Just as the possibility sneaked a smile onto his face, Andrea walked up and gave him a big hug. "Jake! Hey, you made it!" she smiled, looking somewhat relieved herself. "Do you think anybody else will show?"

Jake tried to put on his confident game-face. "Yeah!" he assured, but inside his heart he was reeling even more. He hadn't thought about the possibility of just he and Andrea showing up. If Amy had been upset the morning before, this would send her into convulsions—that is, if she still cared at all.

Jake and Andrea both looked slowly around, watching for the others, and then finally sat down awkwardly on the damp lawn. The pair could not have looked more incompatible. Andrea had her hair in two braids and wore another tie-dye shirt with a brown suede jacket. Jake had seen pictures of his parents' hippie days, and he wondered if Andrea had stolen clothes from their closet. Jake's usual jeans, T-shirt and team jacket with his name embroidered in the left-hand corner posed a stark contrast.

As they sat in silence, munching on their lunches, Jake felt the eyes of the school boring holes in his back. And then, as if that wasn't enough, the dark clouds opened up at that moment with a ray of light like a laser beam focused on Jake's face. Jake awkwardly shifted his weight—sitting cross-legged hadn't been comfortable since third grade. He kept praying that at least one other student would show up.

"You don't have to stay...if you're uncomfortable," Andrea said, without even a hint of discomfort. She unzipped her flower-print backpack and pulled out an apple.

"It's just that I forgot a drink. I thought I might get—"

Andrea pulled two sodas from her bag. "I knew someone would forget, so I brought two." She smiled and handed one to Jake. She turned to her tuna sandwich on white bread and took a king-sized bite. For a petite girl, she was a voracious eater.

"Thanks." Jake nodded, prying the can open while watching Andrea inhale her food. It was kind of nice to see a girl with a healthy appetite.

When Andrea realized she was being watched, she looked up at Jake with bulging cheeks and wiped a remnant of tuna from her chin. Her eyebrows raised and her eyes widened joyfully, her stuffed mouth shooting into a smile as she spotted something over his shoulder. Jake turned around and saw a pack of at least ten others from the youth group walking up to join them.

There was that African-American kid, Billy, who had made the Mom-joke and who Jake now recognized from the freshman basketball squad. Then there was Natalie and Carla, Andrea's friends who he had met the week before. They smiled politely in unison as they grabbed a seat on the grass. Two others, a brother and sister, gave a round of high-fives to everyone. Every few seconds, Jake was forced to scoot back again in order to allow one more into the circle. Before he knew it, at least twenty students had gathered and spilled over onto the neighboring slab of concrete.

Andrea made sure everyone was formerly introduced, and Jake did everything he could to keep up with all the names and faces. He'd never met so many new people in such a short amount of time, but it was awesome. Minutes ago, Jake had been obsessed with what the rest of campus was thinking, but that obsession had been squashed by the realization that he was actually having fun.

When Carla noticed that a junior named Karl had come without a lunch, the group pelted him with their extra sandwiches, cookies, chips, apples—more than he could eat. Jake wished he had something to throw, but he was pretty sure the guy wouldn't appreciate an open Coke being chucked at him.

Billy was quite the comedian and had the group rolling with laughter with his impersonation of Jake from the morning before. He stood up in the middle of the circle and shouted, "There are people starving on this side of the circle, and you're chugging soda through a sock!"

Jake still wasn't fully comfortable with his outburst from the morning before, and his cheeks flushed with heat. But a chorus of "we-love-you-Jake" and "that-was-really-awesome" from around the circle, paired with a few more high-fives, set him at ease again. Billy leaned over with a big smile and a fist bump. "Impersonation is the greatest form of flattery," he whispered. Jake nodded and grinned.

Another girl wandering alone through the quad caught the group's attention, and they begged her to join them. Jake watched her face light up as she took her place with the welcoming bunch, as if she belonged there from the start.

He sat back and soaked it all in. The laughter, the sharing, the warmth were like nothing he'd ever experienced before. He'd worked hard to carve his place in the elite circle of Pacific High's most popular clique, but here, the only criteria was that you showed up. And he hadn't had this much fun at lunch since he was in grade school. For the first time in a while, Jake forgot about acting cool—and it felt good.

As he settled in further, he happened to glance over to the north side of the quad, where his normal group congregated in a tight huddle. Jake could make out Amy, Doug, Matt, Tony, and the rest of the gang, and even from afar he could sense their disgust. But Jake ignored their coldness. He knew none of them would ever be caught dead with his new friends, but he'd keep on inviting them just the same. If they knew what they were missing, they might want in.

Halfway through lunch, Kelsi and Danny walked by the group hand-in-hand, accompanied by their usual pothead friends. Jake's group could not have been more friendly, almost harassing Kelsi and Danny to join them, but the couple barely acknowledged the group with rolled eyes and sniggers. Jake was beginning to get the full picture: Maybe some stu-

dents in the youth group were fakers, but they didn't spoil the whole bunch.

Clyde Will walked by the newly formed circle on his usual lunch patrol, and he stopped for a moment to take in the eclectic group sitting in the center of campus. When his eyes hit Jake's, it looked like he did a double-take, but then Jake thought he saw the tough guy smile.

As Jake's eyes followed Clyde, his attention jumped to a student sitting by himself at a nearby picnic table. The kid wore a black hoodie, which blocked Jake's view of his face as he focused intently on a notepad in his lap. Amidst all the lunchtime activity, the kid was clearly alone, and Jake could not bring himself to look away. He wasn't sure where the feeling was coming from, but something was pushing him to go talk to the guy.

Why not? It wasn't like Jake was doing anything inside his comfort zone today. He glanced around the animated circle, so full of acceptance and smiles. Maybe this loner kid would want a piece of the action.

Jake nonchalantly stood up and walked across the pavement to the hooded stranger. Five yards away, a terrifying thought entered Jake's mind: *What am I gonna say?* Jake was used to people approaching him, but this was different—he had to start the conversation this time. What was he supposed to say to this kid? *"Umm, are you a loner?" "Do you want to be friends?"* Jake rehearsed a couple cheesy greetings in his head. His feet propelled him forward while his brain kept searching for something to say. Finally, when Jake was standing a foot from the table, the kid slowly looked up and made eye contact with him.

And then Jake recognized him. Those eyes were unmistakable. This was the kid who had showed up to that party dressed in a wizard costume. The one Doug had mercilessly taunted and teased. The one who had locked eyes with him that night. Would he recognize Jake's face?

"Hey!" Jake stammered and automatically grabbed a seat across from the hooded kid. The boy's long unkempt hair hung down over his eyes, which squinted to block out the finally emerging sun.

"Hey," the kid grunted back, turning his eyes to the sketchbook in his lap. The page was covered with dark, sinister figures, and his pencil rapidly added hair to one of them—a running girl being chased by a robed figure. Then he seemed to sense Jake watching him—he covered the page with his arm and turned to a half-eaten piece of lasagna in a cafeteria Styrofoam plate. His fork stabbed it until the noodle crumbled and the red sauce oozed out.

Jake leaned forward with a new boldness. "Me and some friends are just eating lunch over there, and I thought you might want to join us."

The kid quickly glanced over to the group, still yapping away across the quad. His eyes turned back to Jake, and he stared at him cautiously, as if he expected some cruel joke. Then he looked back to the sketchbook. "I really need to finish this," he mumbled.

Jake drummed his fingers on the table top, then stood back up. He wasn't used to making invitations and even less used to being rejected. "Um, well, I just wanted to say hi. I'm Jake." He reached out to shake the kid's hand.

"I know," the kid said without looking up. Jake pulled his hand back and shoved it into his pocket. Then, unexpectedly, the kid muttered, "I'm Jonny Garcia."

Those three words hit Jake like a punch in the stomach. The picture from Roger's MySpace flashed in his brain. "Were you friends with Roger?" Jake gasped.

Jonny's head tilted up, a look of fear plastered across his face. He slowly nodded and put his pencil down. The two stared at each other in silence.

"Hi, I'm Andrea," the familiar perky voice chimed in from behind Jake.

Jake recovered quickly, flashing a smile like they had just been shooting the breeze. "This is my new friend, Jonny," he introduced.

Andrea reached her hand to shake his and this time Jonny reciprocated. "So are you gonna join us or not?" She cut straight to the punch.

"Jonny's got homework," Jake answered for him.

Andrea ignored Jake and waited for Jonny to answer. Jonny helped Jake out: "Yeah, I got a test."

"Well, we'll be here every day," Andrea smiled, pointing to the group as she danced away.

Left on his own again and unsure how to proceed with Jonny, Jake decided to make his escape too, although he was sure he wouldn't look so graceful. "Seriously," he concluded, "come join us sometime."

Jonny looked back blankly as the bell rang, bringing an end to this anything-but-normal lunch period.

25

JAKE NEVER REALLY took an off-season from basketball. There were always ways he could improve his game. Plus his dad reminded him at least once a week that what he lacked in height and speed, he would have to make up by working harder than everyone else. So, ever since ninth grade when he'd decided to give up all other sports, perfecting his basketball skills was a 365-days-a-year commitment. He ran and did extra sprints before school to increase his stamina, lifted weights after school to increase his strength, shot a hundred extra free-throws a day to increase his consistency, and studied the playbook until he could run through it blindfolded.

Yet, in the last few weeks, Jake hadn't thought much about the game he loved. It wasn't that he'd lost his passion for it; there were just more important things demanding his time these days. He reasoned that, after his years and years of hard work, he had earned a short vacation. He'd even run the idea by his coach, who fully supported a short rest before he started preparing for college ball. He'd surely be ready to go by the time he moved to Louisville for summer practice.

But Louisville was the least of his worries at the moment. His current source of pain came from the 215 pounds he attempted to bench press in the corner of the Pacific weight room. He lowered the weight to his chest, inhaling deeply, then exerted all his strength to push the bar back up for his final two reps. Earsplitting heavy metal music and the foul odor of teenage boys filled every inch of the small weight room, but Jake was oblivious. As he applied the final heave of his hour-long workout, his pecs screamed with pain and his veins bulged along his forearms. An eager freshman guard named Bobby spotted him from behind, encouraging him in a prepubescent voice. Part of Jake wanted to laugh, but he knew that would mean a cracked rib.

Jake willed the bar up until his arms were fully extended. He inhaled and exhaled twice more and slowly lowered the bar back down for one final rep. Sweat dripped from his white knuckles, and his hair lay drenched across his forehead. The bar paused above his chest, and Jake closed his eyes and gritted his teeth, psyching himself up for one final push.

He sensed commotion above his head and opened his eyes in time to see Doug shove the freshman aside and take over spotting duties. His concentration shattered, Jake's arms started to shake violently. The bar stalled in mid-air, halfway to the finish line, and the weight began to slowly descend back to his chest. Alarmed, Jake looked to Doug for help, but he just smirked at his struggling friend with his hands behind his back. In panic, Jake fought the bar, trapped underneath its heavy mass. After a good five seconds, but what felt like an eternity, Doug casually reached down and lifted the weight back up on the stand.

"What the hell?!" Jake sat up and shouted. He panted with a combination of exhaustion and rage.

Doug laughed and tapped Jake's cheek like he was a little kid. "Are you allowed to say 'hell'?"

Jake jumped up, slapping Doug's arm away to get right in his face. "I could have cracked a rib!" he yelled, bumping his chest up against his "friend" and pushing him backward.

"Cry me a river." Doug shot back that same cocky smirk that never left his face. His six-inch height advantage allowed him to look down on the infuriated Jake.

"What's your deal, man? I'm just trying to work out!"

By now, the other weightlifters had noticed the escalating clash and had surrounded the feuding teammates to break it up.

Doug's smile was replaced by clear annoyance, and he spat down into Jake's face, "Are you sure you got time? Don't you have Christian club or something?"

"What do you care?" Jake tried to brush him off. He and Doug had never settled things since the beer pong party over two weeks ago. Jake had left several messages on his cell, but none had been returned. And the new lunch-time arrangements hadn't really helped the reconciliation process.

Matt appeared and took a step between them, but both boys glared at him until he took a step back again. Doug jabbed his finger sharply into Jake's sweat-drenched chest, leaning in to talk in a foreboding whisper. "Ever since you got religious, you suddenly don't have time for any of your friends," Doug snarled.

In some ways, it was true. Jake had tried to invite them along on his journey, but the requests had fallen on deaf ears. He had never meant to hurt anyone, but he knew his recent decisions had consequences, and most of them were felt by Amy and Doug. "I've invited you to have lunch with us every day," Jake tried to reason.

Doug shook his head, and perspiration dripped from his mop. He laughed sardonically, "Us? Jake, we've been best friends since sixth-grade soccer. It's always about you. Jake Taylor, the prom king. Jake Taylor, the MVP. You know it's true!"

Jake stood there silently. What was he supposed to say? "Sorry for being more popular and talented than you?" Doug was the one always searching for the limelight. Anyway, who was he to be preaching about loyalty? The gossip around school was that Doug and Amy were already hooking up, and it had been hardly a week since he and Amy had their fight. What kind of friend does that? Jake glared at him, his fists

clenching and unclenching at his sides. He didn't want to go down that road, but if Doug didn't watch it, Jake was going to pop him hard.

They stared each other down, neither willing to make the next move. Finally, Doug turned gruffly and walked away, bumping Jake hard into the weight bench. Jake sprang up and shoved Doug in the back, knocking him into the mirrored wall. Doug's large frame hit the glass hard, and it cracked all the way down to the floor. He peeled his arm off the mirror, revealing a two-inch gash down his right tricep. Watching the first drops of blood fall onto the mat, Doug sneered, and his lips curled into an evil grin. A look of silent fury washed over him. They both knew better than to fight at school, but Jake still braced himself for another blow.

Clutching his right elbow in his left hand, Doug leaned forward and whispered loud enough for all to hear, "Guess who's banging Amy tonight?"

Eyes darted back and forth as the other guys in the room waited breathlessly for Jake's response. Worse than a punch, Doug's words had knocked the wind out of Jake, and he hunched over, his fingers curling uncontrollably into a fist. Hatred oozed out of his every pore. He'd tolerated this jerk for far too long. How much could a guy expect to take?

As Jake's fingers stiffened and twitched, Doug taunted even more. "C'mon, church boy. What are you gonna do about it?" Now Jake's entire body trembled with rage, but still he resisted. He knew he should just walk away, but he wanted to hurt Doug so bad.

Finally, Doug shrugged nonchalantly with a condescending wink. "I guess it's about time she had a real man."

Jake uncurled his fist and pointed a hostile finger in Doug's face. "She'd never do that. She's better than you!"

BAM!

Doug's sweaty fist connected with Jake's face, knocking him back a few steps into the surrounding crowd. Jake lunged to reciprocate, but Tony held him back while Matt and another teammate jumped in between and restrained Doug. Both fighters struggled against their restraints, as blood from Doug's arm and Jake's nose spattered freely to the floor.

Slowly, Jake's anger began to drain, and his body felt very tired. He yanked his arms free and picked up his towel next to the weight bench, pressing it to his mouth to staunch the flow of blood. All eyes were on him as he plodded to the exit, tossing his red-soaked towel at Doug on his way out. His body slammed angrily through the back door. It took all he had to ignore Doug's parting shot: "That's right. Keep walking, Taylor!"

As the door clicked shut behind him, Jake swore under his breath and kicked a trash can next to the door on the sidewalk. He charged toward the parking lot, a new surge of anger propelling him relentlessly. The afternoon ocean breeze sent chills down his sweaty back but didn't cool down his spirit. He hadn't been involved in a fist-fight since junior high, and that was over a video game. He tore off a piece of his shirt and wadded it up in his nostrils while he pinched his bridge. What a sight he must be.

The moment his hands touched the cold metal of his truck's door handle, he discovered a new problem. In all the commotion, he'd left his gym bag in the back corner of the weight room with his keys, wallet, and clean clothes.

He kicked the front tire and swore again, irritated at his stupidity, then suddenly he remembered the spare key-holder his dad had installed when he got the truck on his sixteenth birthday. Now, if only he could remember where he'd put it. His fingers felt along the underside of the front bumper with no luck. *Maybe it fell off already*, he dreaded. Skeptical, he moved to the back end, and almost immediately his fingers struck gold on the little black magnetic box. The faintest smile flitted over his now-puffy face.

With windows rolled down, Jake roared out of the Pacific High parking lot, his truck thumping with the rattling bass of some rap song. The rapper spat out irate lines and fiery rhymes about the signs of the times, and Jake let the song's anger flow through him. He tilted his head against his head rest, and the rhythm pulsed through him as he sped home.

That he even noticed the hooded kid walking by himself on the side of the road was remarkable, but there was something about him that riveted Jake's attention. The kid clutched a half-dozen books to his chest as he ambled slowly down the street. As Jake zoomed past, he caught a glimpse of the guy's face, and he recognized him at once: It was Jonny. Impulsively, Jake pulled over a few yards in front of the preoccupied kid.

"Jonny!" Jake yelled through the rolled-down window, but there was no response. He was only a few yards away. *How does he not see me?* Jake muttered to himself.

Jonny kept walking, oblivious.

Jake pushed on the emergency brake and jumped out. On stiff legs, he jogged back to him.

"Hey, need a lift?" Jake shouted.

Startled, Jonny spun around, dropping some of his books at Jake's feet. Their eyes locked for a moment, and Jonny seemed to be trying to evaluate the situation. Underneath his hood, white wires led from his ears down to his pocket, which explained his prior oblivion. He pulled one ear bud out and continued to stare at Jake for a few seconds before finally blurting, "Dude, your face is bleeding!"

Jake fingered his lip, having forgotten how ghastly he must look, and bent down to grab Jonny's books off the ground. "Yeah, but she was tough," he explained with a straight face.

Jonny grunted a quick laugh, then quickly knelt down to his books. "You don't have to do that." He brushed Jake away, picking up the remaining two texts off the ground. He reached to take the others from Jake's hand, but Jake pulled them away and stepped toward his truck.

"Let me give you a ride," Jake offered again.

Jonny remained motionless as his stuff was dropped in the bed of the truck. Jake forced a smile and opened the passenger-side door. "Come on, get in," he commanded, trying to quell the anger still simmering inside from his fight. He didn't want to scare the kid, but he was giving him a ride whether he wanted one or not.

"You really don't have to," Jonny protested, still hanging back from the open door.

"I want to." Jake left the door open and walked briskly around to the driver's side.

Jonny tentatively got in, keeping the last two books safely on his lap. Although he stood over six feet tall, his slender frame barely made a dent in the upholstery.

Jake put his seat belt back on and got directions to Jonny's house. They rode along in silence. Jake hadn't thought of a plan; something inside him just told him to pull over and pick this kid up. What was he supposed to do now?

"What's wrong with your face?" Jonny asked, breaking the stillness.

Jake looked at himself in the rear-view mirror for the first time and almost slammed on his brakes. No wonder Jonny hadn't wanted to get in the car with him. His face was a crusty, swollen mess. He had a fat lip covered in dried blood, his nose was still stuffed with bloody remnants of his shirt, and his puffy right cheekbone looked like he was going to get a shiner. "Bloody nose," Jake lied, but nodding matter-of-factly.

"It matches your shorts," Jonny replied, staring straight ahead.

Jake glanced down at his shorts, which matched his torn and bloody shirt, too. Jake chuckled and reached over to knock knuckles with Jonny, who instinctively raised his hands over his face and bumped his head against the glass like he was being attacked. Jake looked down at his hand, which was also streaked with gore. He quickly jerked it back to the steering wheel. "Oops, sorry," Jake said.

After another awkward silence, Jonny blurted out, "You knew Roger?" His eyes still focused completely on the road ahead.

Taken aback, Jake hesitated, then said, "Yeah, we grew up in the same neighborhood together. I hadn't talked to him much over the past few years, though."

"Oh," Jonny replied.

More silence.

"I was on Roger's MySpace page, and I saw your name. Were you guys friends?" Jake took his turn at asking a question.

Jonny turned his face toward Jake for the first time on the ride. His dark bangs hung down over his eyes. "We played video games. Not in person, over the Internet." He tucked his hair underneath the black hood. He had an innocent face. His dark green eyes darted around, every once in a while meeting Jake's, but not lingering.

"Did you know he was gonna...you know?" Jake probed. It was weird to be sitting next to someone who knew something of Roger.

It was almost like a whisper barely escaping from Jonny's mouth. "I swear I thought he wasn't serious."

"You knew!" Jake exclaimed, not meaning to speak so sharply.

Jonny wasn't defensive. "I saw some stuff he wrote."

"And you didn't tell anybody?" Jake's voice rose in volume again. His earlier anger was feeding his response, but he couldn't help it.

"I—I didn't know. I didn't know he was gonna—I swear." Jonny buried his face in his hands, knocking the side of his head lightly against the passenger-side window.

Jake watched speechless, feeling empathy and relief. All this time, there was someone else at his school carrying guilt for Roger's death, too. "I'm sorry. I'm not mad at you," Jake said softly. "I just want to know what happened."

Jonny pointed to his mobile home park on the right, and Jake turned in. An image of Jonny's MySpace page flashed into Jake's mind. He'd only glanced at it for a second after he read Roger's suicide note, but he could picture it very clearly now. It was dark, like Roger's, minus the note telling the world that he was going to kill himself. Was that the same path that Jonny was on? All of a sudden, Jake felt desperate to help.

"You ever think like Roger?" Jake asked.

Jonny looked up with squinted eyes and a scowl. "I'm not gonna shoot up the school, if that's what you mean."

"I wasn't saying—"

"I'm not Roger." Jonny pointed flippantly to his home, a run-down trailer in terrible need of new paint and a gardener. A tattered hammock hung from the side of the trailer to a tree that had no business holding up anything. A hint of black mildew emanated from the walls.

Jake pulled in the empty driveway and Jonny immediately got out. Jake started to pull away, frustrated that he'd botched it up again.

"Wait!" Jonny yelled, and his arms stretched out over the bed of the truck to grab his remaining books. Jake slammed on the brakes, and Jonny's arm slapped against the back window. The sleeve of his sweatshirt slid down off his arm, and the inside of his wrist pressed against the glass.

Jake was startled. Jonny's brown skin was covered with dozens of long, deep scars. Some of them were fading, but some were definitely fresh. The moment screeched to slow motion: Their eyes met, Jake desperately wanting to say something, to do something. Jonny pulled the sleeve down, grabbed his books, and turned back to his house. Jake watched him stumble toward the door, the books clutched against his chest.

Jake had seen some movie where a depressed girl had cut herself, but he'd never seen the results so up close and personal. What was he supposed to do? Should he tell somebody? Could he pretend like it never happened? Before he knew what he was doing, Jake threw the truck into park and ripped off his seat belt. "You said you like video games?" he shouted after Jonny.

Jonny stopped at the top of the stairs to the trailer's front door. He turned around and just stared. His eyes squinted against the remnants of the late afternoon sun, and he slowly nodded his head.

"Got any good ones?" Jake's grin sent pain searing up his face but, for the first time today, he felt good. Jonny nodded again and stood waiting as Jake started toward the trailer.

JAKE HAD BOASTED of being an expert at *Halo 3*, but after a three-hour thrashing by Jonny, he finally had to plead for mercy. In all his years on the basketball court, he had never heard so much trash-talk. His new friend was hilarious—apparently his mouth had not come with the standard filter the rest of humanity was born with, and it didn't take long for the emo kid to really open up about all kinds of random stuff. During one of their brief breaks, Jonny had given Jake the full tour of the decrepit trailer, including a lengthy description of how he knew the place was haunted. Jake didn't quite follow the explanation but was pretty certain Jonny's mind was a complex place. With his face still throbbing from Doug's punch, Jake tuned in and out of Jonny's never-ending commentary.

Before Jake knew it, he was looking at darkness through the trailer's cracked front window. He quickly allowed his game character to be killed for the three hundredth time and thanked Jonny for his hospitality. The truth was, the talkative sophomore had never even offered a drink of water, and it was Jake who had finally asked for a sink to clean off his bloody face. He figured Jonny wasn't used to having company. Jake noted that in his three-hour visit, Jonny's mom had never walked in or called.

By the time Jake walked in his own door, it was well past eight. He knew he should have called his mom to tell her he'd miss dinner, but he figured it might be easier to ask for forgiveness than permission.

For the first time in a long time, Jake took a long look at his house, noting its stark contrast to Jonny's. Where Jonny's cramped living room was covered in stained carpet and dusty mismatched furniture, Jake's house was spacious, exquisitely furnished, and immaculate. Jonny's entire trailer could have fit into the Taylor's newly remodeled kitchen and breakfast nook, which had been redesigned to allow the morning sun to shine more brightly through the custom windows. Usually, Jake didn't give his surroundings a second thought, but he was suddenly struck by how lucky he had it. He really *did* enjoy the fruit of his dad's hard work.

He walked tiredly into the kitchen, where his mom was bent over cleaning the black granite counters with a Miracle Sponge she'd bought off the home shopping channel. Her eyes were glued to the 27-inch flat-screen installed above the microwave. Ty Pennington from *Extreme Makeover Home Edition* was handing keys to a weeping single mom as the bus moved out of the way of her new mansion. Pam's eyes were moist as she mechanically scrubbed away on the sparkling counters. She was always cleaning.

"Hi, Mom." Jake greeted her from the kitchen doorway.

"Oh!" She jumped, startled. She wiped her wet eyes with her apron. "I'm so pathetic, this episode is a rerun." She dropped the apron and got her first good look at Jake. "Oh my goodness! Jake, what happened to you?" Pam looked in horror at Jake's swollen face, placing her hand on his cheek to get a better look.

The cleaner on her hands stung Jake's cuts. "Ouch!" he yelled, and she reactively dropped her fingers.

"Who did this to you?" she demanded, on the verge of tears.

"Doug."

"Doug, your friend?"

"It's a long story," Jake dodged, throwing his backpack on the black granite to head for leftovers in the fridge. He knew his mom meant well, but he didn't feel like getting into it. Besides, she never was good at dealing with hard reality—he'd learned it countless times growing up, watching her wear a smile regardless of the problems she was facing. That was her solution to everything: Push it down and put on a smile.

"Well, where have you been?" His mom followed him to the fridge and pulled out a cold enchilada casserole to heat up in the microwave.

Jake grabbed the milk and chugged straight from the carton. Then he pulled a Gatorade from the fridge door and spun off the cap. "I was at a friend's house." Jake walked over to the trash compactor and threw the empty milk carton away. "Where's Dad?"

She leaned up against the sink next to Jake and placed her arm around his shoulders. "Please call next time."

Jake took another gulp of Gatorade, carelessly splashing some onto the pristine surface of the counter. Before he could even apologize, Pam had already grabbed a paper towel to wipe it up.

"An Andrea called for you. Who's Andrea?" she inquired, handing Jake a piece of paper with a number on it from next to the kitchen phone.

"Why does Dad always have to work late?" Jake changed the subject and forked up a bite of enchilada. Over the years, he'd found that ignoring his mother's questions was a nicer way of saying "None of your business," and she usually went for it.

"I guess he's just really busy at the office." Pam grabbed the sponge and resumed her counter cleaning. Jake was pretty sure it was already spotless, but cleaning to his mom was like basketball to Jake: a therapeutic escape. Jake had seen her take out her frustrations with his dad countless times on a barely visible stain in the rug. With both hands on the sponge, she looked back up at her son. "I haven't seen Amy for a while."

What a loaded statement. It had been over a week since her kiss goodbye. He'd seen her every day at school, but despite myriads of glances, neither had made a move to approach the other. At first, he'd rationalized that she was the one who walked away, so she should be the one to return, but now with Doug in the picture, it was all a moot point. He would have to accept the obvious. "We broke up." Jake scooped his second enchilada from the plate.

Pam spun around to face Jake directly. "What? Oh, I liked her. She was good for you." The pained expression on her face looked like she was the one who'd been broken up with. She grabbed Jake's plate out of his hands while he was still chewing and washed it in the sink.

"It's not a big deal," Jake lied. "I think we're just on a break. We'll work it out." It was easier to deny than explain.

"What happened, honey?" His mom squirted dish soap on the plate while she waited for the sink water to get hot.

Jake stepped away from the sink, giving his mom room to work. He eyed his bulging backpack lying on the counter, representing several more hours before he'd be able to crash into bed. "I don't know. We'll work it out. I got homework." Jake grabbed his bag from the counter and headed toward the stairs.

"We'll talk about this later?" his mom pleaded after him with a frustrated edge. From the base of the stairs, Jake heard her sigh, dump out his half-full Gatorade bottle into the sink, and throw it in the recycle bin.

27

JAKE FINALLY CLOSED his last book a little after midnight, leaving him far less sleep than he preferred. Chatting with Andrea for an hour in the middle definitely hadn't helped. He trudged wearily onto campus the next morning, wearing big sunglasses he hoped would attract less attention than the black eye they were covering. Of course, nothing could cover his fat lip.

After stopping by the weight room to pick up his bag (which, surprisingly, was still intact, wallet and all), he headed down Senior Hall. He used to make fun of the guys who were too cool to take off their shades inside, but now he was the one sporting the look. He could almost tangibly feel the ridicule of the people he passed. But it amounted to nothing compared to the surprise he had waiting for him at his locker.

Hearing that his former best friend and girlfriend were officially hooked up was one thing, but seeing it with his own eyes was a shock Jake wasn't ready for. After dumping off his books, he shut his locker door just in time to see Amy give Doug a mocha and a kiss on the cheek just seven lockers down from his. Until two weeks ago, Jake was getting the morn-

ing coffee and kiss—how quickly he had been replaced. Amy reached up to fold her arms around Doug's neck, revealing the belly button ring that even now drove Jake crazy. Jake tried hard not to stare but failed miserably. Doug reached in and kissed Amy on the lips, and she protested in the squealing way girls do when they really don't mind. Jake was pretty sure they knew he was there, which made it worse.

Jake wished his locker door was still open, so he could at least slam it shut to express his feelings. But all he could do was walk away. Last night's pep talk from Andrea about staying positive was quickly wearing off, and the first bell hadn't even rung yet. When he glanced back at them, trying to appear casual, he locked eyes with Amy, who seemed to be watching him walk away. He quickly turned back around the corner toward Mr. Gil and English.

"Did you hear Chris got in trouble?" Danny's drawling voice abruptly crowded into his irked thoughts. He put his arm around Jake's shoulder, smiling like they were old friends.

Danny was another guy Jake had no interest in being around, but with all the people he wanted to avoid, it was impossible to evade them all. In some ways Jake despised Danny even more than Doug. At least Doug didn't pretend to be some kind of saint around certain people.

"What?" Jake responded, trying to seem as disinterested as possible. He glanced down at his English homework, subtly swinging his shoulder to get Danny's arm to fall off.

Danny ignored the effort. "That time you were cussing," he laughed. "Man, that was awesome!"

To Jake, Danny's whole life seemed like a lie, so why would he be telling the truth now? Nevertheless, Jake found himself bothered that Chris might really be in trouble. Danny had to be wrong. Jake stopped mid-stride to face him in the center of the crowded hallway. The aroma of pot-concealing cologne jumped off Danny's skin, assaulting Jake. "You're full of it," he snapped, turning his head to breathe.

"I'm serious," Danny shot back, his eyes still dancing with merriment.

Jake couldn't believe he was even having this conversation. "He didn't say anything to me."

"Of course not," Danny smirked, and Jake could almost envision him twirling a villainous mustache. "Star athlete coming to our church. Chris doesn't want to mess that up."

Jake wanted to get away. Danny's cologne and personality repulsed him to the point of gagging. If only Danny's dad knew what his son had become. *How could the apple have fallen so far from the tree?* "What are you talking about?" Jake demanded.

"I've seen it before. That's how these guys work." Danny patted Jake on the shoulder, as if he'd just done him a favor, and then left as suddenly as he had come. Jake watched Danny's retreating strut, a numbness washing over him.

✚ ✚ ✚

With images of Doug and Amy replaying like the movie of the week in his brain, and Danny's story about Chris colliding with them in a frightful smashup, Jake struggled through his morning classes. In just a few weeks, he had lost his girlfriend and his best friend, and he was now possibly responsible for a good guy losing his job. And then, of course, there was Roger. *Will that ever go away?* What if he just took Amy's advice and let it go? *Would that even work?*

Lunchtime did not come soon enough. The bell awakened him from his thoughts. Jake gathered his books and headed for his new place of solace: the center of the quad with his odd new group of friends.

The circle had become a mix-match of all kinds of students looking for a friendly place to have lunch. Joining the eclectic group were punkers, skaters, preps, jocks, and nerds, as well as more than a few who were just impossible to label. Jake threw his backpack down on the cement and let out a loud groan. Before he could even take a seat, he was surrounded by sympathetic faces. "Everything okay, Jake?" Andrea asked, handing him a bag of Doritos that was being passed around.

Jake smiled and took a chip. "I've had better mornings," he confessed under his breath, not wanting everyone to hear him complain.

Billy scooted in on the other side, grabbing an entire handful of chips. "You know what they always say?"

"What?" Jake smiled, waiting for one of Billy's unusual punch lines.

"Sometimes you're the dog... sometimes you're the fire hydrant." He laughed contagiously.

Jake tousled Billy's new braids as Billy retreated back to the other side of the group.

At least forty students now sat around the circle, each engaged in conversation, each accepted by all. Jake had seriously thought the group would die out before the first week's end, but here they were, growing closer with every passing day. "Who are all these people?" Jake chuckled, scanning the crop of new faces.

"I don't know, but isn't it awesome?" Andrea laughed.

A light tap on the shoulder forced Jake to turn around. There stood Jonny, his head half-blocking the blinding sun—hoodie, sketchpad and all. Jake jumped up to greet him, knowing this was probably killing the kid. A look of relief swept Jonny's face when Jake slapped him a high-five and made room for him to join the expanding circle.

"No homework today?" Jake asked with a grin. Even with all the garbage he'd endured today, he couldn't contain a smile. He introduced Jonny to the students in the group one by one. Jonny was a far cry from the non-stop chatterbox Jake had visited the night before. But, by the end of lunch, Jake caught his new friend explaining the real possibility that several of the Pacific High faculty were actually vampires. A couple of students played along, adding their opinions of which teachers lived off human blood.

At least for the moment, the pain of losing Amy seemed less difficult. Jake knew she was probably watching him hang out with the same group of people they had once ridiculed, and he didn't care. As he looked at Jonny carry on about the difference between vegetarian and carnivorous vampires, somewhere in the back of Jake's brain he knew that something very cool had just happened. Today wasn't his best day ever, but all of a sudden, it wasn't his worst.

AFTER JONNY'S FIRST LUNCH with the group, Jake had been pretty sure the boisterous circle had scared Jonny away. Jake had even planned on apologizing later on, when Jonny astonished him by asking what this Souled Out thing was all about. Jake eagerly offered him a ride, promising to come a little early for another butt-whipping at *Halo*, and Jonny had enthusiastically accepted.

With trepidation, Jonny followed Jake into the packed youth room. At the picture of Roger, he paused and bit his lip. "Did Roger come here?" he asked quietly, his eyes intent on Roger's face.

A few steps ahead of him, Jake turned back to the picture as well. "He came once," Jake whispered. "He left quite an impression." The first several times Jake came to youth group, he too had always stopped to look at the photo—Roger was, after all, the person who was ultimately responsible for him being there.

After a few moments of silence, Jake put his arm around Jonny's shoulder and turned him to face the rest of the room.

Even Jake was blown away by what he saw. There were new faces everywhere, many like Jonny who had become friends through the lunchtime circle.

As funny and talkative as Jonny was in private, now he looked like he wanted to disappear. Jake could see the anxiety growing in his new friend's eyes as he introduced him to stranger after stranger.

"Okay, you can forget everybody else's name except this guy. This is Chris," Jake explained as they zigzagged through the new faces en route to the stage. Chris was arranging papers on a small music stand, but he immediately dropped them to greet the new student.

"Nice to meet you, Jonny!" Chris extended his hand to him. "If you're here with Jake, then you are immediately cool by association."

Jake had overheard Chris use that line on at least five other people already, but it always made him laugh. Before Jonny could respond, Andrea appeared from the crowd of students.

"Oh my gosh, Jonny! You're here!" she exclaimed as she reached up and gave him a big hug. "Remember my name from school?" she teased. Her arms were embraced by two serpentine copper bracelets that wound up from her elbows to almost her armpits. They coordinated well with her sari-like maxi dress in a brown tribal print that flowed around her slender body like coffee.

"Andrea," Jonny croaked out with a smile, his cheeks flushing faintly.

Her hug pulled his hood down his back, and instinctively he moved to pull it back on, but Andrea's hand stopped him. "You look better with it off," she said sincerely and pulled Jonny away. "Come on, you gotta meet the band."

Jonny shrugged at Jake and followed Andrea, his long black hair plastered to his head. Although it was just a hoodie, Jonny looked like a completely different person with it off. He had looked so dark and mysterious decked out all in black, and even in his house playing video games he had kept it on. Now his posture straightened a bit, his demeanor lightened, and a shy glimmer even sparked in his eyes as Andrea jerked him forward to yet another group of students. Jake laughed as Jonny rigidly accepted a bear hug from one of the varsity football players.

Jake turned his attention back to Chris, who was watching and chuckling along with him. "I don't know how you did it. This place is different because of you," Chris remarked as he glanced around the room.

He was right. Even with all the new faces, a spirit of community pervaded the air. When a student walked through the door alone, he'd get swarmed immediately by a host of welcoming classmates. The ratty old couches had been taken out and replaced with more chairs to hold the influx of additional bodies, so there was no longer that cliquey corner. Laughter abounded, but there were also heartfelt conversations and even a few scattered tears. It seemed like real life was taking place there, uninterrupted.

Jake absorbed Chris' compliment. He had received tons of praise over the years for his contributions on the court, but this felt different—better, more significant. Something tickled at the back of his throat, like something had lodged itself there. Except with Amy, Jake was not the touchy-feely type and preferred to maintain his personal space. But now a warm flood of gratitude rushed over him, and before he could stop himself he hugged the youth pastor for the first time.

Chris hugged him back, patting Jake as he whispered, "I love you, man."

Jake fumbled for a response. He couldn't remember the last time a man had said those words to him. "Thanks," he finally said, scrunching up his face.

Then, over Chris's shoulder, Jake saw Danny enter. His bizarre claim had plagued Jake all day, and he couldn't stand it anymore. He turned back to Chris seriously. "You know when I kind of cussed at everybody a while ago?" Jake stammered in a barely audible voice. "Did I get you in trouble?" He stuck his hands in his pockets and dug his toe into the carpet.

Chris rubbed his chin methodically as if searching for a response. "Well, Jake, the church fired me."

"What?!" Jake burst out. "Are you serious? But I'm the one who said it, and it's not even really a cuss word, maybe a B-level word at best! Believe me, I could have said a lot worse, like—" Jake rambled frantically.

"Jake!" Chris interrupted, placing his hand tenderly on Jake's shoulder. "I'm just kidding, bro." He rolled his eyes and laughed out loud.

"You weren't fired?" Jake asked, much quieter.

"No, I was just messing with you." Chris smiled. "Jake, I've been doing this for a long time, and that morning when you stood up was the coolest thing I've ever seen. Don't you worry about me."

Jake caught his breath and leaned his head back as an invisible weight thudded off his shoulders to the floor.

"I really gotta start this thing, but later I'd like to hear your explanation of how one word makes the A-list and another gets B-listed," Chris said with a grin, grabbing a microphone.

Whether Danny's claims were true or not, they didn't seem to matter anymore. For the first time in his life, Jake felt like someone was truly on his side. Sure, his parents would probably do almost anything for him, but Chris was different. Somehow in just a few short weeks, Jake had a bond with him that he hadn't experienced with anyone since childhood.

Chris tapped on the microphone to get people's attention. "Hellooooo!" he warbled in a falsetto voice as a hundred students around the room wrapped up their lively conversations. He cocked his white Adidas visor to one side, then tested, "Checkety-check, yo, is this thing on?" Then he busted out into some corny beat-boxing.

Jake hopped off the stage, then turned quickly for one last thing. "Chris?"

Chris looked down at him, chanting, "Wiggida wiggida, what's up, dude?" He covered the mic for a second and looked at Jake with compassionate eyes.

"You have no idea," Jake faltered. "You and God are all I got." With that, he turned and joined the rest of the group.

✚ ✚ ✚

Youth group ended at 8:30, but it was almost 9:15 when Jake, Jonny, and Andrea finally exited the church. Somehow, the draw of homework didn't usually send students racing home afterward, and kids just liked to hang in the room when it was over. In fact they'd stay until the stroke of midnight if Chris didn't finally turn off all the lights and herd them outside.

It had been an amazing night. They did an exercise called Affirmation, where students partnered up with someone they didn't know well and got a minute to brag about themselves. That was hard enough, but then the partner listening was instructed to jump on their chair and shout back at the top of their lungs all the great things they'd just learned about that person. Jake had been partnered with a shy Chinese girl, a foreign exchange student who was visiting the group for the first time. Jake wasn't sure he'd interpreted her broken English properly, but after he thoroughly embarrassed her by shouting her praises to everyone, she had hugged him. And he almost keeled over when she shyly proclaimed to the room that "he like to play with his balls."

Jake had promised himself that he wouldn't let Jonny out of his sight, but it turned out to be tough to keep tabs on him. Jonny was wandering all over the room in random conversations, appearing to enjoy himself even more than Jake and making enough friends to cause a traffic jam. After Andrea's earlier comment, he never did pull his hood back on, but Jake wondered if the long sleeves would always remain. He knew he could never tell anyone about what he had seen under those sleeves. It made Jake wonder how many other people he saw every day were hiding something.

After the meeting, the three jumped into Jake's truck. It would have only made sense to have the smaller Andrea sit in the middle, but she talked herself into the window seat instead, leaving the lanky Jonny sandwiched between her and

Jake. Jonny was a good sport about it—how could he say no to a cute girl?

For some reason, being all smushed together put a damper on their conversation, and as they drove, all three just stared straight ahead, letting the radio fill the silence. Jake didn't mind. For him, it was a pleasant break from the constant noise of all the crazy teenagers packed into that tiny youth room. Maybe when he got back home, he'd go shoot some hoops and let his thoughts simmer down.

Jonny's voice broke the lull. "How often do girls shave their legs?" he asked, matter-of-factly.

Jake and Andrea exchanged glances. "What?" Jake asked, amazed. Andrea tried to conceal her laughter, unsure whether Jonny was serious or not, but it just came snorting out her nose.

Jonny couldn't understand what was so hilarious. "I just have always wanted to know," he stated calmly, his sincerity provoking another burst of laughter.

Jake rolled down his window and let in the fresh air. Honestly, he didn't know the answer to the question. It had never occurred to him to ask Amy, but even if it had, he was pretty sure it would not have been worth the risk—Amy would have likely thought Jake was accusing her of having hairy legs. But now that he thought about it, he supposed this actually could be valuable information. He turned to Andrea as the only one with authority on the issue. "Seriously, how about it?"

Andrea just looked at them, as if she still wasn't sure they were serious. At length she replied, "Well—it kind of depends on the girl."

What kind of answer is that? Jake thought to himself. He tried to hide his interest by looking out the open window, but he still listened for more, just in case.

"That's what I figured," Jonny answered simply, never once breaking into a smile.

Jake sighed and shook his head, amused and baffled by Jonny's complex simplicity. He thought about explaining to him what a socially acceptable conversation looked like, but it felt a little like telling Picasso to only color inside the lines, so Jake decided to keep his mouth shut.

With women's legs certainly on everyone's mind, again the truck grew silent. Jake had read in a book somewhere that every conversation experiences awkward silence at least once every seven minutes. He was spending this particular silence trying to ignore an urge to reach over and touch Andrea's leg. It wasn't so much out of attraction—it was just how a guy's mind worked.

Fortunately, Andrea stepped up this time. "Speaking of THAT...did you have fun tonight?" She addressed Jonny, breaking not only the silence but also Jake's focus.

"I normally avoid big groups," Jonny confessed, now leaning much closer to Andrea than Jake. "I guess I'm just really self-conscious—but I'm really glad I came."

"You get embarrassed easily?" Jake piped up as they drove through downtown Oceanside to get to Andrea's house.

Jonny laughed as if he had a story to tell, but he kept it to himself. Even so, he smiled as if he'd already delivered the punch line.

As the truck slowed for a red light, it pulled up next to a red convertible full of gorgeous college girls. As Jonny stared ahead, lost in thought, Jake had an idea. He knew a gag could have destructive effects on his insecure new friend, but he just couldn't resist. Jake's arm rested along the back of the bench seat, and he slyly tapped Andrea on the shoulder and motioned for her to crouch down in her seat.

With Andrea now below the girls' view through the window, Jake nonchalantly pulled his arm tight around Jonny's shoulder and drew him closer to his side. Jake made eye-contact with two blondes in the convertible's back seat and nodded with a huge smile. They giggled at the sight of Jake and Jonny, sitting alone in each other's arms in the cab of the truck.

Jonny noticed the girls and smiled back, naively waving at them. He turned to Jake and whispered, "Hey, I think those girls like..."

Jake gave Jonny a flirtatious eye and drew him even closer with his arm.

"Jake, man, what are you..." A look of horror flooded Jonny's face as he struggled to pull away from Jake's embrace. His eyes begged Andrea for help, but she was now tucked completely out of sight almost on the floorboard. So he shot a glance back at the girls, who were now pointing and laughing at the boys. "No, no—it's not what you think!" Jonny yelled to the girls just as the light turned green. "We're not—there's a girl here!" He frantically tugged on Andrea's shirt as the convertible started to pull away. "Andrea, sit up! They think—" he shouted. Andrea was now giggling uncontrollably. Jonny yanked on her, but it was too late. The girls were gone.

Andrea finally straightened herself up, and Jake removed his arm as they both laughed shamelessly.

"You got me," Jonny admitted, grinning sheepishly.

Andrea patted him on the arm. "Jonny, you're so cute."

Jonny scooted closer to Andrea, now leaving a healthy gap between him and Jake. "No offense, bro. You're just not my type," he kidded, then added, "Do you really think those girls were digging us?"

"Oh yeah, Jonny, they were digging," Jake scoffed good-naturedly, making a shoveling motion with his right hand.

"Take a left here into Shadowridge," Andrea pointed. Shadowridge just happened to be the wealthiest neighborhood in Oceanside. Each house was a castle with an amazing view of the ocean; the most-prized properties actually opened up onto the beach. Jake considered his family to be rich, but people who lived in Shadowridge were on a whole different level. Judging by Andrea's wardrobe, Jake would have never guessed that she lived around here. He shot a glance over at Jonny, mesmerized by the row of mansions. Jake had to admit they made Jonny's trailer look more like a port-a-potty than a place to live.

Andrea's gorgeous house sat at the end of a long cobbled driveway bordered by up-lit shrubs and a gurgling fountain. Andrea seemed oblivious to the size and magnitude of her home as she thanked Jake for the ride and apologized to Jonny for the prank. Jake and Jonny were awestruck.

"Andrea, your house is...is ginormous," Jake stuttered.

Andrea nodded her head without enthusiasm, holding the truck door open with one arm. "It's a big house, way too big."

"We can trade sometime if you want something smaller," Jonny suggested.

Andrea shut the door and spoke through the window. "If that's what it would take to spend time in the same room with my parents, I'd trade you in a second." Her usual smile was gone, replaced with an apathetic shrug.

Dumbfounded, Jake wanted to reciprocate the comfort she'd given him over the past couple weeks, but nothing came out. All he could muster was a simple, "I'm sorry."

Andrea shrugged again. "Life's not perfect. That's why I love God." Her sweet smile returned, and she waved goodbye over her shoulder and walked up the long driveway.

The two boys didn't say anything to each other for a few moments as they backtracked through the neighborhood. Jake already admired Andrea, but now he was pretty sure she was an angel. He'd have to ask Chris about her.

"You have a lot of friends," Jonny broke the silence as Jake crossed a set of train tracks that literally separated Jonny's neighborhood from Andrea's.

"So do you—now," Jake responded, a bit distracted by his thoughts about Andrea. The night air chilled him, and he rolled up his window.

"Yeah," Jonny considered. Then, after a pause, he added, "I think Roger would have had fun tonight." Now the ensuing silence was not so much out of awkwardness as out of the sadness they both felt.

After Jake dropped Jonny off at the bottom of his driveway, which now looked nonexistent compared to Andrea's, he sat there for a few minutes thinking about Roger. Jonny was right; Roger *would have* had fun. The guilt had melted into a milder

remorse, but still he pounded his steering wheel. "Roger!" he yelled, wishing yet again he could go back in time.

He pulled the truck away and turned up the radio to drown out his thoughts. Some song by some group Jake didn't even know the name of crooned some lyrics about love at first sight. Jake attempted to sing along as loud as he could. It didn't help.

WHILE JAKE'S TRANSITION to a completely new group of friends was an unexpected twist in his last semester of high school—it was turning out to be as refreshing as one of those surprising fruit juice combinations, like kiwi-mango-lime or white-cranberry-peach. True, the loss of his friendship with Doug, Matt, Tony, and the others was still painful, and Jonny Garcia wasn't nearly as "cool" as Doug Moore, but at least Jonny was real. And both Jonny and Billy could run Matt over in a comedy routine any day. None of his new friends were going to be named "Most Likely..." in the yearbook; they probably wouldn't even show up on any page other than the mug shots. But these friendships were more authentic than any Jake had ever experienced, and he'd never laughed so much in his life. After only a few weeks, Jake could honestly say that he preferred his new life to the old one in all respects, except for one: Amy.

Jake expected his feelings for her to dissolve like they had for everything else he used to think was important, but that couldn't have been further from reality. Jake seemed to see Amy draped on Doug around almost every corner of the

school, and the feeling in him that started as denial was morphing into anger and frustration. But as much as it hurt to see Amy and Doug together, not seeing her at all was worse. Her face was the last image in Jake's mind as he dropped to sleep each night, and his longing for her plagued his days. It had seemed easy enough for her to move on, but for Jake, it was anything but.

It crushed Jake that he had become just another name in the long line of guys who couldn't live up to her standards— yet another name she had crossed off her shopping list. During their more than three years together, Amy had repeatedly assured him that he was different, but by the looks of her kisses with Doug, being different didn't count for anything. As much as Jake wanted Amy back, he also longed to rip Doug's face off. He knew it wasn't the answer, but imagining a faceless Doug seemed to bring him momentary relief.

Yet even in his anguish over Amy, Jake also found himself smiling more. Nothing was predictable anymore, and instead of feeling nervous over it, he felt exhilarated. Like when Mr. Tough Guy Clyde surprised his ever-growing lunch group with an armload of foot-long subs one day. Or when Jake and twenty of his new crew rocked the house at a chess tournament. Jake hadn't even known the school had a chess team, but he had the time of his life cheering on a member of their group to get a checkmate (or whatever it was called). They had brought in cardboard cutouts of a huge "D" and a picket fence, chanting "De-Fence" while the opponent pondered his next move. Both teams were so surprised by the huge turnout that they had to bring in more chairs from another classroom.

Then there was the time they all got together to get Billy a cake for his birthday. It was covered with big red frosting lips and the message, "Your Mom's Hot." Before Andrea could even finish passing out pieces to everyone, a huge cake-fight broke out, leaving everyone plastered with frosting. Jake got his first tardy in weeks when the entire group decided to stick around to clean up the huge mess.

He felt safe in the presence of Andrea, Jonny, Billy, and the others, much more so than he ever did around his basketball friends—there was an undeniable freedom to be himself and not always worry about saying something stupid or appearing to have it all together. Every day, at least one or two people showed up with a new friend, and the group grew to almost a hundred students. Dozens of people Jake had ignored in the halls for years were now considered friends. By far, his favorite part of the day was walking through the group at lunch saying hello to everyone. He'd adopted Chris' "cool by association" line and used it way too often. He practiced Andrea's knack for cutting through the surface when someone looked like they needed more than just a hello. And he'd learned from Jonny not to care so much about what people thought of him.

But probably the biggest surprise for Jake had to be the ease with which he began to believe in God. There wasn't one thing or one moment that made it happen, but one night, sitting in the church parking lot with Chris, it all just clicked. He had always believed that Jesus Christ was God's son, but he'd never fully understood why it mattered or what it meant to have a "relationship" with him. After watching Chris, Andrea, Billy, and so many others living their faith out together, he knew that's what he wanted, too.

One week later, Jake found himself standing up to his waist in the frigid Pacific Ocean. With Chris next to him and a ton of his friends cheering from the beach, Jake was baptized, officially joining God's family and announcing to everyone that he was going to do his best to find out God's plan. Immediately after Chris dunked him in the water, he was mobbed by bodies rushing and splashing into the surf. A mesh of tackles and hugs went on for at least ten minutes as his body grew comfortable with the cold water and his heart grew warm with love. He later learned that the sopping-wet hugs were a Souled Out tradition after a baptism, but they had added the tackling just for Jake.

Jake was home.

AS GREAT AS JAKE FELT whenever he was with the church gang, the feeling ended the moment he walked in his own front door. Going to church hadn't helped the home situation much. He'd invited his parents to the baptism, hoping it would help them understand, but just like basketball season, they were too busy with their own thing.

Jake shared his frustration with Chris, who counseled him to honor his folks even when they didn't deserve it, but this was much easier said than done. Jake made it a point to tell his folks when he was going to be out late and where he was going, and he even stayed in a couple nights to just watch television with his mom. But she seemed far more interested in the fictional characters on the screen than him. Jake felt like his household was a constant battlefield; sometimes coming through the front door felt like storming the beaches of Normandy, and other times it was like the middle of the Cold War. Even when his parents weren't there, the tension they left behind was inescapable.

As he walked in the house the evening after his baptism, Jake quickly assessed that tonight looked like a World War II

night. He could hear his parents shouting in their bedroom upstairs, as if fighting behind closed doors ever hid anything. Jake leaned against the open front door, ready to leave this mess behind him, but something kept him listening just a little longer.

"We're not done talking!" Jake heard his mom try to assert herself.

"Why do you always bring this stuff up when I've got to get to a meeting?" His dad turned the blame.

"Another meeting? Are you serious? At nine o'clock at night? Come on Glen, I'm not stupid! What's her name?"

"How dare you accuse me of that while I'm out there working hard...for you!" There it was, that line Jake was all too familiar with.

"Well, what else am I supposed to think?" Pam seemed to be wilting.

"I can't even debate this with you. You've already made me too late!" Glen swung open the bedroom door.

"Don't you dare walk out that door..." she weakly gave one last effort, but Glen ignored her. He grabbed his briefcase at the top of the staircase and stormed down the stairs, rushing toward the front door. It was then that Glen noticed Jake leaning up against his escape route. He froze with a startled look. Jake glared venomously at his father and pushed himself off the door.

"You just get home, Jake?" his dad asked gruffly.

Jake nodded his head with resentment.

"You heard that?" His dad sounded more accusatory than apologetic.

"I've *been* hearing that, Dad," Jake shot back.

"What? A little arguing? It's nothing; your mother just gets over-excited sometimes."

Jake shook his head as his mom came to the railing. Her eyes were red, and she held a wad of Kleenex in her right hand.

"Jake, really, it's okay. Just a little disagreement," she said softly.

There she went again, lining the minefield with fluff. She was just as bad as his dad, refusing to acknowledge that things were so clearly not okay.

Still in a rush, Glen approached the guarded front door and lightly slapped Jake on the face. "Don't worry about us, son," he said calmly. "You just keep worrying about yourself. I gotta run."

Jake stepped aside only slightly, forcing his father to squeeze through a small slot in the doorway. He walked briskly down the front walk toward his red Porsche waiting in front of the house.

"It's not worth it, Dad," Jake called out to him as his dad stuck the key in the car door to leave for who knew how long. With a dismissive wave of his hand, Glen jumped into the car and roared off without a second glance. Jake turned back to his mom at the banister, but she had disappeared back into their room.

Jake sighed. *Welcome home.*

Jake dropped his bag on his bedroom floor with a thud and flopped down on his bed. He lay there motionless for a moment trying to get a handle on his jumbled thoughts. *Is every family like this?* His parents sure looked like they had the perfect life: a big house, fancy cars, and all the luxuries you could ever dream of. But Jake knew better—he was pretty certain his parents would have divorced years earlier if it weren't for him. He first started to notice their fights when he was in junior high, and they had gotten uglier as the years went by. Jake had once suggested counseling, and they looked at him like he owed them an apology. Seeing a counselor would be equivalent to admitting they had problems, and that was the one thing their marriage still had: the façade of perfection. Jake just had to laugh.

He glanced slowly around the room at his closet full of name-brand clothes, the sliding-glass door that led to his private balcony, an entertainment unit covered with thousands of dollars worth of presents from his parents. In that moment, lying on his bed watching the ceiling fan spin shadows across the walls, he couldn't feel any of the love those gifts were supposed to demonstrate. In fact, he'd give it all away for a normal family, if one even existed. He began to understand exactly what Andrea had meant when he had dropped her off from youth group a few nights earlier.

He glanced at his bedside clock, watching the digital numbers click from 7:58 to 7:59 to 8:00 P.M. He thought about calling Andrea, but he didn't really even feel like picking up the phone. He looked down at his backpack on the floor; it wasn't going anywhere, which meant neither was his physics homework. His eyes roamed his walls, where even the Louisville posters demoralized him. As awesome as those dreams were, they demanded so much of him. *What if I can't live up to what they expect out of me?*

Jake felt like his head was about to explode. He flailed his fist against the mattress, jumped up, grabbed his basketball, and ran back down the stairs and outside, pounding the ball into the pavement. As usual, basketball offered him a much-needed escape. Not the basketball where thousands watched to see if he would succeed or fail, but the basketball where no one was watching. So Jake headed down the street to spend yet another night on the neighborhood court.

He faked right, jabbed left, sky-hooked, jump-shot, free-throwed and three-pointed away his anxieties. He sweated through the range of emotions as he let his mind freely ask the questions exploding from it.

Jake missed Amy. He missed the times when they would just talk and talk about anything, or about nothing at all—about parents, worries, frustrations, whatever was on their minds. Andrea had been great lately, but he didn't share the same history with her. Amy had been good at listening, too (emphasis on *had been*). She, too, had always brought him hope. She, too, always understood him...*So why doesn't she understand now? Why can't she just give me time to figure things out? Why did she jump so quickly over to Doug? How could she do this to me?!* If their parents' examples were typical of relationships, then what was the point anyway?

But then Jake remembered Chris. From what Jake could tell, Chris and Cari still loved each other very much, even after several years of marriage. Jake had caught the two eyeing each other across the room on several occasions when they thought nobody was looking. Jake had noticed how they still held hands when they walked together, and how Chris would never finish a phone call with her without saying "I love you." Chris was constantly bragging about how hot his wife was, and he always made family time a priority. Their son Caleb was probably the cutest kid on the planet, and though they didn't spoil him with toys and gadgets, he was spoiled with love. Jake had never been drawn to little kids, but ever since the Costco adventure, Caleb had taken a liking to him, and Jake couldn't deny that the feeling was mutual. All that love just couldn't be a sham. If it were possible with the Vaughns, then it had to be possible for others. *If Chris only knew how much hope is riding on his marriage,* Jake mused, sinking another ten-footer—his seventh in a row.

As the swooshes surged and the stresses seeped, Jake sensed this shoot-around was different than those of the past. The conversations within his head felt more like they were with someone else, and he didn't feel totally alone. There seemed to be somebody listening to every concern he had. *Is this prayer?* he chuckled to himself as he drained a third straight three-pointer from the right corner. Just the thought made the hairs on his arms stand up straight. He made a mental note to ask Chris if God played basketball.

He was winding down from his workout when he noticed a familiar car pull into the driveway across the street. All the clashing thoughts that he'd been working out of his mind for the past hour were suddenly silenced. The silver Toyota Camry was a newer model than the one that had carpooled Jake and Roger to countless soccer games, birthday parties,

and sleepovers, but he knew immediately who was behind the wheel. While Jake had seen that very car pass dozens of times over the years without a second thought, tonight he found himself crossing the street.

Esther Dawson pulled herself wearily out of her car and opened the trunk to unload her groceries. The last time Jake had seen her was at the funeral, where he had been unable to utter a single word of consolation or apology. Now, by the glow of a single street light, Jake watched the exhausted woman make her first trip up the driveway toward the front door. She wore a dark skirt suit with white Nike tennis shoes, the perfect attire for a middle school administrator. Jake remembered years long gone when she would take him and Roger to school with her on Saturday mornings, using her all-purpose key to let the boys shoot hoops in the gym. Now, as she walked into the house, Jake jogged over and waited for her at the open trunk. He tossed the ball on the front lawn and scooped up the remaining groceries.

"Jacob!" Mrs. Dawson's startled face lit up as she approached the car again. "Oh, you don't have to do that." She motioned to the grocery bags, now covered in Jake's sweat.

"Hi, Mrs. Dawson," Jake said cheerfully, as if they met like this all the time. "I don't mind."

"At least stay for some cookies, then. You still got a sweet tooth?" she smiled through her tired voice.

"Sure do," Jake said, ignoring the hours of homework still waiting for him in his bedroom. Physics had waited this long; what was another couple minutes?

A wave of sorrow washed over Jake as he entered the home where he had spent so much of his childhood. He hadn't been back since that fateful night after the basketball game, when he'd chosen a date with Amy over his plans with Roger. The walls were still painted beige, but the carpeted floors had been replaced with hardwood, and there was new furniture arranged in a new layout in the front room. But the smell was the same. Jake took a deep breath, inhaling the unmistakable aroma of freshly baked bread. Mrs. Dawson made the best sourdough, and memories of he and Roger eating clam chowder in her homemade bread bowls on a rainy day invaded his consciousness. The Dawsons had always been so good to him.

He walked into the kitchen and dropped the bags on the counter. Everywhere Jake looked flooded him with memories—like he and Roger waking up early to watch Saturday morning cartoons in the Dawson living room; Friday night root beer floats and Monopoly; building forts in the family room with every blanket, sheet, and pillow they could find in the whole house; and countless dinners with the family around the dining room table. Even when Mr. Dawson left during their sixth grade year, Roger's mom always kept an extra chair around the table, just so Jake knew there was a place with Jake's name on it any time. More than once, Jake had shown up on the Dawsons' doorstep unannounced, with his sleeping bag and a toothbrush, during a thunderous fight at the Taylor home. Sometimes she had stayed up and talked with him; other times she simply opened the door and let him fall immediately to sleep on Roger's upper bunk bed.

Jake took another deep breath and tried not to think so much. Mrs. Dawson poured two glasses of milk, then pulled out a package of Double Stuf Oreos. His own mom refused to buy them because they were too unhealthy, but Roger's mom always had them.

She handed Jake one of the glasses and led them to the living room couch, the only piece of furniture that hadn't been replaced. She placed the cookies on the coffee table and grabbed two for herself. Jake unscrewed his Oreo and held the two pieces gingerly, unable to swallow. He carefully put the two halves of his Oreo back together, stared at it for a second, then dunked it in his milk.

On the coffee table was an old photo album labeled, "Roger: 4th grade—8th grade." Jake fingered the cover, almost afraid to look inside.

"Oh, sometimes I like to escape down memory lane." Mrs. Dawson smiled sadly, picking the book up off the table. "Would you like to stroll with me?" She laid the album on Jake's knees.

Jake gingerly lifted the cover. The first two pages were filled with Roger's school pictures. He only had one look in

those shots: a giant smile. Jake reached for another cookie, crunching it in two bites each as he sat captivated.

Mrs. Dawson turned the next page, and staring back at Jake was a picture of the two boys on the first day of fifth grade. They stood side-by-side with their arms around each other's necks. For some reason they thought it was cool to wear the same bright orange shirt from a camp they'd gone to that summer. Jake just stared at the picture. It summed up their early childhood so well—inseparable.

"I know he was really happy there." Mrs. Dawson spoke resolutely.

No doubt there had been many tears before, but tonight Jake could tell that she was choosing to focus on the good memories. He attempted to do the same, but each turn of the page pulled him deeper into sorrow and depression. She turned another few pages, and suddenly Jake could not find enough air to breathe as he viewed a picture of himself in the hospital room with Roger after the accident. They were both grinning widely, and Jake had his arm around his best friend who showed off his full-leg cast.

That should have been my accident. The car should have hit me, Jake's conscience screamed at him.

"That cast was his badge of honor," Mrs. Dawson shook her head, turning the page like it was any other. *How can she treat it so casually?* Jake thought. *Doesn't she know how much that picture matters?* Or maybe she did, and that was the reason for the quick page turn.

"Why don't you keep this one? Roger would want that," Mrs. Dawson was saying as she pulled out a happy picture of the boys in their soccer uniforms.

"Thanks," Jake whispered. It had been a few minutes since he had said anything. "But could I have the cast photo?" he asked sheepishly.

She squeezed his hand and turned back with shaking fingers to pull the old picture out from underneath the plastic covering. He delicately held it in his hand, not wanting to leave the smallest fingerprint or smudge. Life had been so much simpler then. What happened? But he knew the answer already... Popularity happened. Amy happened. The parties happened. Cooler friends happened. And none of it included Roger. If only he could go back...

Again, Mrs. Dawson broke into his regrets. "Jake, thank you. I've missed having you around." They had come to the end of the album, and she placed it back on the coffee table and closed up the half-eaten package of cookies.

Jake couldn't stop staring at Roger's smile and cast. His hand was shaking, and his throat was tight.

"Mrs. Dawson," he stammered. "I'm sorry I wasn't a better friend to Roger. I—I didn't know." He couldn't even look her in the eye.

Mrs. Dawson turned to Jake and grabbed his trembling hand, knocking the picture to the floor. As Jake bent down in front of her to retrieve it, she touched his shoulder and looked him in the eye.

"None of us did. And I was his mother. He was my son," she whispered. Tears flowed down her cheeks as she tried to pull herself together, and Jake looked away. Whatever pain he was experiencing, it must be nothing compared to what she was going through. She'd already had a husband leave her, and now she'd lost a son. Impulsively, Jake reached out to hug Mrs. Dawson, wanting to make up for the pathetic embrace he'd given her at the funeral. For several minutes, they held each other tight mourning their mutual loss together.

It was in that embrace that Jake came up with an idea. After he shared it with Mrs. Dawson, she was more than happy to lend Jake several of Roger's old photo albums. Although Jake had not been there for Roger in his greatest time of need, his best friend's life would not be forgotten.

Sitting in his bedroom at 2:00 in the morning, his physics book still unopened, Jake scanned a stack of pictures into his computer. On the screen was Roger's new MySpace page. In bold letters next to Roger's senior picture, Jake had typed "Make My Life Count." Even if no one ever clicked on the page, this simple exercise was transforming Jake's clouds of guilt into a fiery passion to not let anyone else make the same mistake.

31

NORMALLY WHEN JAKE got less than his standard eight hours of sleep, he was a walking zombie the next day. Today, however, the weight he had been carrying around for weeks had diminished to nearly nothing. He was so ecstatic about the new Web site that he'd stayed up until almost four the night before finishing off physics. But no one would have guessed he was surviving on only two hours' sleep. The roughest part of his day was keeping his project quiet, but he was determined to just watch and wait to see what might happen. He'd let the site speak for itself.

After physics (where Jake scored 16 out of 17 on the homework), Jake met Jonny outside his sophomore bio class, and they headed together through the Pacific High quad to their lunch spot. Everything about Jonny had changed dramatically over the past couple weeks. His days of wearing that same black hooded sweatshirt were gone; now he looked like any other guy in his jeans and T-shirt—not that Jonny would ever be like everyone else. Jonny had his quirks that sometimes drove Jake up the wall, but he also had the ability to make Jake

laugh like no one else could. What had started with Jake just trying to be nice had blossomed into the most genuine friendship Jake had enjoyed since Roger.

Jake was most excited when Jonny started wearing short sleeves. Far more than just a response to the weather heating up, they represented a shift in Jonny's perspective, and they demonstrated that scars really can heal. Jake and Jonny were united on a deeper level because of Roger—they could share their sadness and regret as well as funny stories and fond memories of him. They were just good for each other.

As they walked together through the quad, Jonny babbled on about the risk of genetic mutations to the flu virus, and how it could turn our pets into giant freaks like the Teenage Mutant Ninja Turtles. Jake just smiled and played along, asking questions like what would be the best dog food to feed them, and if buying a turtle would be a wise investment under these circumstances. It wasn't like Jonny believed all this stuff; he just enjoyed exploring all the possibilities.

Jonny suddenly blurted out, "You think it's okay to wear underwear with hearts on them?"

Nothing that came out of Jonny's mouth should have surprised Jake anymore, but he really hadn't seen this one coming. "What?" Jake whispered harshly, hoping his friend would get the clue that there were some questions he shouldn't announce to the world.

But it wasn't gonna happen. Jonny pulled up his shirt and hiked up his underwear, revealing white boxer shorts covered by sparkly pink hearts. "My mom bought these on a clearance rack yesterday," he explained too loudly as he stretched them out further. "I hope they're not used." His face looked worried, as if it were a genuine possibility.

Jake glanced over at a group of skaters passing by, who had started snickering. He yanked Jonny's shirt down so rapidly that it knocked off some of the glitter.

"Hey, my sequins!"

Jake put his arm around his friend and pulled him quickly away from their growing audience. "Dude, what's it like in there?" Jake chided, playfully strangling Jonny as he knocked on his melon. The more Jake corrected Jonny, the more he realized that Jonny really didn't care how others saw him—a feat Jake was continuing to master.

"What's it like in where?" Jonny asked innocently, wriggling out of the loose choke-hold and rubbing his head. Jake just shook his head and smiled.

Cutting across to the center of the quad, Jake caught a glimpse of Danny and Kelsi heading over to their pothead gang hiding out underneath the stairwell. Jake watched them and imagined the cloud of chemical euphoria they'd be lurking in. Jake may have smoked his share of weed over the years, but now the whole thing just looked so gross: hiding out in the shadows of campus with a tiny clique, lighting a roll of paper on fire and sucking in the smoke, waiting for the high that always went away. Jake got way more of a rush out of his new lunch gang. It was much more than just a fleeting high. It stuck with you.

"Aren't they in the youth group?" Jonny interrupted Jake's thoughts.

"Yeah, kinda," Jake admitted, focusing his eyes back on Jonny.

"You seem different than them," Jonny commented matter-of-factly.

He had no idea that those words were the highest compliment Jake could imagine. Jonny didn't need a response, but Jake answered anyway, "I'm still trying to figure this whole thing out." After all, it had only been two months since Jake had been in Jonny's shoes making the same observations.

The boys passed by a giant sign advertising the upcoming, first-ever flannel pajama dance. Jake rolled his eyes. The Pacific High Social Club had apparently run out of ideas. But as Jake blew it off, Jonny stopped to read every word. He turned to Jake with an uneasy look on his face.

"What's up?" Jake asked.

"You ever ask a girl out before?" Jonny's eyes grew wide.

"Like on a date?" Jake played along, whispering back like this new topic was top-secret information.

Jonny nodded, his eyes glued to Jake.

"Yeah, I've asked one or two," Jake answered, acting like an expert in the field. The truth was, he'd only ever asked Amy, and it was only after she took the first step. But Jake didn't see the need to add these details to the conversation at present.

Jonny stared at the ground for a moment, deep in thought. "You think Andrea would go with me?" he finally mumbled.

"Andrea?" Jake repeated, shocked. His first thought was that she was way out of Jonny's league. But really, it made perfect sense. By nature she was affectionate and was probably the first girl to show Jonny any kind of attention. While Jake was kicking these thoughts around, Jonny's face had blanched white and looked like he had forgotten to breathe. Jake snapped out of it and slapped Jonny on the back. After all, Jonny didn't need someone to tell him to get real—he needed a wingman.

"You got a game plan?" Jake asked with a wink and cocky smile, ideas already forming in his mind.

Jonny shook his head. "No. What's a game plan?" he whimpered apologetically.

Jake propped his elbow on Jonny's shoulder, and the two put their heads together as they walked slowly to the lunch group. "You see," Jake said, grinning like a guru. "If you can make them feel like a million bucks, then they're like putty in your hands." Jake rubbed his hands together and pointed his index finger at Jonny for effect. "And let me say, I got the perfect idea for you, my friend."

Jonny's goofy smile erupted, and his eyes twinkled. "Okay, but...are you going to be there?"

"Of course—" Jake straightened his back, then poked Jonny in the ribs. "—Not! You gotta fly solo on this one. But I'll help you train."

They arrived at their spot, and Jake watched Jonny settle in next to Andrea with a whole new understanding. She gave him a big hug, having no idea what her warm embrace was probably doing to his insides. Or maybe she did. Jake smiled, imagining the possibilities.

DING DONG.

The gong-like doorbell reverberated through Andrea's entire house. Sitting on the doorstep was a large block of ice with a hammer leaned up against it. Quaking with fear, Jonny raced back a few steps to hide behind a well-manicured bush, the perfect place to watch and not be seen.

He and Jake had spent the better part of the afternoon concocting this plan. Jake had given his 100 percent guarantee that it would turn Andrea into putty. Jonny wanted to give it some time, but Jake had reassured him that the longer he put off asking her out, the harder it would be.

Jonny peeked through the leaves and wiped his sweating hands on his jeans. Suddenly, he heard soft footsteps, then the creak of the large oak door opening just ten feet from where he was hiding. He held his breath and wiped a new layer of sweat from his hands.

"What do we have here?" an unfamiliar and much older voice resounded.

Jonny trembled and stood up slightly so he could see over the shrubbery. Standing there was an older version of the girl of his dreams. It was Andrea's mom.

She picked up the hammer, and Jonny gasped. He leaned into the prickly bush, panting for air and scolding himself under his breath. He closed his eyes and tensely crouched into a ball, as if he was waiting for an explosion. "Stupid Jake, this better not be another prank..." he muttered. "I swear I'll smash his windshield with that hammer..."

But Andrea's mom just turned back toward the house. "Andie, do you know what this is?" She shouted back through the doorway.

Then Jonny heard Andrea laugh, and he looked up to peer back over the bush. There she was, wearing that lacy tank-top she'd worn at school, but not the cowboy boots. Her cute little feet rested bare against the cool entryway tile. Jonny sighed and relaxed a little, drying his hands yet again on his now-soaked jeans.

"Let's check it out!" Andrea took the hammer from her mom and swung it forcefully into the helpless ice block. Jonny's eyes opened wide as ice chips flew everywhere, and the contents inside the block became more and more visible. After one final gargantuan swing, the entire block crumbled, leaving a wilted daisy lying all by itself on the Stephens' welcome mat.

At that point, Jonny took a deep breath and started to stand, but then he hesitated. Jake had clearly explained that the exposed flower was his cue to step out from hiding and deliver the line, but Andrea's mom was still standing there, watching in the doorway. On quivering legs, Jonny finally stepped out from behind the bush into the walkway. He instinctively pulled a white 3x5 card from his back pocket and began to read as Andrea tenderly picked up the gift.

"Ummmm...now that we've broken the ice, how about going on a date with me?" Jonny nervously recited, his eyes fixed on the card. Andrea's mom looked at him with curiosity. Her gaze did nothing to help Jonny stop shaking.

Silence.

One-one thousand.

Two-one thousand.

Three-one thousand.

It seemed like three years. Jonny let his hands drop to his sides, and he heaved another deep breath. His left foot slowly dragged slightly behind him, as if he was getting ready to turn about-face and take off running down the street.

Andrea's mom elbowed her speechless daughter in the side, and Andrea blurted out, "Oh my gosh, how sweet!" She giggled a little. "Ummm, of course!"

Jonny's shoulders finally unhunched and his hands relaxed as Andrea cradled the wilted daisy like a newborn baby, the hammer still clutched in her right hand. Her mom stood next to her, also smiling.

"Okay then, let's go!" Jonny quickly turned to leave.

"Right now?" Andrea looked to her mom, who appeared equally surprised. But Mrs. Stephens just nodded approvingly.

"Make sure you're home by ten."

Andrea's smile dipped almost imperceptibly as she took a step back. "Let me go grab some shoes," she chirped and bounded away.

Mrs. Stephens abruptly turned toward Jonny, her smile completely gone. "Where are you taking my daughter?"

Jonny automatically looked down at the card, as if it would help him come up with the words that escaped him. There was nothing. So he just stared blankly at Mrs. Stephens.

"We'll just go for a walk," Andrea interjected from behind her, returning to the doorway with flip-flops in hand. Jonny smiled eagerly to agree with the brilliant and timely suggestion.

Sitting in his truck a few houses down, Jake couldn't hear the words, but when Andrea returned to the door with her shoes, he stealthily drove off down the road. Jonny was on his own now.

✤ ✤ ✤

Jonny and Andrea walked slowly down the Oceanside pier, each licking an ice cream cone from a nearby shop. Andrea's house was just a short half-mile walk to the beach, so without a car, it was either the pier or...really there were no other options. He fingered the change in his pocket from the twenty-dollar bill Jake had loaned him. Jonny had proudly handed the ice cream shop employee enough money to pay for both cones, like he was taking care of his girl like boyfriends are supposed to.

That confidence, however, was overshadowed by the mess he was making. As they walked, Jonny helplessly watched more and more ice cream drip down his hand. Walking and licking at the same time was awkward enough, but he also had to keep up with Andrea and appear attentive to her conversation. As she chatted about thrift-store bargain hunting, he wiped the sleeve of his sweatshirt across his mouth with one long swipe, erasing the marble fudge off his face. He glanced over at Andrea's cone, which could not have looked more different. Her strawberry swirl had been perfectly manicured into a gentle pink lump, and she continued gracefully licking her dessert like a professional while maintaining an engaging conversation. Jonny couldn't help but shake his head, impressed.

They walked through the Oceanside Harbor, with rows of boats docked on one side and rows of souvenir shops and restaurants lining the other. The Beach Boys played in the background from a nearby bar and grill as the sun set over the Pacific Ocean behind them. Happy couples of all ages strolled hand-in-hand through the narrow promenade. Jonny's fingers twitched, and he reached for Andrea's hand as she walked, but he pulled it back before she noticed. He kept scratching his head—he either was searching his brain for exactly the right response, or he'd forgotten what she had said altogether in his anxiety about the ice cream mess.

"You want to sit down?" Andrea sweetly asked, breaking the twenty-third moment of silence for the evening. Jonny nodded, taking a seat on a wooden bench next to a sleeping older woman wearing a garbage bag for a poncho. Andrea was small, but there was no way she was fitting in between them. Jonny looked up, clueless, as the poncho lady awoke from her nap.

"What if we sit over here, so we can both sit down?" Andrea laughed, taking a seat on another wooden bench only a few feet away, this one empty. She patted the bench with her hand.

Jonny smiled sheepishly. He waved goodbye to the dozing and now drooling old woman and joined Andrea on the other side of the walkway. She had left plenty of room, but Jonny plopped himself so close to her that their shoulders and knees rubbed. Andrea smiled and barely shifted her legs while crunching into her waffle cone.

"You like your ice cream?" Jonny asked, his eyes casually following a group of surfers carrying their boards down to the beach.

"You've already asked me that four times," Andrea laughed, playfully elbowing Jonny in the stomach. She pointed at the red crumbs on his marble fudge. "I've never heard of anyone bringing their own toppings to an ice cream shop."

"I've just always loved bacon bits," he laughed nervously, pulling a plastic shaker out from his sweatshirt pocket to sprinkle more on his cone. "You sure you don't want to try?" he offered. Jake had strongly discouraged him from bringing the bacon bits, but Jonny refused to go anywhere without bringing along his favorite topping. Judging by the huge smile on Andrea's face, he confidently shook the container harder.

Andrea shook her head and covered the remainder of her cone with her hand in a kind but adamant refusal. Jonny teased her, pretending to accidently drop some on her lap. Glancing down, he noticed the marble fudge smears up and down his gray sleeves and instinctively pulled them up to hide his mess. As he did so, Andrea suddenly stopped laughing.

Her eyes were focused on his wrist: the same wrist that he had cut into with a razor blade for years, the same one he etched only a few weeks ago after his mother had come home drunk and screamed at him for a half-hour after he'd already had a lousy day at school. Jonny hadn't cut since the day he met

Jake and Andrea at lunch, but the series of scars lined up horizontally on the underside of his wrist were still clearly visible.

Andrea reached over and stroked the long scars with her petite fingers, and Jonny froze. She didn't seem to mind the scars at all, but instead looked oddly peaceful. She tapped the scars lightly, her eyes zeroing in on them. Jonny quickly pulled his sleeves back down and moved her hand out of the way.

Andrea spoke slowly, more seriously than Jonny had ever heard from her. "You know, I used to be a cutter."

Jonny instinctively looked away as ice cream dripped freely from his cone onto his opposite hand, but his eyes grew wide and his jaw dropped. "You?" he whispered.

She nodded. "Parents got divorced when I was in eighth grade. I thought it was my fault." Andrea looked back at Jonny compassionately, like she knew all the pain he had felt. "It was before I met God," she continued. "He saved my life." She delicately pulled his sleeve up a few inches again, and Jonny let her. She wrapped her tiny hand around his entire wrist, covering the wounds.

"Scars are supposed to heal, you know," she said warmly.

Her big brown eyes gazed deep into his. The nervous quivering in his legs was gone, and he didn't look away this time. Jonny leaned forward, forward, forward, his eyes drooping shut, his ice cream-sticky lips puckered slightly.

Andrea glanced up from Jonny's arm just in time to reactively raise her own cone in front of his face. In slow motion, his nose ran straight into her strawberry swirl, knocking the sculptured scoop onto her lap. Startled, Jonny jerked back, and his own sloppy scoop toppled to her lap as well. The scoops sat there, slowly melting into her denim skirt as Andrea and Jonny stared at each other in horror.

"Oh, Jonny! I thought we were just friends," she gasped. "I'm sorry!"

She stared at the creamy mess on her skirt, then frantically tried to knock it to the ground with her bare hands. In a state of panic, Jonny grabbed his lump of half-frozen ice cream with his bare hand and stuck it back on his cone. Andrea dropped her cone into a garbage can behind the bench and dabbed at the mess on her lap with a wilted paper napkin. Jonny attempted to help her, feebly wiping it off with his still-sticky hands.

"No—oh, uh—that's okay, Jonny." She brushed his fingers away.

Both sat motionless, staring blankly ahead for what seemed like an eternity. Jonny helplessly sat with his hands in his lap, afraid to look at her. He watched longingly as a small yacht cruised slowly out of the harbor, as if he wished he could join it on a trip to some deserted island where he could die of starvation.

Crickets chirped, the seconds ticked by, and drips of vanilla and chocolate again seeped down Jonny's hands. He looked down at the red particles floating down his knuckles. What else could he do? With a shrug, Jonny eyed his well-traveled ice cream scoop, and instinctively his tongue shot out and took a lick.

AFTER WATCHING JONNY land the date with Andrea, Jake couldn't have been prouder of his young protégé. At the same time, he had to admit he was wishing for someone to spend Friday night with, too.

He stopped by the gym on his way home. Ever since the fight with Doug, Jake had done his weight workouts at the local YMCA. He much preferred the smaller and more familiar Pacific High weight room, but it just wasn't worth the risk of dealing with Doug again. He'd have to endure the packed family fitness center—with all its middle-aged men wearing spandex—for the short time he had left until he packed his bags for Louisville.

So, while his old friends were most likely at the party of the weekend, Jake pumped iron and took out his aggression on the bench press. The feel of the cold iron resting in his palms as he did rep after rep of squats, bench, curls, lats, and tris turned out to be more than enough company for a Friday night. A couple hours later, he drove his truck into the Taylor driveway, feeling a good kind of tired.

Until he saw Amy.

There she was, sitting all alone on the curb in front of his house. She was wearing Doug's lettermen's jacket over a little red dress Jake used to love. Doug's black Jeep was parked haphazardly along the curb a few feet in front of her, but there was no sign of Doug. Jake glanced all around to make sure.

Jake parked his truck and hesitantly got out, a whirl of emotions flurrying around him as he approached her. Amy's face was smudged with mascara and tears, and as Jake got closer, he could detect the all-too-familiar scent of alcohol mixed with perfume.

"Amy? Are you okay?" Jake tentatively took a seat next to her on the cold curb. She didn't object.

"I missed you at the party," she mumbled, without looking up from the gutter.

"I haven't been to one in over a month," he reminded her.

"I know."

Jake looked at Doug's jacket. It was nearly identical to his, with all the same championship patches and pins, minus two very significant ones that Jake took pride in: an extra varsity emblem, and a league MVP patch. The only real difference he noticed tonight, though, were the four insulting letters embroidered across the front: D-O-U-G. Jake winced. "Where's Doug?"

"The party. Probably passed out," Amy snorted indifferently. She jangled Doug's keys. "I stole his Jeep."

Jake couldn't help laughing. The two just sat in awkward silence. It wasn't cold tonight, but the breeze against his sweaty workout clothes made Jake shiver. But even in the stillness, it just felt good being near Amy again. Whatever reason Amy was there tonight, Jake was grateful.

Eventually, he stole a glance at her. She was looking right at him, as if she was waiting for his head to turn in her direction. This was the first time they'd been this close since the day she had said goodbye at church, and his heart throbbed, waiting for Amy to speak.

And then she dropped the bomb.

"Jake, I'm pregnant," her voice cracked.

An invisible, giant fist punched him in the gut, and he gulped desperately for air. He searched her face, waiting for a punch line, but it didn't come. Jake's eyes burned, and he hunched over to stare flaming darts into the dried-up gutter. He knew Amy was waiting for a response, but he could only stutter, "Are you sure?"

She slowly nodded, her voice now even quieter than before. "I missed my period, I took four home tests. I'm sure."

The previous anger Jake had felt toward Doug was nothing compared to the rage that welled up within him now. Jake and Amy had almost always been careful, making sure that something like this could never happen. And in only a few weeks, Doug had swooped in and taken complete advantage of her. *Why did she have to come here and rub it in my face?* Jake felt like crushing something, someone, but could only clench his fist tight upon itself. His knuckles turned white and the tendons in his forearms popped out as a scream rose in his chest and lodged in his throat. He could seriously kill him.

And then, as if she were reading his mind, Amy looked straight at him. "It's yours, Jake," she said weakly.

Again, the wind was knocked out of him by some invisible force. "What about...Doug?" Jake stammered.

"We never..." Amy whispered, trailing off.

Jake grabbed his knees and leaned back on the cold sidewalk, trying to make sense of it all. He felt great relief that Doug and Amy had never...but it didn't remove the weight of the situation. His breath escaped his lungs with gale force, unable to verbalize any intelligent thoughts. "Wow. Does your mom know?" Jake fumbled.

Amy stood up from the curb and paced. "She would kill me," she squeaked, her volume rising with panic. "She was my age when she had me. I can't tell you how many times she's warned me to be careful." She wiped her hand across her cheeks, smearing more mascara into her soft skin.

Jake was reeling in the darkness like a meteor hurtling in space. If he didn't slow down, he was going to rip apart. He wanted to say more, but all that came out was another "Wow."

"Yeah, you said that," Amy shot back, her voice gaining strength. "Look, I know it's more than either of us need to deal with right now, so I've decided not to keep it." She turned resolutely to go. "I just wanted you to know."

"That's it?" Jake shot to his feet to face her. The last thing he wanted to do was get into another fight with Amy, but the finality of her decision was more than he could handle.

Amy nodded firmly. "I grew up without a dad. I'm not gonna allow—"

"I get that, Amy," Jake interrupted, "but isn't that a decision WE should make?" He took a step toward her, lowering the volume and tone of his voice.

"WE, Jake? We haven't talked in a month, and YOU are going to Louisville soon," Amy shot back loud enough for the neighbors to hear. "You're going to take your little birdie bag and move on with your life—even more than you already have."

"But what about...?" He cut himself short. *She's not coming to Louisville?* He had been secretly hoping for the day when they could reunite in college, hundreds of miles away from Doug and the rest of their problems. He took a step back, trying to make sense of it.

"Jake, I'm not going to have this baby!" Amy ignored his question. She pulled the Jeep keys out of her pocket and began to fiddle with them in her hand.

"I'm not trying to tell you what to do, but this is my..."

"It's not your choice." Amy brushed past Jake's shoulder toward the Jeep.

"Amy, wait!" Jake pleaded, jumping up to follow her.

She spun around, her face screaming resentment. Jake jogged up alongside her. "Amy, I just think this is something we should talk about." He spoke calmly but firmly.

Amy shook her head with one hand on the door handle. "It's my body, Jake, my future," she declared.

Jake placed his hand tenderly on her shoulder. "I know, I just don't want you to rush into this."

"Do you know what would happen to me if I kept it?" She ignored his hand, opening the door and getting into the Jeep.

"What?" He tried to block her from shutting the door.

"Have you ever seen someone pregnant? It's kind of hard to hide," she snapped. Then she whispered, "Don't do this to me, Jake."

She released the emergency break, and the car rolled forward with the door open. Jake took a step closer, placing one hand on the back of her seat. He whispered, "What about the baby?"

Amy attempted to slam the door shut, but Jake grabbed her hand, pulling her grip off the handle. "Great!" she moaned through a rush of tears. "Why don't you make me feel worse than I already do!" She turned the engine over with the door still open and shifted from neutral to first while staring venomously at Jake. "I'd thought maybe your religious thing might make you more sympathetic, but I guess I was wrong."

This was the knockout punch. Jake staggered back, releasing the door, completely at a loss. He didn't want to fight with her. If only she'd let them talk this out.

"Wait. Amy, I'm sor—" he whispered.

Amy slammed the door shut and yelled through the window, "Stay away from me, Jake!" The car peeled out down the street. Jake stood alone on the sidewalk.

"Amy, I'm sorry," he pleaded again under his breath, watching her fly around the corner.

Dazed, Jake trudged up to his front door, aiming for the safety of his bedroom. At least there, he wouldn't be able to mess anything else up. He would give anything for another shot at the last fifteen minutes, but even then, he wasn't sure what he would do differently.

Before his fingers even reached the handle, the door flung open, and his mother stood frozen in the doorway. Her eyes were red from crying. In one hand, she held her small brown travel suitcase, and in the other, a trembling tissue.

"Mom?" Jake stared at her in a fog. She failed miserably at a weak smile and brushed by him toward her BMW in the driveway. Jake stepped out of the way to let her pass. "Mom, what's wrong?"

She looked back at him for a moment, then came back and placed her hand on his shoulder. She kissed him tenderly on the forehead. Still no words spoken, she walked back to her car.

"Wait, Mom! Tell me what happened," Jake begged, half-hoping she wouldn't say anything. His parents had gone through many fights, but he'd never seen one of them come to this. The look of complete resignation on his mother's face scared him.

His mom turned to face him, looking like she was about to say something, but no words came out. Fresh tears ran down her cheeks as she opened the back door and threw her suitcase in. She climbed in the front and spoke hoarsely through the open door. "Honey, I just can't right now." She closed the door, but just before it clicked, she mumbled, "I'll be at your Aunt Judy's."

Jake stood there in the driveway, dumbfounded, for the second time that night. He watched his mother pull out of the driveway and down the street, the same path Amy had taken just moments before. As he watched the tail-lights disappear around the corner, Jake's confusion and sadness slowly built into anger. With Amy, he was the one at the root of the problem, but with his mom, he knew exactly who the culprit was.

"Dad!" Jake yelled, marching into the house, slamming the front door behind him. He stormed down the hall into his dad's office. Behind the large mahogany desk, Glen sat in the dark, a shot glass in his hand and a nearly empty bottle of Jack Daniels by his side. He was a wreck: his hair was disheveled, his tie lay on the floor, and the contents of his briefcase were sprawled all over the desk.

"What did you do to Mom?" Jake accused more than asked, standing on the other side of the desk looking down at his father.

His father put the glass down and leaned forward, running his hands sloppily through his hair. His eyes remained averted, avoiding Jake's angry stare. "She's pretty mad this time," he slurred.

"What happened?" Jake angrily leaned on the desk, bending over to get in his dad's face. Jake was finally on the other side of the firing squad, and he was in no mood to offer mercy.

Glen took a few moments to get his words out. When he finally spoke, they came out broken. "Your mom caught me with another woman." He shifted his eyes away from Jake's condemning glower and sunk back in his expensive leather chair.

"She what?!" Jake shouted.

"She wants me to leave."

The words hit Jake like a wrecking ball to his guts. He felt disemboweled. He took a few steps back and collapsed against the door frame. "How could you?"

"I don't know...But it's a two-way street, it's not just me," his father feebly defended himself.

Jake looked at his dad in disgust. The man who always had all the answers, who always felt free to dole out unlimited advice, even now was trying to spin some of the blame on his mom. *Pathetic.*

"How long?" Jake shot back, his blood boiling at the thought of his dad with another woman. The thought of his parents getting a divorce had never seemed that big a deal, but it was revolting to think his dad would actually sleep with someone else.

"Year and a half. But it was over already. We'd decided to end it. I tried to tell your mother, but she wouldn't listen."

How dare he do this to us? Jake thought about how he had wanted to grow up to be just like his dad when he was a little kid. Now he'd rather punch him. "You're unbelievable, you know that?" Jake spewed, shoving the papers on his dad's desk so they flew all over the room. "I don't even want to look at you!" He stuck his finger inches from his dad's nose and let it linger there as he seeped as much hatred as he could across the

gap. But after a minute, Jake's exhaustion took over. His hand dropped to his side, and he weakly turned to the door.

"Jake!" his dad yelled angrily from his desk.

Jake stopped in the doorway, refusing to turn around for his father's last words: "I'm sorry son...I never meant to hurt anyone."

Jake shook his head. "Too late for that." He charged up the stairs, leaving his father sitting in the office, his footsteps echoing through the empty house.

Jake didn't sleep much that night, or much of the next, or the next. He lay hopeless in bed, wondering how his life had taken such a major dive. He clenched his pillow in his fists thinking about his parents, then crushed it against his face as he groaned about Amy.

How could I have been so stupid?

How did they let this happen?

How could Dad do this?

What do I have to do to make up with Amy?

Why won't Mom call me back?

Should I even try to call Amy?

Round and round his mind chased him, stopping only to confront him with tormenting images of Amy with Doug, his dad with a stranger, even Jonny with Andrea.

Hours crawled by with no respite, except the mind-numbing thump of his stereo and tedious monotony of the television. Holed up in his darkened room, Jake retained no sense of when night turned to day, then turned to night, then turned to day again. He even skipped church for the first time since he started going. The weekend dragged on, leaving Jake crumbled in its wake.

34

MONDAY MORNING FINALLY ARRIVED, and Jake trudged through the Pacific parking lot in a daze, his books feeling like hundred-pound dumbbells. As much as he didn't want to be at school, two days straight in his room had started to feel confining, and his mind was ready to be distracted from the horror story his life had become. Even Mrs. Holmes' annoying voice in physics class would be better than the plaguing voices in his head. He caught a glimpse of himself in a reflection of a car window—he looked terrible. He had just thrown on a crumpled T-shirt and jeans that morning; he hadn't even combed his hair or brushed his teeth. Any task beyond breathing just seemed so trivial and tiring now.

Jonny frantically ran up from behind Jake, jolting him out of his lethargic stupor. "Jake! Jake!" Jonny tugged on Jake's shirt. "I got huge problems!"

Jake smiled mechanically and kept walking. *Huge problems—wasn't that the fad of the week.* What could Jonny's be? Maybe he'd forgotten his locker combination again, or even worse, had gotten stuck on a video game level. Jake was in no mood to be his rescuer. He picked up his pace.

Jonny followed suit, his lanky stride matching Jake's without a second thought, his voice rising in intensity. "It's Andrea, I totally screwed up!" he moaned. "I should have never brought the bacon bits...but that's the least of my worries." Jonny went on and on and on, explaining in great detail the catastrophe of two nights ago. But past disagreements with Amy and lectures from his dad had taught Jake the skill of nodding without really listening. Three minutes in, he had no idea what Jonny was even talking about. Jake just stared ahead into the distance and turned the corner toward English.

"...I kinda tried to kiss her," Jonny implored. "I mean, she grabbed my hand or at least my arm, and oh, I thought she was...I'm such an idiot! Jake, what should I do?" Jonny waved his hands wildly.

Jake just heard something about a kiss. Helping Jonny score the date with Andrea had happened in another world at another time, and Jake's brain couldn't think back that far. He kept walking in silence next to the despondent Jonny through the crowded halls. Finally, he realized it was his turn to say something. "Whatever," he muttered, never breaking stride.

"Whatever? Whatever! Jake, this is huge! I just blew my one chance," Jonny exploded, jumping in front of Jake. "You got to help me out, man!" His lower lip quivered, and his eyes were wide. But Jake just stopped abruptly in front of his classroom and stared blankly back. "What's wrong with you today?" Jonny persisted.

Jake looked at the ground, trying to focus. The rage that had been simmering inside all weekend started to boil again, and before he gave them permission, words spewed out of his mouth. "You want to know what's wrong? I'll tell you what's wrong," Jake snarled. "It doesn't matter if you screwed up. It doesn't matter if she doesn't like you. It doesn't matter if she never speaks to you again. It's all so stupid, man."

"What?" For the first time, Jonny was rendered speechless.

"Dude," Jake continued relentlessly, "I guess she doesn't like you. Oh well! It wouldn't have worked anyway." He patted Jonny on the back as if he had somehow done him a favor.

Jonny shrugged Jake's hand off his shoulder and scowled, his glance flickering over the crowds of students milling around them. "You suck as a friend," he mumbled quietly.

Jake knew the words were spoken more in pain than in malice, but Jake was already maxed out, and they sent him over the top. Did Jonny seriously have no idea the kind of sacrifice that he had made to become his friend? "Yeah, I suck," Jake erupted. "That's why I picked you up. That's why I'm always defending you. That's why I helped you get a date in the first place—a date that *you* screwed up." He vomited the words mercilessly at Jonny as he felt all the anger and fury he had stuffed down rush from all parts of his body toward his mouth. "That's why I didn't tell anybody about..." Jake's voice dropped to a whisper, "...your little problem." He sneered and made unmistakable slicing motions on his arm.

With each cruel jab, Jonny flinched and shrank back. But Jake's anger was contagious and finally Jonny shouted back. "I don't need you, man! I was just fine before you ever bothered me!" He pushed his way through the throng of students, breaking into a run the moment he hit a clearing.

Jake watched him go, his every stride stabbing Jake with guilt. He staggered into English, avoiding the dozens of eyes gawking at him.

On the other side of campus, Jonny finally made it to his locker, heaving deep breaths of desperation. His fingers trembled as they spun the dial, taking four tries before they got the combination right. When he finally opened the locker, his violent drawings covering the inside walls received him with a dark, sinister welcome. He had left them up out of neglect, but now he stared at one particular picture in the corner of the locker door: a bloody man sinking into the ground, or rather being absorbed, hopelessly reaching up with all his strength for help that wasn't there. He had drawn that picture over a year ago, and Roger had posted his adaptation on his MySpace page the night before he had...Jonny closed his eyes

and leaned backward as if in pain, bracing himself against the cold strength of his locker.

A detached voice startled him. "At least you're finding out now."

Jonny spun around, covering his dark shrine. It was Danny Rivers, that kid from the youth group who was always smoking pot and had bullied him for years. He approached like they were old pals. Jonny slammed the door shut. "What?" he snapped.

"Chris just told him to be nice to you. You were kind of his little project," Danny laughed. He leaned in close, staring spitefully into Jonny's eyes. "I guess he failed that one, though, huh?" Danny slapped Jonny on the back and carelessly walked away. The late bell rang and he nonchalantly called back over his shoulder with a sneer, "Didn't know you were an artist."

35

JAKE MECHANICALLY PLODDED through his morning classes, moving from one room to the next without a single conscious thought. Somehow his body found the way to his usual seats, and he made it through the first four periods without anyone bothering him. Maybe his disheveled appearance kept everyone away. Regardless, Jake was in no condition to endure the lunch gang, so after Physics he just kept walking, all the way to the parking lot.

Once he got to his truck, he was confronted with a new dilemma: Where would he go? He definitely didn't feel like going home; he'd been locked up there for the last two days. Besides, the thought of running into his dad made his blood boil. So he just climbed in and wandered into the stream of traffic, blindly passing stoplights marking unobserved cross-streets. Before he knew it, he found himself parked down the street from the Vaughn's house.

In a T-shirt and gym shorts, Chris was playing soccer with Caleb in the front yard. Caleb sported a Superman shirt with a red napkin tucked into the back of his collar like a cape, and he leaped and tumbled all over the lawn like a hyperactive

superhero. Jake watched the patience with which Chris kept retrieving Caleb's poorly placed kicks, and how he smothered the kid with hugs and kisses in between them. Jake had to chuckle aloud when Caleb put so much effort into one swing that he missed the ball altogether and toppled, giggling, onto his back. Chris scooped him up into his arms and tossed him in the air, Caleb squealing with delight.

Jake debated breaking up their special time. With one hand still on the key in the ignition, he decided to leave them out of his mess and get out of there. But just as his fingers started to twist the starter, Caleb sent the ball flying in his direction. Chris lunged to catch it, spotted Jake, and waved him over with a huge smile, then he lightly drop-kicked the ball back to his son. Reluctant but relieved, Jake got out and trudged up to the driveway.

"Shouldn't you be in school?" Chris teased as he scooped up the returning soccer ball, his eyes studying Jake. He quickly bent over to his son's level. "Hey Caleb, buddy, how about you go help Mommy inside for a bit?"

Caleb didn't take the hint and rushed to Jake with hands reaching up like claws. "Roar! I'm a lion!" He threw the full force of his body into the side of Jake's leg, knocking Jake back a few feet, then latched on and pretended to gnaw on his jeans.

"Uh oh! Are you going to eat me?" Jake asked, shaking Caleb around on his leg as he tickled him from above.

"No! I like cookies!" the three-year-old exclaimed.

"I bet Mommy will give you a cookie if you go help her," Chris interjected with a wink toward Jake. Caleb stood motionless for a moment, as if considering the offer, then ran inside flapping his arms like a bird. Chris waited for the front door to shut and then came alongside Jake. "Are you okay?"

Jake's throat closed up, and he could only shake his head.

"Come on inside," Chris invited, reassuring Jake with a strong arm around his shoulders.

Caleb sat at the counter, contentedly munching on a gooey mess that covered his face and hands with chocolate. The coloring page in front of him was also predominantly brown. Cari stood at the sink and smiled hello while she cleaned up the cooking chaos. The unmistakable aroma of freshly baked chocolate chip cookies hung sweetly in the air.

Jake had only been to the Vaughn's house once before, a few weeks earlier, when they'd hosted a dinner for all of the graduating seniors from the youth group. Their home had been warm and tidy that night, but today they clearly weren't expecting company—books, toys, and blankets were strewn all over the front room. Even so, the clutter embraced Jake with comfy relief, so different from his own sterilized home. He sank into a chair at their dining room table while Chris poured them each a glass of milk and Cari stacked a plate of cookies for them. When Chris joined him at the table, he waited patiently for Jake to speak when he was ready.

Jake took a sip of the ice-cold milk, then dunked a cookie and munched it slowly. "I'm in trouble," he finally offered vaguely.

"What's wrong?" Chris prodded in a relaxed voice.

"Everything," Jake sighed.

Chris chuckled to himself. "Hmm...how about a few more specifics?"

From anyone else, Jake would have resented the laugh, but Chris' settling nature actually helped him stay calm and think more clearly. Jake covered his head with his hands and stared at his pathetic reflection in the glass table. "Well, I went off on Jonny in front of the whole school," Jake started. Chris winced, but said nothing. Jake continued, "And my parents are getting a divorce, 'cuz my dad got caught cheating on my mom..."

"Jake, I'm so sorry." Chris' words were warm and sincere, and pain reflected from his eyes as he waited for Jake to elaborate.

Jake braced himself for the fallout of the third bomb before he added, "And Amy's pregnant."

Chris paused, peering at Jake across the table. Then he breathed, "Wow."

"Yeah, that's what I said." Jake grimaced, remembering Amy's cold reaction.

Cari walked in from the kitchen, drying her hands on a dish towel. She walked behind Jake and rubbed his back. "How's Amy?"

That wasn't the question Jake was expecting. "She wants to get rid of it," he answered, averting his eyes to the floor.

"Oh." A sigh escaped Cari as she sat down at the table next to the guys, but her voice was gentle and unjudging. "Has she made up her mind?"

"I don't know." Jake trembled. He rested both elbows on the glass table and leaned forward. "What can I do? She won't even talk to me."

"Jake." Cari took his hands and looked directly into his eyes. "She needs to know that she won't be alone, that you'll be there for her."

Jake shook his head and sneered a little. He had *always* been there for her. *She* was the one who wouldn't give him time to figure things out. *She* was the one who broke up with *him*. *She* was the one who had moved on so quickly. He flicked his glass of milk with his fingernail, and condensation dripped to the table. "I've dreamt of going to Louisville my whole life. She knows that."

Cari leaned forward, lowering her voice to barely more than a gentle whisper. "And you think she dreamed of getting pregnant at eighteen?" She looked at Jake with compassion.

Jake took a deep breath, crossed his arms, and leaned back in his chair, the smell of cookies still thick in the air. "Well, what do I do?"

"Have you talked to God about any of this?" Chris suggested.

"God?" Jake scoffed. "I don't even want to talk about Him." He knew that Chris would eventually bring the big guy into this, but Jake just wasn't in the mood.

"God didn't do this to you," Chris said in an even tone.

"Well, he didn't stop it. Here I am, going to church, reading my Bible, all that crap, and *this* is what I get?"

"Jake, God's not punishing you." Chris's eyes never veered from Jake's.

"Well, it sure feels like it! Look at my life—it's falling apart!" Jake's anger started to build again, this time at God, the one guy who wasn't supposed to let him down. "This God-thing, it isn't working! It's not worth it!"

Chris paused, opening his mouth, then shutting it again. Finally, he offered, "Jake, God's not some genie, or a vending machine, or someone who magically solves every issue for you. And He's not 'worth it' because He makes your life all better and all your problems disappear. That's not how He works." Chris paused again, then continued, "But God *is* on your side, Jake."

Jake shook his head vehemently. "It doesn't feel like it."

Chris reached out and rested his right hand on Jake's shoulder. "Whether you're feeling Him or not, it doesn't change the fact that He's here for you."

"Then why is my whole life falling apart?" Jake asked, a tear slowly trickling down his face. He had not cried in front of anyone since he was a little kid, but he didn't try to hide it.

The youth pastor's words stung: "Maybe it already was falling apart, and you're just now starting to care."

"My life was fine." He knew it was a lie before the words even came out, but it's what he'd been telling himself for so long.

"God wants so much more for your life than just 'fine.'" Chris asserted.

"Like what?"

Once again, Chris's response wasn't what Jake expected. "I don't know, Jake. I'm not God. But I promise you, it's awesome. You just gotta trust Him through this."

That word "trust" was a hard one for Jake. "I just don't know, man. I don't know if I can," he said.

An understanding smile formed on Chris' face. "Well, besides God, I'm here for you, no matter what." He lightly punched Jake on the shoulder. "It's your call, Jake. You and I both know where the other roads lead. You gotta decide for yourself. But let me ask you—what else are you going to do?"

Jake had to admit that Chris had a point. He sat back in his chair and sighed deeply.

THE CLOCK NEXT to his bed read 1:43 A.M. Jake lay wide-awake on his back, staring at the ceiling. His eyes probed the darkness and noticed several spots the painters missed years ago—he'd never seen them before. His mom still wasn't answering his phone calls, and his dad's Porsche was gone. He had absolutely no desire to talk to his dad, but he still found himself waiting for the unmistakable creak of their front door. There had been no sound from downstairs, except the annoying grandfather clock that signified another hour of aloneness. He longed to fall asleep, but his mind kept replaying the conversation with Chris over and over again. He hated to admit it, but Chris was right. Jake wanted to blame his whole mess on God, but who was he to be blaming anyone? He was the one who had made poor choices—just like his dad.

Jake sat up on the edge of his bed, staring at the pictures on his bedside table. His eyes lingered on the happy snapshots of him and Amy. He missed her so much. Her final demand that he stay away from her echoed through his head, but he ached to say just one word to her: *Sorry. I'm sorry, I'm sorry, I'm sorry!* He groaned to himself, wishing Amy would just give him a chance.

His eyes skimmed over all the Louisville stuff on his walls: pennants, posters, and a cover of *Sports Illustrated* with an image of the Cardinals parading a trophy around the court. It had always been a source of comfort and excitement. But tonight, the décor felt more like a burden he wasn't sure he had the strength to carry.

He glanced back over to he and Amy's junior prom picture, sitting on the dresser in the frame she'd given him. She was right, and he knew it: Why should he get any say about the baby if he was just going to leave in a couple of months? And why would she still be going to Louisville, pregnant or not? She wasn't going to Louisville for herself; she had only been following him all along.

Jake grabbed his letter of intent to play basketball at Louisville out of the top drawer of his desk and held it weakly in front of him. It represented his entire future, but for the first time, it didn't feel totally right. He thought back to the day he'd received it in the mail almost four months ago. It was *everything* to him—the reward for all his years of effort, the answer to all his father's complaints. Now that dream seemed so irrelevant compared to the world that was crumbling around him.

Where did God fit in all of this? Maybe He wasn't to blame, but couldn't He have stopped his dad from having an affair? Couldn't He have stopped Amy from getting pregnant? Couldn't He have stopped Roger? *Wouldn't He have wanted to?*

Jake dropped the letter onto the floor and slid off the edge of the bed onto his knees. His heartbeat reverberated through his ears in the intense silence. Was God really listening? Feeling awkward, Jake pulled himself back up to the edge of his bed, rubbing his clammy palms together methodically. *Why is this so difficult?* He'd prayed before, but tonight was different, like his whole life hung in the balance.

Jake slid back to his knees with no idea what to do. Starting with a trickle, the words began to flow, coming from the parts of his brain he normally tried to ignore.

"Um, God, I don't know if I'm allowed to be mad at you, but I am. All this is happening to me and I'm trying my best to do what's right, but everything just seems to be getting worse. Chris says that I can ask you for help. I don't even know what I need, but I know that I need it. I guess I need you." Tears began to accompany the stream of words. "I'm sorry for a lot of things. I've screwed stuff up bad. I'm sorry for Amy...for Jonny...for Roger...I'm sorry that I ignored him, that I was too good for him, that I wasn't there when he needed me most. I was so selfish. I *am* so selfish. All I know is I can't do this alone. Give me the strength to do what's right."

Jake broke into sobs of desperation. He'd never cried like this before. "Show me what to do!" he pleaded to God under his breath. "I don't have anywhere else to turn." He stayed on his knees for more than a half-hour, gasping for air in the dark. The only light came from his digital clock, which glowed 2:15 A.M.

Finally, Jake reclosed his eyes and just crouched in silence on the floor—not really listening for anything, not really thinking, just being quiet. It wasn't dramatic, but Jake noticed his heartbeat slowly returning to normal, and his hands stopped sweating. The voices in his head slowly eased. He was fully alone, but in a very real way that he couldn't explain, he knew that he wasn't.

He hesitantly opened his eyes, hoping the growing calm was not just because of the darkness. He leaned over and carefully turned on his bedside lamp, but the tranquility remained. He sat back on the edge of his bed and gazed once more around his bedroom. He slid his body underneath the covers and laid his head on the cool side of the pillow.

He shut his bedside light off once again and lay motionless in the darkness. His eyes closed, and he was enveloped in a sense of comfort. Jake wasn't sure what this feeling was, or even if it was all just his imagination—but whatever it was, there was peace.

About one minute later, just as Jake was about to doze off, a sudden thought popped his eyes open again. The idea gradually developed and grew clearer and clearer as he mulled it over. After just a few more minutes, he knew exactly what he needed to do.

LESS THAN FIVE hours later, Jake arrived at Amy's house a few minutes before seven. On the bench seat next to him was a brown cardboard box that he'd packed until 3:00 A.M. Although he knew what he was doing was absolutely crazy, he had never been more sure of a decision in his life. The previous days' agony dissipated into an intense excitement that he'd never felt before, even on the basketball court, and although he was now on his fourth day with almost no sleep, he was wide-awake and brimming with nervous energy.

Jake parked his truck along the sidewalk in front of the small townhouse. He prayed at least fifty times on the ride over that she would agree to just hear him out. After that, if she still wanted nothing to do with him, he could live with it—but he had to try. He gave himself a quick pep talk and a long inhale, then he anxiously trotted up her short driveway. Jake had made this same walk many times before, and he remembered the nervousness he had felt picking her up for their first formal dance, but it paled in comparison to the anxiety he faced now. He knew there was no blushing beauty joyfully awaiting his arrival today.

He stopped at the door, briefly debating the pros and cons of ringing the doorbell versus knocking, when suddenly he heard the distinctive sound of a garage door opening. He turned away from the door and jogged back toward the driveway, where Amy's mom's ten-year-old blue minivan was slowly backing out of the garage. But Amy's mom wasn't driving this time. It was Amy, her long blonde hair unmistakable even from Jake's view, pulling away before he even got his chance! Jake wanted to lunge out and pound on the window, but he decided it would be better not to scare her, so he held back. Suddenly, the van jerked to a stop, and he knew he'd been discovered.

Jake waited a moment and then crept toward the van as the engine continued to run. He cautiously rapped on the passenger window and got his first full look at Amy. She wore an old pair of baggy sweats, she had no make-up on, her eyes were puffy and her nose was red. While Jake knew Amy loathed to be seen like this, he still thought she was the most beautiful thing he'd ever seen.

"Amy," he said, loud enough to be heard through the closed door.

"Stay away from me!" Amy blasted back, both arms on the steering wheel. She didn't even glance in Jake's direction.

"Amy, just please, hear me out," Jake pleaded. "It will only take a minute."

Amy's knuckles whitened on the steering wheel, and her jaw muscles clenched. She rolled the van in reverse, forcing Jake to jump out of the way. "I told you, go away!" she moaned as she looked at Jake for the first time. Her bald tires peeled out backwards into the street and sped away.

Although he thought he had prepared himself for anything, this was far worse than Jake had envisioned. Where was she going? She would never be caught dead at school looking like that. But he hadn't come this far to give up so easily, so Jake sprinted back to his truck and squealed after her.

He roared from third into fourth gear, whipping around a corner to catch up with the van. He spotted it a hundred yards ahead, waiting for a green light to merge onto Cassidy Street, a relatively busy boulevard that cut through the heart of south Oceanside. Jake pulled up next to her in the wrong lane, praying for no oncoming traffic, and yelled through his rolled-down window. "Just five minutes, Amy, please!"

Amy turned to Jake and glared at him as if he was a stalker. She shook her head violently. The light turned green, and Amy's car made the right and sped off again.

Jake banged his steering wheel and screeched to the right, cutting off another car. *God, please, please, please!* he chanted in his mind as he zigzagged through the passing lane. Traffic increased as they neared downtown, and he swerved and dodged, almost spinning out to keep up with her. Suddenly, a signal ahead turned red, and Jake slammed on his brakes and skidded to a stop inches from the car in front of him. He gulped with relief, then leaned out the window toward Amy, two cars ahead in the next lane.

"Please, Amy! I'm so sorry! I'm sorry for Friday night! I'm sorry, I'm sorry, I'm sorry!" Jake yelled frantically over the hum of a dozen engines lined up behind the crosswalk. If she would only look at him, and see that he wasn't angry or psychotic. But she stayed intently focused on the tail-lights ahead of her. Jake grew frustrated and thrust his elbow into his seat back. "C'mon!" he groaned, staring at her in hopes that it would force her to turn his way.

Then he realized she wasn't just ignoring him—she was crying uncontrollably. He could see her shoulders shuddering in the silhouette through the rear windshield, and she kept reaching up to wipe her face on her sleeve. The car behind Jake honked angrily, reminding him that the light had turned green. Amy jerked forward, pulling into the first parking lot on the right. Jake floored it, swinging his truck from the left lane and hurtling into the second entrance of the lot.

Amy parked the van along the back edge of the lot facing an industrial alley. She stayed buckled in her seat with the windows now rolled down, seemingly waiting for Jake to approach. Jake veered diagonally into two and a half spots and screeched to a

stop, just barely bumping into Amy's left front quarter-panel. He jumped out of the car and stood in front of her door.

"What!?" she demanded. Her voice sounded like it was scraping on her throat. Her eyes were bright red, and her sweatshirt sleeves were damp. Her hands were still glued to the steering wheel, as if it were her only source of strength left.

In all the commotion, Jake's perfectly crafted speech had flown out the window, so he just started babbling, afraid she would tear away again before he had a chance to finish. "This morning, I woke up, and I just had this feeling that I needed to see you. I'm sorry about how I reacted the other day, and I don't know what it's like to be you, and there I was making it worse..."

"Stop!" Amy pleaded. She unbuckled her seat belt, slowly stepped out of the van, and stood face-to-face with Jake. "I can't do this," she whispered, avoiding Jake's eyes, as cars zoomed by on the busy street near them.

Jake gently placed his hand on her arm. It was the first time he had touched her in months, and it felt good even through the bulky sweatshirt. "We can."

"You're leaving!" she exploded, finally raising her gaze to Jake's face.

"Not anymore," Jake whispered, taking a step closer to her so they were only inches apart.

Amy didn't flinch, but mumbled under her breath, "What are you talking about, Jake?"

A giant smile spread across his face, and he hustled back to his truck. "Wait a second," Jake called over his shoulder. He had imagined this moment dozens of times over the past five hours, and now it was actually happening. His heart thudded away, threatening to jump out of his throat. He pulled the box from the truck and carried it back to Amy. Without saying a word, he dumped the box out at her feet; it was full of all of his Louisville stuff—posters, T-shirts, pictures, mugs. Colorful pictures flew everywhere, plastic bobble-heads clunked on the blacktop, and a Louisville hacky-sack rolled over to her sneakers.

The two stared in heavy silence at the massive red and white heap lying on the asphalt. Amy gradually turned back to Jake, shaking her head in disbelief. "I—I can't let you do this. It's your dream," she sputtered.

"It's MY choice!" Jake announced, grabbing her right hand in both of his.

Amy covered her face with her free hand, tears flowing once again. "You don't know what you're doing."

"Amy, I do." Jake took a risk and embraced the sobbing Amy in a tender hug. His ex-girlfriend melted in his arms and buried her soaked face in his shirt. He had held her so many times before, but he was certain this was the most vulnerable they'd ever been with each other.

"I just can't be pregnant," Amy softly mumbled into his chest.

Jake held her tighter, then pulled a few inches away so that he could look into her eyes. "You've spent your whole life trying to get people to like you."

Amy's whole body began to shake as tears streamed down her cheeks. "But I'd lose everything," her voice cracked.

Jake pulled her in tight again, tucking a loose strand of her hair behind her ear. He lowered his head to hers and whispered ever so gently, "You won't lose me."

Minutes passed as they held each other tight at the edge of the parking lot in the middle of downtown Oceanside. Jake was sure there was nowhere in the world he would rather be than in this lot, holding Amy while she cried. Her sobs gradually subsided, then she abruptly pulled back to look once again at Jake.

"You don't have to do this," Amy whispered, crossing her arms, as if she expected him to take it back.

Jake knew that she had been hurt too many times before, and he couldn't deny that he was just as scared as she was. He looked back down at the pile of his Louisville dream that he had just dumped out like the trash, then looked back up, his eyes connecting with Amy. "I know, but I want to," he said resolutely. "You're more than worth it."

Amy leaned back against her van. "Jake, I'm scared. I'm not ready to be a mom."

"Neither am I." Jake shrugged, shoving his hands into his pockets.

Amy laughed for the first time. "Is there something you need to tell me?"

Jake looked sheepish. "I mean a dad," he corrected. "I'm not ready to be a dad." Jake stepped over to the van and leaned up against it next to her. They stood side-by-side, arms folded across their stomachs, watching the cars pass as they reflected on the full weight of their decision.

"What about Doug?" Amy turned to Jake and grimaced, scrunching up her nose. Jake's heart automatically skipped a beat. That nose-thing always made Amy look so cute; she was irresistible.

"I'm not really interested in Doug," Jake said with a playful smile but a serious tone. He pushed away from the van and faced Amy, grabbing both of her hands. "I want to make sure you get this: I'm here, no matter what—whatever you decide."

Amy nodded her head, holding back more tears. "Okay. I'll think about it. But I'm not promising anything."

Jake nodded. He slipped his arms around her again and closed his eyes, saying nothing, just feeling her warm and close against him. He understood and trusted her with the decision. Only then did Jake notice the giant green sign directly behind them that read NORTH COUNTY WOMEN'S HEALTH CLINIC.

JAKE BOUNDED THROUGH his front door a little after 1:00 P.M. He had just left a long breakfast with Amy at a little café down the street from the parking lot. He'd pinched himself at least twenty times over the past four hours to make sure it wasn't all a dream. Neither of them had been quite in the mood for school after their emotional rendezvous, which made the breakfast date all the more exceptional. They had talked and talked about everything, from college plans to the whole Doug "thing," over fresh-squeezed orange juice and a tall stack of buttermilk pancakes. Jake had listened intently about how Stanford had offered Amy a partial scholarship, and her mental anguish trying to figure out how a baby fit into all that. Jake had revealed his anger and turmoil over his dad's affair. He also finally explained to her about his God-experiment, and for the first time, she sincerely listened. In all their time together, they had never talked at such a deep level of honesty. Jake savored every minute they had in that corner booth.

The thought of him and Amy possibly getting back together brought an unconscious smile to his face. Jake also enjoyed watching her eat; he'd never seen her devour so much food.

That eating for two was no joke! But it was so cute. As horrible as he'd felt just twenty-four hours earlier, and as real as his problems still were, he now felt there was hope, and he reveled in it.

But those good feelings vanished the moment he entered his kitchen at home. His parents were seated at opposite ends of the breakfast table, and they didn't look happy. Jake's mom's chair faced away from the front door, but Jake could still see her crossed arms as she sat apathetic to a sink full of dirty dishes. His dad was back in his power suit and held a crumpled-up paper in his hand. The tension hung in the air like fog. All of a sudden, the pancakes and syrup didn't feel so good in Jake's stomach.

"What are you doing home so early?" his dad demanded, pushing back from the table and walking toward Jake. "Why aren't you in school?"

Jake turned to his mom, ignoring his father. "What are you still doing with him?" he pointed accusingly at the man he used to call dad. Who was this man to question him about anything?

His mother rose from her seat to intercept Glen, grabbing the crumpled paper from his hand. Before she even revealed its contents, Jake realized what it was—he'd left the letter of intent to Louisville on the top of his bedroom garbage can.

"I was cleaning your room, and I found this," she said, her eyes imploring him to explain.

"Mom, I don't know how..." Jake fumbled. He hadn't even considered how to explain everything to her yet.

Glen's booming voice interrupted. "You don't know?!" He moved closer to Jake and held out an open palm for the letter. "Jake, what's the meaning of this?"

"I'm not going," Jake said absently, still keeping his full attention on his mom. He hated even responding to his dad's question.

"Excuse me?" Glen waved the letter a few inches from Jake's face.

The brief glimpse of remorse the man had shown just a few days ago was now buried in his angry swagger, which caused

Jake's recent peace to evaporate into loathing. This man had been sleeping with another woman for the better part of a year and a half, and now he thought he could be upset?

Jake finally turned to him face-to-face and raised his voice to match Glen's. "I changed my mind."

Glen shook his head in disbelief, and he loosened his tie while firing an accusing glance at Pam. She simply watched with resignation from her seat at the kitchen table.

"Really." He turned back to Jake. "When did this happen?"

"It's complicated." Jake had no intention of explaining the decision. Later on, he could tell his mom, but Glen was no longer in his circle of trust.

The man who had fathered him placed his right hand on Jake's shoulder and took a long deep breath, then lowered his voice. "Jake, this is not the way to get back at me."

Jake felt his blood pressure rising, and he shrugged his dad's hand off his shoulder. Why did his dad think that the world revolved around him? "It has nothing to do with you," Jake growled through his teeth, rolling his eyes.

"Do you know how many guys would kill for an opportunity like this?" Glen raised his voice again, slamming the letter down on the granite counter.

"Like you?" Jake fired back sarcastically. It was time they'd had it out on that point, and Jake was more than ready.

Glen stared at the wrinkled letter long and hard, his fingers playing with the edges, restraining himself from crumpling it all over again. "Jake, think for a second," he said. "This scholarship is the only thing you've got. It's your only chance!"

Jake didn't move. Maybe his dad would have been right two months ago, but not now. "Not anymore," he whispered back barely loud enough to be heard.

Glen threw his arms up and stormed back to his chair on the other side of the table. Jake's head began to throb, tired of pushing down his anger and exhausted by the pressure. *How dare he try to give me advice?* For years he'd endured the

lectures, but now that time was over. Jake hated the thought of retreating from a fight, but he couldn't stand being in the same room with his father anymore. He wiped his hair out of his eyes and wearily turned to leave.

"Jake."

His mom's soft voice made him pause. The easy response would have been to keep walking, but he tried to step into her shoes for a moment. What was she going through right now? He turned and looked at her, hoping she would see his compassion rather than his irritation.

She rose from her seat and walked toward Jake, tenderly placing the palm of her hand on his face. "Honey, I thought this was your dream," she probed. "What's going on?"

Jake studied her face for a second. Her eyes were still puffy from a weekend of tears, but they couldn't hide her concern. She didn't look mad at all, just tired and confused.

"I just can't," Jake whispered back so only she could hear. He really didn't want to hurt her when she was hurting so much already.

She stared back into her son's blue eyes. "Why can't you?" she asked.

Jake really couldn't tell her—Amy hadn't made her decision yet. He fumbled for a decent explanation, but there was none. He looked his mom squarely in the eyes and whispered, "Amy."

Pam shook her head, confused. Jake shot a glance to Glen, who was now leaning in to listen. "What about Amy, honey?" his mom asked.

Jake's heart was pounding like a freight train. He coughed twice to clear his throat, looking back at his mom and then to the ground.

"What?" his father shouted from the other side of the room. Jake shot him a mean glare. If he never heard that man's voice again, he'd be okay with it.

His mom kept asking with her eyes, when suddenly she caught her breath. "Oh." She pulled Jake into her motherly embrace.

"Will someone please tell me what's going on!?" Glen demanded.

Pam and Jake pulled apart, and she brushed her fingers tenderly through his hair. "Amy's pregnant," she asked and confirmed at the same time. Jake subtly nodded his head. Now they knew, whether he liked it or not.

"TELL ME YOU'RE JOKING!" Glen exploded, jumping back up from his chair. He knocked over his briefcase, inciting him to kick it across the room, sending it spinning across the hardwood floor. Jake winced but kept his eyes on his mom. He hoped Amy would have better success with keeping the news from her mother; he prayed this would not ruin things for her. As for him, he'd made a promise to Amy, and he was going to keep it, no matter what.

"She can't force you to stay!" Glen boomed, his anger still increasing.

"It's not like that," Jake spoke directly to his dad. "It's MY choice."

"You're choosing to ruin your life!"

"I guess YOU would know," Jake snarled, jabbing his index finger in his father's face. Glen had no quick answer to that dagger, but turned crossly to pick up his briefcase. Jake savored the reaction, feeling like he'd finally landed a punch where his dad was weak. He glanced over at his mom, expecting to see at least a wry smirk, but she sat still, her eyes glazed over.

Glen picked up the letter from the counter and stomped out of the kitchen, his shoulder bumping Jake so hard that it knocked him back a step. He wadded the letter in his fist and tossed it at Jake's feet. "It's your future," he muttered as he left. Jake listened to his heavy footsteps echo through the hallway and out the front door.

He and his mother stood in silence for almost a full minute. Pam looked as if she wanted to cry, but her eyes had no tears left to give. Jake felt terrible about making her feel worse than she already did, and he committed in that moment to being a better son. It was just the two of them now, and they would

need each other. Jake glanced at the stack of dirty dishes, most of which he probably put there. "You want some help with the dishes?" he offered gently.

Pam smiled slightly and nodded. Jake grabbed the sponge and handed a dry towel to his mom. As he scrubbed the remnants of a burned oven-pizza off a silver tray, he turned to her with wet and soapy hands and said, "Mom, I'm praying for you."

39

AFTER SPENDING the rest of the day with his mom cleaning the house and running errands, Jake was excited to head to youth group. Chris was one of the few people that he actually *wanted* to tell about the morning's car chase. Turning the corner into the youth room, he spotted Andrea passing out name tags from her usual spot behind the welcome table. Most of her bracelets were gone today, but she did sport a four-inch-wide silver plastic band around each wrist. Today's shirt was royal blue with a bold red "W" imprinted right in the middle of a bright yellow shield.

"Where have you been, stranger?" Andrea asked, offering Jake her hand like it was the first time they'd met.

"Oh, I've had some family stuff," Jake answered, reaching across the table to give his friend a hug. "What's the W stand for?"

"Wonder Woman!" Andrea laughed, as if Jake was the only person who didn't know.

Jake grabbed a name tag from the table. "So what are your super powers?"

"Well, I've got an invisible jet, and my bracelets can block

bullets." She flexed her arms out in front of her, pretending to block invisible bullets coming from who knows where, complete with sound effects. "Pichew, pichew! Hoo-yah!"

Jake crumpled up his name tag and tossed it at her head. Andrea's superhero bracelets deflected it back at Jake, who dramatically fell to the ground. Andrea giggled, trotted around to his side of the table, and pulled the much-bigger Jake back to his feet.

"Sorry, I should have warned you," she smiled, turning to write up a new name tag. She slapped it directly on Jake's shirt. It read, "Don't mess with Wonder Woman...trust me."

Jake laughed as she returned to her duties, then suddenly turned serious. "So, have you seen Jonny?"

A group of freshman boys approached the table to write their names in illegible chicken scratch. Andrea greeted them warmly and then turned her attention back to Jake. "No. Friday night turned a little awkward." She cringed. "I haven't seen him since. Haven't you talked to him?"

Jake shook his head. The truth was he hadn't seen his friend since he'd shouted at him outside of first period yesterday. That whole morning was somewhat of a blur, but a stab of guilt rushed through him as he remembered mimicking Jonny's cutting problem in front of everyone in the hallway. With everything else going on since then, Jake hadn't done anything about it until this afternoon, but none of his calls were answered or his texts returned.

"I, uh, kinda took some of my stress out on him yesterday morning when he tried to tell me about your date," Jake admitted. "He hasn't answered any of my calls since."

"Oh my gosh, Jake. This could be bad." Andrea uneasily explained how their conversation had gone awry on Friday night.

Jake winced to think that he had only added to Jonny's shame, and he reached into his pocket for his cell phone. He scrolled down to Jonny's name again and pressed Dial. Jonny's phone began to ring, which was an improvement from the last five calls that had shot him straight to voicemail.

"It's ringing!" Jake nudged Andrea, and they nervously waited to hear Jonny's familiar voice pick up. But after four rings, it once again went to voicemail. Disappointed and now even more worried, Jake began, "Jonny, this is Jake...Andrea and I are here, just wondering where you are. I know I totally botched it yesterday, and I'm so sorry. Listen, I really want to tell you all this in person. Please call me back tonight." Jake was confident there would be no call back, and resolved to pay him a visit after youth group.

✤ ✤ ✤

Alone in the dark of the mobile home, Jonny watched the call go to voicemail. A dusty shaft of light sliced through the dingy drapes, and he let the cell phone slip from his fingers to the ground. He picked up the razor blade again and turned it back and forth in his grip. Pressing it into his flesh, he carved temporary relief on the inside of his arm. At the end of the first cut, he lifted the blade and looked closely at the blood glistening in the moonlight. He sighed deeply and wiped his eyes as he lowered the blade for the next cut.

40

"**I JUST NEED TO GET ONE THING,**" Mark informed his scowling son later that night as they started upstairs to the church offices.

"We're always the last ones here," Danny grumbled. He followed his dad who kept climbing the stairs without a response.

As Mark entered his office, Danny strolled down the hallway, swearing under his breath. He turned the corner and immediately froze when he saw Chris' office light on. Quietly, he edged up to the window and peeked inside. Jake was visible through the partially open blinds, sitting on the couch talking with Chris. Danny looked around and then pressed his ear against the door.

"So, how you holding up?" Chris asked.

"Well, I'm never having sex again," Jake sighed.

"Don't say that. Your wife will be miserable," Chris laughed, throwing an armful of books into his backpack. "Did you talk to Amy?"

Jake leaned forward on the couch out of Danny's sight, but his words came through loud and clear. "I think Amy's gonna keep the baby."

Danny's eyebrows shot up and he smiled, pressing his ear even harder against the door.

"Your parents know?" Chris asked.

"My mom cried. Like she needed anything else to worry about."

"Your dad?"

"I don't care what he thinks anymore." Jake slouched back into Danny's view, crossing his arms and flicking his hair out of his eyes with disdain.

Chris leaned back in his creaky office chair, folding his hands behind his head and chewing his lower lip. "Okay," he conceded, then sat forward and leaned his elbows on his desk. "I've got something I want to run by you and Amy."

The click of his father's office door locking behind him jerked Danny away from his eavesdropping. He crept back down the hallway with a broad smile and followed his father downstairs.

As Jake walked the halls of Pacific High the next morning, it felt like everyone knew something he didn't. The long stares, hushed laughter, and whispered secrets between friends all seemed a little too coincidental. He'd discreetly checked to make sure his fly was up and had even stopped by the bathroom to see if there was anything embarrassing on his face. Everything seemed to be normal, but with all the drama going on in his life, he figured maybe he was imagining things. Since the beer-pong incident and his new choice of friends, his popularity had definitely waned. He had gotten what he had (kind of) wished for—he had become just another face in the crowd. But today seemed different.

As he made his way through Senior Hall toward his locker, he turned the corner and all his intuitions were fully justified.

There, in the center of the hallway, a large crowd had circled, and in the center Doug's attacking voice was unmistakable.

"IS IT TRUE?" Doug bellowed.

Jake pushed people aside and found Amy cowering in tears as Doug waved a blue flyer in front of her face. She nodded discreetly, and Jake knew it was out.

"YOU SLUT!" Doug bawled at her. Amy dropped her head in shame, avoiding Doug's menacing snarl and the condemning gaze of the crowd. They all seemed to be waiting for a response from her, but she gave none. She simply turned to escape, charging right into Jake.

"What's going on? Are you okay?" Jake grabbed her face in his hands. Amy ignored the question, angrily knocking his hands away and pushing through the mob, finally vanishing around the corner. Speechless, Jake watched in confusion as she disappeared.

The hair on his arms stood straight up and he turned his attention to Doug. The growing mass of students surged back a step, creating a small arena for the two jocks to have it out. "Man, what's your problem?!" Jake challenged, stepping into the center.

Doug shoved the flyer into Jake's chest. Jake looked down at what was unquestionably a comic sketch of him and pregnant Amy. His stomach lurched at the twisted image.

Jake crumpled up the flyer and threw it to the ground. "Where'd you get that?" he growled. His mind raced through who could have found out. No one knew except for his parents and Chris.

"You tell me!" Doug shoved Jake.

"It's not like that!" Jake pushed back hard.

Doug stepped forward, throwing his chest into Jake's. "It's not like *what*, Jake?"

"You know what I mean, Doug." Jake glared at Doug, their noses only inches apart, their chests heaving almost in unison.

"Oh, I'll tell you what I know, all right." Doug grabbed a fistful of Jake's shirt and laughed sarcastically. "I knew she was a sl—..."

BAM!

Jake's right fist slammed squarely into Doug's face before he even had time to think. "DON'T YOU EVER CALL HER THAT," he yelled at Doug, now doubled-over. With blood oozing from his nose, Doug lunged at Jake, throwing him hard against the lockers. Jake winced as a lock dug into his shoulder blade.

"What? Don't call her what?!" Doug spat in his face. "A SLUT?" Doug socked him hard in the stomach. "'Cuz that's all she is! A slutty whore!"

Bent over in pain, Jake furiously charged Doug, hurling him back against the opposite bank of lockers. Doug's body crunched on the rattling steel, and he gasped for air, but he managed to drive his knee up into Jake's face. As Jake stumbled, Doug pounced and knocked him to the ground.

"You're a fake!" Doug shouted, standing over Jake with his fists clenched. "You got your little Jesus lunch group doing whatever you tell them to do! But you're the biggest fake of them all!" He spat venom into Jake's face as blood continued to drip from his nose. "Well, no one's fooled, Jesus-boy! No one's fooled..." Doug's rant faded as he started to back off, rubbing his bleeding face with the back of his hand. He rocked back and forth, his fist ready to uncork at the first sign of movement.

From the hallway floor, Jake glanced around at dozens of riveted faces, all waiting for him to retaliate. But with a throbbing face and aching back, Jake realized he didn't really want to fight with Doug at all. Honestly, the way things looked, Doug's rage was understandable. Besides, he had only one thing on his mind right now: Amy.

The first bell didn't ring a moment too soon, and Clyde's gruff voice could be heard from around the corner, herding kids to class. Doug unclenched his fists and nudged Jake hard in the ribs with his foot. "You're not worth it," he sneered, strutting away with his crew—the guys that used to have Jake's back. Matt looked at Jake and shrugged, a trace of sympathy on his face, but Tony and the others didn't even give him a second glance. The swarm of students followed suit, tearing themselves away one by one from what could have been the fight of the year. Jake recognized many of the parting faces, ones who used to greet him like a hero in the halls, and others who only recently he'd shared lunch with. *How they all turned so quickly.* Soon, Jake was left alone in the hallway.

He groaned as he pushed himself off the worn floor, his entire body protesting his every move. He dabbed at his forehead, shocked that there was no blood. He brushed his hair out of his eyes and staggered forward, and then his foot kicked something that caught his attention as it rolled away. Bumping up against his locker a few feet ahead, a scuffed-up old penny landed tails-up. Even though he was sore, Jake couldn't resist scooping it up—he rattled it around in his hand as he remembered the first talk he'd heard from Chris, about how pennies "aren't even worth picking up." He clutched it tight for a second, then he slipped it into his back pocket.

On his left, the gigantic school announcement board, where countless news articles and photographs of him had been plastered over the years, was now completely covered with hundreds of the malicious flyers in a rainbow of colors. The nearby rows of lockers were also plastered with the same cruel joke. If nothing else, the perpetrator was dedicated. Jake peeled off a fistful of flyers only to find a second layer. He frantically began pulling them down with both hands, discovering more with every swipe. The flyers floated down to the ground until he was standing in a pile, and still there were more. After thirty seconds, he realized he wasn't even making a dent. He looked down the hall, away from the entrance—they were everywhere, on every locker, on every wall, even the floors were strewn with them. Whoever did it must really hate him. Infuriated but weak with helplessness and pain, Jake finally punched the board and stumbled away.

41

SNICKERS AND JEERS followed Jake everywhere he went, not only about the pregnancy gossip, but about how he'd fought Doug like a girl and gotten pummeled. His swollen left cheek didn't help. And now Jake couldn't find Amy anywhere. He'd texted her a dozen times, but she wasn't responding. Of course, how could he blame her? Even after all they'd talked through yesterday, he knew all her worst fears had come true before she could even fully choose what to do. And deep down, Jake couldn't help thinking he was to blame. He seemed to have a knack for ruining people's lives lately.

Lunchtime came, and Jake wandered aimlessly: He had nowhere to eat. He hadn't been welcome with Doug and his old crew for months now; and after what had transpired that morning, he was quite certain the new lunch crew didn't want him around either. He roamed through campus searching for a little corner where he could sit unnoticed and watch for Amy. It was the only thing that kept him at school—the gut feeling that she was still there somewhere. As lonely misery twisted his stomach in knots, he wondered how many students faced this same friendless dilemma every single day of their lives.

What a horrible way to live. This was how Jonny had felt. This was Roger's life. Jake's heart ached with frustration. Maybe this was all just the cruel lesson God wanted him to learn.

He finally found a secluded bench against a building at the corner of the quad. From there he could see his normal lunch circle, today trimmed down to only a handful of students. He could see Andrea in her favorite neck-tie skirt, her back facing him but engrossed in conversation with Carla and Natalie. She must have felt more betrayed than anyone, having been the one who'd first stood up for him. Jake pulled out his lunch and nibbled on his sandwich, but he wasn't very hungry. He closed his eyes and groaned to himself, leaning his head back against the wall behind him. The sun radiated warmth across his face, adding to the feverish ache in his jaw.

"The circle's over here, Taylor." A familiar voice broke through his agony. "We're a little small today, and we were hoping you'd join us." Jake opened his eyes to see Andrea's silhouette standing directly in front of him.

"Don't tell me you don't know," he said, raising one eyebrow.

Andrea shrugged. "We know."

"Then what are you doing here? You don't want to ruin your rep by being seen with me." Jake started to get up, but Andrea put her hand on his shoulder.

"Jake, it doesn't matter. Anyways, like, who am I to judge?"

Jake smiled sardonically. "Well, for one, you're...like, perfect."

"Oh no, I'm not perfect. If you had the dirt on me..." Andrea adamantly shook her head.

"Whatever." Jake shrugged, weary and wary.

"Jake, there's different kinds of dirt," she began, but then she paused as her eyes focused on something over his shoulder.

Jake spun around to see Amy angrily approaching. He braced himself, ready to apologize profusely. Amy glared at Andrea, who took a few steps back so the couple could talk alone.

"How could you let this happen?" Amy half-demanded, half-cried.

"Amy...I am so sorry..."

"I knew this was going to happen!" Amy melted into sobs. "Everybody hates me!"

"No, they don't," Jake replied, folding his arms around her shaking body. "Hate *me*? Maybe. You? Not so much." He smiled, then whispered tenderly in her ear, "Amy, it's gonna be okay." The words were as much for himself as for her.

Andrea cautiously took a step toward the embracing couple. Amy abruptly turned to her and scowled, "What?!" Andrea meekly held out a tissue from the packet in her pocket. Amy broke into fresh sobs, her annoyance dissolving as she reached out to accept the gift. "Thanks," she whispered.

"I've got a whole pack, if you want them," Andrea offered softly.

"Why are you being so nice to me?" Amy asked, dabbing her eyes.

"I guess I just know what it's like to feel alone. It sucks, right?" Andrea handed her another tissue.

The three just stood in silence for a few moments, supporting each other with their presence as Amy continued to weep on Jake's shoulder. Finally, Billy approached tentatively, stopping five feet away. "You guys gonna join us for lunch?" he asked.

Amy looked to Jake and breathed in deeply. "Sure, why not?" She grinned bashfully through her streaming tears.

Andrea erupted in a smile, taking Amy's arm to lead her back to the lunch spot. Jake turned to Billy and winked. "Only if your mom's gonna join us."

CHRIS HAD GOTTEN THE CALL midway through his second lap of Costco samples with a few teens he mentored weekly. Mark's request that he stop by his office as soon as possible interrupted a lively discussion about whether there would be sex in heaven—and right before the tasty Philly cheesesteak sandwich table. An "urgent" meeting with Mark was never a good thing, so after dropping the guys off, Chris nervously knocked on Mark's office door, prepared for another list of complaints.

"Come on in, Chris." Mark's deep voice echoed through the door.

Chris let himself in and smiled at Mark, who sat gruffly behind his desk. "Grab a seat." Mark pointed at the only option in the room: the low-rider chair. Chris uneasily grabbed the seat and waited.

Mark shot straight to the point. "I was deeply disturbed to hear from my son last night that one of your students got his girlfriend pregnant."

Chris dropped his jaw a little and raised his eyebrows. He

shook his head and took a deep breath, grabbing the arms of his chair to make sure he stayed seated. "Where did Danny hear this?"

"He overheard you two talking in your office last night," Mark calmly responded, as if he collected information this way all the time.

Chris was incensed. Since when was eavesdropping on a private conversation acceptable? And now he was in trouble? Chris chuckled to himself in order to keep his cool, but it was all he could do to not verbally explode. He'd had enough of Mark, and Danny. "Your son had no right to listen to our private—"

Mark cut him off. "You're right, but he did, and now I know. I'm just not comfortable with this kid being around here."

Unable to stay seated any longer, Chris jumped to his feet, now towering over Mark. He planted both of his hands firmly on the desk. "Not comfortable! Mark, you judge this kid, but you have never even bothered to get to know him! You don't have a clue of what he's dealing with in his life! I'll tell you what—Jake Taylor could teach us a thing or two about what it means to follow God!"

Mark sat in silence, motioning with his right hand for Chris to sit down. Chris slowly lowered himself back to the edge of the seat, but remained ready to spring again.

"I can tell you don't always think highly of me, Chris." Mark gave the accusation in a subdued tone. "While I'm far from perfect, I'm doing the best I can." He paused, then added, "You need to decide if you're able to respect and follow my leadership."

Chris stared at him, speechless. So this is what it had all come to? He'd served faithfully as New Song's youth pastor for almost a decade, and now Mark was all but asking for his resignation? Chris shook his head methodically in disbelief, stood up, and walked out of the office in a daze without another word.

Chris walked right past his own office to the church parking lot and jumped in his car. He didn't want to be anywhere near Mark Rivers at the moment. With the engine on and windows rolled up, he shook his fists in frustration. "Ahhhhhhhhhhhh!!!" he screamed into the steering wheel.

A torrent of thoughts tore through Chris' consciousness on his ten-minute drive home. It enraged him that Mark refused to see all the good that God was doing in the youth ministry. Chris had never seen kids loving God more, loving each other more, and just doing things that made a difference in life. If Mark didn't see that, then maybe he didn't deserve it. Maybe all he deserved was a group of kids like his precious Danny! *Talk about fishing for the splinter in someone else's eye while smashing everyone else with the plank coming out of his own,* Chris grumbled to himself as he turned the corner onto his cul-de-sac.

He parked his car at the bottom of the inclined driveway and yanked hard on his worthless parking brake. He marched into the vacant house and opened his laptop on the kitchen table. He immediately opened a new document and started typing, the click of each key stabbing him like a needle.

Dear New Song Church Leadership Board,

It is with great sorrow that I must inform you that my service as youth pastor here has come to an end, effective immediately. Due to differences in ideology and vision for the future, I will now seek employment elsewhere. I am grateful for the opportunity to serve here the past ten years.

Sincerely,

Chris Vaughn

Chris pushed back from the table and sighed. Balancing his chair on two legs, he glanced around his house. The walls were plastered with framed reminders of students and events gone by: super bowl parties, ugly sweater Christmas parties, birthday parties, bonfires, graduations, weddings, mission trips. He looked out the windows into the yard, remembering the Slip'n'Slide wars they'd duked out on the back lawn, the toilet paper and forks they'd cleaned up from the front lawn, and the Ultimate Frisbee games they sweated through in the park behind their house. Stu-

dents' faces flashed before his mind's eye, and he wondered what would happen to all of them. "Ughhhhh," he sighed.

Chris saved the letter and was closing his laptop just as he heard Cari and Caleb at the door. Caleb, sporting a Burger King crown and a gigantic grin, ran into the house and tackled his dad.

"Daddy, I'm king of da world!" Caleb announced, holding the crown snug to his bouncy curls. Chris snatched the miniature royalty in his arms and held him tight.

"Hey, honey." Cari looked at Chris quizzically, coming over to rub his back. "You're home early. Everything cool?"

Chris nodded half-heartedly and placed Caleb on his shoulders. "Let's talk over dishes." He smiled wryly as he kissed her, meaning this should wait until Caleb was asleep for the night.

"I'm on my trone!" Caleb squeaked from his perch. Chris paraded him around the house, bouncing up and down wildly as his son clutched his head. He decided to let his worries rest for a few hours.

Later that night, over dirty dishes and soap suds, the Vaughns held each other and cried. They agonized together over countless pros and cons and the implications of each, the worst of which was how to break the sad news to the students. They were Chris' kids. Leaving them felt like abandoning family. After wearing themselves out weighing the options, they spent an hour together talking and listening to God on the subject. Finally, just before going to sleep, Chris printed the letter, stuck it in a manila folder, and placed it in his backpack to take to work the next day. He and Cari agreed to continue praying about it for the next week, but outside of a miracle, Chris knew the letter was all but delivered.

43

MAYBE IT WAS the telling baby bump that people couldn't stop staring at, or maybe it was the rumors people were whispering as she walked by. Whatever it was, Amy couldn't escape the evidence all around her that her social standing had taken a serious dive. She watched longingly as groups of girls that used to look at her with envy now turned their backs when she approached. The guys just looked at her, some with disgust, some with a bizarre interest, as if she was so obviously a sure thing. Amy could only wipe her nervous hands on her maternity pants, but even as she touched them they reminded her of just one more place she couldn't fit in.

And so she walked alone. Fighting through the crowds down the hall to Calculus, the stares of her classmates boring into her bulging belly nagged her, along with the whispers and sneers. She walked head-down to hide the tears stinging her eyes, her books clutched close to her chest. Suddenly, out of nowhere, an arm slipped through hers, and a cheerful voice asked her if she wanted some company.

Amy turned and saw Andrea strolling next to her, shielding her from the prying eyes and giggling masses. As they walked

together, Andrea kept Amy engaged in conversation, filling in the gaps with bubbly chatter when Amy was too overcome to speak. Andrea asked her all about the growing baby, offering plenty of ideas for names and gushing about how great she looked. She even asked if Amy would help her with her Geometry homework sometime.

Amy stood outside her Calculus class and stared disbelievingly after Andrea waved goodbye. And for the first time in a long time, Amy smiled—just a little.

✚ ✚ ✚

Chris' behavior had been erratic all day, and now as youth group began, the kids were asking him what was up. He laughed them off and continued with the fun and games as usual. But when he mounted the stage to give his talk, Jake noticed Chris looked pale, almost nervous. Chris dragged a huge wooden cross—about ten feet tall and made of rough wood—up to the center of the stage. Everyone sat in rapt attention as he skipped the introductory banter and started right in, his eyes heavy and bleak.

He spoke about the friends of a paralyzed man who burrowed a hole in someone's roof so they could get him in front of Jesus. Chris pleaded with the packed room of students to do whatever it took to show their friends the love of God. As he concluded, the usual restless shifting, bored whispering, and stealthy texting was noticeably absent, and the room felt alive with focused energy. Jake leaned forward intently, his elbows resting heavily on his knees.

"So we're going to end tonight with a response time," Chris explained, taking a seat on his favorite teaching stool. "Some of you came tonight bearing scars. You've got junk, baggage, whatever you want to call it. Your response: Let God heal you." Chris paused for a moment, then he added, "Can I just give you some good news? Love wins! Seven days a week, and twice on Sunday!" He grinned. "So let the junk go. You'll never miss it..."

Quietly and unnoticed by Jake, Amy slipped through the door and found a seat on the floor along the back wall.

"...And some of you came tonight feeling totally alone. Your response is to simply let God love you. The rest of us may try, but we will fall miserably short. Only God is the friend who will never let you down, whose line is never busy..."

Amy looked up, her eyes locked on Chris.

"...And maybe some of you came here tonight hurting for someone else. You want to know your response? Show them God's unconditional love. You be His hands and His arms. It might not be easy—but don't give up. You know why? Because LOVE WINS!"

Jake thought of Jonny. He had blown it so badly with him. How could he be God's arms when he couldn't even get Jonny to talk to him? *Will he ever trust me again?*

"...Whatever your response, write it on a piece of paper, put it at the foot of this cross here, and let God's love win!" Then he walked over to the edge of the stage and sat down against the far right wall.

The band got up and started playing a song that Jake knew pretty well by now. As he let the words sink through him, he wrote one word on his slip of paper: *Jonny.* Whatever it took, he needed to make things right, and he felt driven—almost inspired—as he walked to the cross and laid it down. Then he kneeled next to it and lowered his head, begging God to help him. A flood of other students lined up and gathered around to lay down their scars and insecurities and concerns at the foot of the cross, surrounding Jake as he kneeled there.

As Jake got up to return to his seat, the lone figure seated against the wall in the back caught his eye. Instantly, he recognized Amy, looking so fragile and alone. His heart pounded, and he sped past his chair to take a seat next to her on the floor. Wordlessly, Amy placed her head on his shoulder and then collapsed into soft sobs on his chest. Jake said nothing, but embraced her with both arms to hold her tight. Andrea and Billy both noticed her as well and came back to sit by her on the other side. Andrea, again, provided the tissues.

Thirty minutes later, Jake stood on Jonny's porch. The trailer was dark, and no cars were parked in the driveway, but Jake persisted at banging on the door, pleading for an answer. This was his fifth attempt since last Tuesday night; he even fell asleep on the steps Saturday night waiting for someone to come home. But tonight, Chris had renewed his hope, and Jake was ready to try again.

"Please, Jonny. I'm sorry," Jake implored again and again through the door. Finally, desperate and out of ideas, he leaned on the door and slid down to the ground. "Please, God," Jake whispered. A pen poked into his leg from his front pocket, and he pulled it out with his church notes. A new plan suddenly popped into his head, and he scribbled a written apology and stuck it in the crack of the door.

On the other side of the trailer, Jonny sat on the floor in his bedroom, leaning against his unkempt bed, headphones blasting music through his head. He scrawled words fervently on his sketch pad, pushing down so hard on his pen that it soaked through to the next page. Sitting on his bedside dresser was a bottle of pills he'd stolen from his mother's medicine cabinet. He grabbed the bottle in his right hand and shook it, the tablets rattling like candy inside. He sighed to himself—his mother didn't even know he'd skipped school all week; she hadn't even been home since Friday. He thumbed the bottle's cool plastic smoothness as he focused on the blood oozing from freshly sliced skin on his left forearm.

44

JAKE AND ANDREA weren't the only ones who missed Jonny at school. Danny had noticed as well, but for completely different reasons. Danny sat next to Jonny during fourth period biology, a course that Jonny excelled in while Danny, the only junior in the class, struggled. Since three weeks after school started, Jonny had involuntarily helped Danny sustain a passing grade. The deal was simple, they would "compare answers" on their homework during the first few minutes of class as Mr. Ventor, who was nearly blind even in his inch-thick glasses, took attendance. As the year progressed, Danny did less of his own work and more copying; he'd even extended his arrangement to include tests. He was careful never to correct all his answers, just enough of them to keep a strong C. Jonny had feebly resisted at first, but finally he yielded, allowing Danny a clear view of all his answers on a daily basis.

That all changed, however, after Jonny started going to youth group. That next day, Danny had routinely reached for Jonny's notebook, but Jonny had snatched it away and refused to share. Danny pushed and prodded and barraged him under his breath with derogatory names and racial slurs, but Jonny

never said a word, and his work stayed hidden. It also stayed concealed during the next test, which was worth 20 percent of their grade. Danny was unprepared as usual, and his grade in the class plunged to an F.

From that day forward, Danny did whatever he could to make Jonny's life a living hell. Danny bombarded Jonny with as much torment as he could get away with—flicking spit wads at him across the aisle, subtly sticking out his foot to trip him, whispering cruel comments for only his ears to hear. Of course, he never did this at church or around Jake, where he could be stopped. He confined his bullying to the limits of fourth period biology.

Jonny never complained, never fought back. But he also never again let Danny cheat off him. This irked Danny to no end, but he couldn't think of much more to do until the fortunate Monday a week ago, when Danny witnessed Jake's verbal offensive and Jonny's resulting retreat. When Jonny didn't return to school or youth group, it looked like Danny's well-timed words at Jonny's locker had hit the mark.

When Jonny finally entered their classroom again a week later, Danny smirked at him with malice. Jonny's dark eyes stayed focused on the ground as he shuffled toward the back row. While most wouldn't have given Jonny's tall but unassuming figure a second glace, Danny stared at him relentlessly, sure there was something dramatically different about him today. Back again was the black sweatshirt that hid his troubled face inside its hood and his scarred arms inside its long sleeves. The old Jonny had returned.

Just as he got to his seat, Danny flicked his foot out. Jonny stumbled and fell into the chair, dropping his backpack on the ground. "Long time no see," Danny whispered. Jonny didn't even flinch, ignoring the snide greeting and instead staring blindly to the front of the room where Mr. Ventor was delivering a monotone explanation of the miracle of photosynthesis.

As usual, Danny was far from interested in the science of life, but he did find appeal in the study of his relapsed neighbor. His eyes surveyed Jonny from head to toe, where they lingered on the spilled contents of the unzipped front pocket of Jonny's backpack. Lying there amid a couple pencils, some index cards, trash, and a pack of gum was Jonny's battered cell phone. Danny studied the stuff, then stealthily slid his foot out into the aisle. Jonny's head remained inertly preoccupied, so Danny slyly nudged the phone under his desk. With one eye on Mr. Ventor's shiny bald head and the other on Jonny's shabby hood, Danny slumped down in his seat, grabbing the phone and slipping it into his pocket.

"I gotta use the bathroom!" he proclaimed to the whole class, interrupting Mr. Ventor mid-sentence.

The teacher scribbled out a pass without skipping a beat in his lecture, and Danny was gone.

Fifteen minutes later, as students hungrily counted the minutes dragging by before lunch, the Pacific High emergency alarm bell rang loudly across campus. Annoyed teachers, their instruction interrupted by yet another drill, led hordes of students from every direction into the deserted quad. The shrill, pulsing siren pierced the air, and people everywhere covered their ears for relief. They all knew the routine: Stay in line and head toward the middle of campus. But Clyde Will barked out reminders just the same: "Get back in line! Hustle up! Stop messing around! This is your final warning!"

In spite of the seriousness in his voice, and in spite of the trauma that had shattered their routine just a few months ago in Senior Hall, students still joked and goofed, enjoying their early escape from class. The tidy lines disintegrated once they reached the wide expanse, and clusters of friends regrouped, shouting over the ear-splitting alarm as teachers uselessly attempted to call attendance and maintain order.

Suddenly, a fleet of Oceanside police cars sped around the corner and screeched to a halt in front of each of the school's entrances. Two fire engines followed closely behind. Against teachers' orders, students pressed against the chain-link fence to see what the commotion was about.

"Get back in your lines!" Clyde yelled into a megaphone while teachers echoed the same demands. Together they worked to herd grumbling students away from the fences.

In the center of the chaos, Jake finally found Amy. "You know what's going on?" Jake asked, cupping his hands around her ear.

"I heard some girl talking to her mom on her cell. Our school is on the news for some kind of bomb threat," Amy hollered back. Billy and Andrea joined them, offering silent greetings instead of battling the screeching siren.

Then, just as quickly as it had started, the alarm was abruptly replaced by the soothing sound of silence, until lively conversations everywhere quickly filled the void. Clyde climbed the steps to the second level of the D building and flipped on the siren on his megaphone. All heads turned toward the tall security guard who now mandated their attention.

"Students, this is not a drill. This is real!" Clyde shouted into his megaphone. "A bomb threat was reported on our campus. The police are searching the school. You will remain here in your lines until I tell you differently." Clyde sternly scanned the mob of faces and warned, "Let me make this perfectly clear—anyone caught trying to leave this area will be immediately suspended with a recommendation for expulsion. This is not a joke—especially at this school."

Students rustled around, uncomfortably silent, waiting for someone to say or do something. Could there really be a bomb on campus? And if so, had anybody thought about the stupidity of keeping them all trapped here?

As Jake observed the scene around him, Danny Rivers caught his attention making his way up to Clyde. He whispered something into his ear. Jake wasn't the only one who noticed him—hundreds of eyes watched, and a new murmur rippled through the crowds. Did he know something? Was he confessing to the crime? A knot tightened in Jake's stomach; anything Danny was involved in couldn't be good.

Clyde pulled two officers over, and Danny repeated his message. Seconds later, the group headed briskly away toward another part of campus.

Out of sight from the school body's inquisitive eyes, Danny led Clyde and the officers directly to locker number 1779.

They were joined by the principal, who unlocked it with her master key after the sniffer dog didn't detect anything worth barking about. The senior police officer delicately opened the door, and they all peered in to investigate the locker's contents. Violent pictures covered the inside like wallpaper. One pictured a kid riding a bomb into Pacific High. In another, a knife dripped blood on a crowd of students.

The lead officer pulled out a black spiral notebook and thumbed through more sadistic drawings, scribbles, and poems. His face registered concern. He was flipping back toward the front cover when his radio crackled to life.

"Yeah, we have a trace on the cell phone used to call in the threat," the voice squawked on the other end.

"Ten-four, what do you got?"

Garbled static filled the airwaves while the officer spotted a name scripted in graffiti-like letters across the first page. "The number belongs to a—" He held the writing up for his partner to read aloud in perfect unison with the radio.

The curious murmur rustled through the students again when the investigating group returned. Jake's eyes locked on the action, and his sick feeling returned when he watched Danny head blithely over to his buddies, a smug smile on his face. Clyde led the officers over to Mr. Ventor and showed him the front cover of a notebook. His eyebrows furrowed and his lips pursed as he searched around and pointed to a lone student sitting in the back of his line, several yards away from anyone. His back was to them, hunched over as he sat on a planter. Clyde and the cops made their way through the throng of students and surrounded him.

"Jonny Garcia?" the lead officer questioned.

Startled, Jonny jumped up, ripping his headphones out of his ears. "What?" he mumbled, suddenly aware that he was the center of attention—in a really bad way.

Jake, Amy, Andrea, and Billy watched the officers from across the quad. "It's Jonny! He's here!" Andrea gasped. Jake sprang up from his seat. None of them could hear what was going on, but it looked serious.

"We need to take a look at your cell phone, son," the lead officer directed Jonny. He sullenly pulled his backpack around and unzipped the small pouch in the front. His fingers dove in, but paused when they came up empty. Dismay covered his face as he frantically scoured through the other pockets. He even turned the bag upside down to shake everything out. There was no phone. "It's—it's gone," he muttered.

With one hand on his gun, the lead officer stepped closer to Jonny, placing a handcuff on his wrist. "You're going to need to come with us," he growled, yanking Jonny's other arm back and fixing it in the cuffs. One of the other cops stuffed Jonny's belongings back in his bag and escorted him back through the mob of students.

Jonny's head hung low while hateful stares and sneers seared into him. Then, as if by fate, he raised his head right at the split-second he passed Jake. Their eyes met, an eternity passing in a millisecond.

Immediately Jake's mind transported him back to his final eye-contact with Roger. He had tried to talk him into putting the gun down as their eyes spoke silent volumes to each other. The hairs on the back of Jake's neck shot straight up as he remembered the last conversation he had with Roger that horrible, terrible day.

"You don't want to do this, man," Jake reasons.

Roger's stare is relentless. "Too late, Jake..." and then those four words: "Like you ever cared." He raises the gun to his chin, and—

The reverberations of the gun in his mind shot Jake back to reality as Doug, who was standing behind him in line, piped up, "It's always the quiet freaks you gotta watch out for."

Students around him chuckled but remained stunned by this new student terrorist.

Jake wanted nothing more than to turn around and deck Doug. Instead, he stood paralyzed. *Was this really happening again?* The blood started surging through his veins, pushing him to act, to move, to care. "There's no way," Jake whispered, his eyes following Jonny's journey of shame. "He wouldn't do this." He glanced around the quad to clear his head and saw Danny laughing with several of his pothead jerk friends.

Suddenly, with no clue where it came from, Jake had an idea. He pulled out his cell phone and scrolled down to Jonny's name, knowing full well he wouldn't answer, but with a feeling of who might. Sure enough, even from a distance, there was no denying it. A second after Jake pressed Talk, Danny nervously jumped, plunging into his pocket. He pulled a phone out, scowled at the caller ID, and silenced the accusing ringtone. Jake seethed.

"He didn't do it. We gotta do something!" Jake exclaimed to his friends. He looked back at the squad car where the officer was pushing Jonny's head in to cage him like an animal. After conferring on his radio, the driver then walked around and got in the front seat. Jake's mind raced, knowing that every second that ticked by was moving him further from being able to right his wrongs. "I've got to stop that car!"

Amy placed her hand on his shoulder. "Jake, you'll get expelled." Jake didn't even hear her.

But Billy piped up, "I got an idea!" The four quickly huddled together and excitedly identified their roles. Twenty seconds later, Billy took off sprinting in the opposite direction, screaming at the top of his lungs, "FREEDOM!"

Two surprised security guards chased after the black kid on the run, leaving the exit they were guarding completely unmanned. Jake covertly made his way through the scattered students and snuck out the gate en route to the front entrance with relative ease.

Across the yard, Clyde saw him slinking out and instinctively rushed after him. As he raced to the opening, Amy in-

nocently stepped in his path, causing Clyde to lightly push her to the side. Amy then delivered an Oscar-worthy melodrama. "Ohhhh!" she moaned, stumbling to the ground, clutching her pregnant belly.

"Oh my gosh!" Andrea shrieked from nearby, dropping to assist her. "She's pregnant! And you just pushed her!" she screamed accusingly at Clyde.

"Ohhhh!" Amy continued.

"Is it coming?!"

"Ohhhh!"

Immediately Amy became everyone's primary focus, causing every maternally minded teacher to glare sharply at Clyde for his utter carelessness. Clyde attempted to placate the worried crowd that now trapped him while turning to his megaphone to stop the fleeing Jake.

"Taylor, get back here now!" he barked.

Jake heard the command but kept running. It wasn't too late. He had to save Jonny. From a distance, he could see the squad car pull away from behind the school, heading toward the front entrance.

Inside the squad car, Jonny painfully but slyly worked a bottle of pills out of his sweatshirt pocket. He managed to prop the bottle up between his knees. He had come to school that morning with feeble but fresh hope. When his mom had finally come home last night (almost sober), she had slid Jake's note under his door, and he convinced himself to give it all one more chance. He leaned forward and went to work carefully unscrewing the bottle cap with his teeth.

Clyde disentangled himself from the crowd around Amy, handed his megaphone to another guard, and ran toward the open gate.

Jake sprinted through the packed parking lot toward the entrance. He had to stop the car. He had to make it right.

The cap popped off, and Jonny slowly tipped the bottle forward into his mouth. Pills spilled down into the crease of his legs, and he scooped as many as he could into his mouth.

Five yards before the entrance, Clyde caught up with Jake and tackled him to the hard ground. Jake scrambled to his feet, but Clyde grabbed him and wouldn't let go. Jake tried vehemently to shake free, but 230 pounds of muscle was a formidable opponent.

"Jake, this ain't cool!" Clyde yelled, out of breath.

Still struggling, Jake looked up at Clyde with panic in his eyes. "Please, let me go, Clyde!" he begged." I got to make things right!"

The police car sped toward them, fifty yards away...then forty...then thirty...then twenty...suddenly Jake noticed a slight weakening in Clyde's grip, and he threw his arms apart and down. He was free! He staggered toward the squad car and threw himself in front of it with his arms up to get it to stop.

BAM!

Jake's body slammed off the hood onto the rough pavement as the car squealed to a stop

Inside, Jonny whiplashed against the seatbelt, spewing the pills out of his mouth all over the back seat. The officers jumped out of the car and surrounded Jake from both sides.

"Put your hands up so we can see them NOW!" the officer closest to him ordered.

From his crumpled position on the ground, Jake slowly raised his cut hands above his head. "He didn't do it! I know who did," he pleaded fearlessly.

Clyde approached from behind, putting his hand on the officer's shoulder to diffuse the situation. "Jake, what are you talking about?"

Two other cops hurried over and lifted Jake to his feet, pinning his arms behind his back. They pushed him over to the hood of the car, where they sprawled him over the dent he had just created. Jake looked through the windshield directly into Jonny's eyes and called to him, "Things are different now!"

DANNY SAT ALONE in the cramped Pacific High detention office with an armed police officer just outside the door. He'd been left alone in the empty room for over an hour, which had given him plenty of time to count the number of tiles in the ceiling as he lounged on the cold metal folding chair awaiting his fate. His shaggy brown hair clung to his neck and forehead—this had to be the only non-air-conditioned room in the whole school—and he grumbled and cursed and pouted and whined with no one to hear. He leaned forward and banged his head against the steel edge of the table, muttering about how stupid he was for holding onto Jonny's cell phone after he'd made the call. He'd tried to ditch it when Jake made all his commotion, but a security guard spotted him throwing it away and he was busted.

A few muffled voices outside the door made Danny turn around as Chris and Jake entered the room. The officer shut the door behind them. "Why'd you bring him?" Danny jumped up and pointed angrily at Jake.

"Why am I here and not your dad?" Chris shot back sharply.

Danny shrugged. "Just hurry up and get me out of here. I didn't do anything," he insisted.

Chris shook his head in amazement and silently turned back toward the door.

"Where are you going?" Danny challenged.

Chris paused and half-turned, jeering over his shoulder. "Doesn't sound like you did anything wrong."

Danny leaned back on the conference table, throwing his hands up. "It wasn't my fault! Somebody set me up." Danny glared at Jake. "I don't deserve this."

Chris continued toward the door. "They found you with his cell phone, Danny; you're not fooling anybody." He knocked, and the officer immediately opened the door.

"You can't just leave me here!" Danny threatened, standing up with fire in his eyes.

Chris didn't even turn around. "I'm not leaving you *here*—they'll take you downtown 'til your dad finds time to pick you up." He motioned to Jake to leave, but Jake didn't budge. "It's up to you," Chris shrugged as he walked out.

Danny shouted after him, "Are you insane? You can't do this...I'll get you fired!" Chris kept walking down the hall, and Danny kept watching him as the door slowly closed. "Okay, okay, what do you want to me say?" he called after him. "What? That I'm not perfect, that I screwed up?" Danny kicked his chair, sending it crashing against the opposite wall. "It was an accident. I panicked!" The door completed its slow arc closed. Chris never looked back. "Okay, okay! I know I lied, and it's my bad! I'm sorry! Chris, it was just a little prank! Just come back!" Danny pleaded at the top of his lungs. The only answer was the click of the door. Chris was gone.

"I'll stay," Jake offered, still standing just inside the door.

Danny collapsed against the wall, pounding his fists against the painted cinder block, and he slid to the ground. With his head in his hands, he mumbled just loud enough, "Why are you doing this?"

"I'm not sure," Jake honestly admitted. Staring at Danny sitting morosely on the floor, his heart began to fill with pity.

Danny slowly raised his head to look at Jake, a flash of defiance igniting his eyes. "Y'know, I was the one who made that flyer."

Jake slowly joined him on the ground. "I figured."

Danny looked sidelong at him. "So why are you still here?"

"I just couldn't let it happen again."

A minute passed in silence. Then Danny asked quietly, "Let what happen?"

Jake stretched out his still-bloodied knee. "I let Roger down, and that's something that will haunt me forever." He picked at a few pebbles of gravel still embedded in it, then continued, "I couldn't repeat that mistake with Jonny...or with you."

The seconds ticked by like heavy grains of sand filling their lungs. With his eyes focused squarely on the opposite wall, Danny's broken voice squeaked to life. "I did it."

Jake stopped fiddling with his knee and waited for him to continue.

"I was there that Sunday Roger came." Danny sounded like he'd never even admitted it to himself before. "I-I walked in late, and he was sitting in my seat. So I whispered in his ear, 'You don't belong here.' I didn't mean he had to actually *leave*. I just wanted my couch. Roger didn't say anything, he just stood up and left. I would have run after him if I knew he was gonna... I swear I didn't know..." Danny turned to Jake, now with tears rimming his eyes. "It was my fault! It was me!" he confessed.

Jake sat motionless, old emotions stirring up with a vengeance. Part of him wanted to ram Danny's head into the concrete wall, but instead, he took a deep breath and rested his shaking hand gently on Danny's shoulder. "It was all our faults," he whispered softly.

Jake stayed with Danny for another hour. Not in a million years would Jake have thought he would spend that much time with Danny Rivers—and certainly not by choice—but a voice

in his head pestered him to stay put. They even prayed together in short sentences, asking God for forgiveness and freedom from their guilt. Mark finally showed up to take his son home.

Later that night, after spending a few healing hours with Jonny, Jake staggered into his bedroom and turned on his computer to check out the Lakers' score. He was pleased to see they had stomped Sacramento and were now three and nothing in the playoff series, but in light of the events of his day, these trivial details didn't really pique his interest.

His hand moved the mouse to his Favorites at the top of the screen, and he hesitantly clicked on Roger's MySpace page. He hadn't been back since he created it, and he felt a little nervous as it loaded. He would be bummed if no one had taken an interest in it—but then again, what did it matter? Today had been a great reminder of how much he had changed and learned since Roger's death, and a silly web site couldn't take that away from him.

The blue background washed over the screen like a wave of peace, and the boxes and images and words quickly followed. Jake moved the mouse to the left. The notice said he had friend requests. He clicked on it, wishing randomly for seventeen. What he saw nearly knocked him out of his chair. There were 2,736.

Jake scrolled through the thousands of pictures, many of which included a short message:

Roger's Friend Requests	
Listing 7 of 2736 comments	Prev | Next
Jamie APPROVE DENY	Roger, I'm so so sorry I wasn't there 4 U. Your page has inspired me to live life differently.

Tyler APPROVE DENY	I've bin there, fo show, but I ain't no mo. Thx bro!
Ro-ro APPROVE DENY	I'm a cutter but I'm now going to get some help. Thanks.
Roxanne APPROVE DENY	I wuz lookn for a site on how to kill myself and instead I found UrS. U SaVeD mY LiFe.
Master Malcom APPROVE DENY	My sis threatens to commit suicide, Ima not gonna ignore her ne more
Shaniah APPROVE DENY	Roger, you have no idea. Thank you.
Train APPROVE DENY	Praying for your family.

Overwhelmed with the response, his heart skipped in his chest. Jake scrolled and scrolled and they just kept coming, unknown face after unknown face. After thirty minutes, his fingers got stiff, but there were still more. Finally, he made it to the end and clicked the Check All box, and then clicked Approve.

An hour later, Jake fell asleep, still smiling.

ALTHOUGH HE DIDN'T always get to do it, Chris loved to practice his talks in the youth room before the students showed up. He would picture each of their faces in the seats and pray that his words would not fall on deaf ears. Tonight, he prayed especially hard.

After seeking wisdom or a sign or *something* for the past few days, he and Cari had officially decided that their time at New Song Community Church had come to an end. He planned on delivering his resignation letter that night after youth group. It was one of the most excruciating decisions he had ever made in his life. As much as he hated leaving these students that he had poured his life into, he knew he couldn't work for a man he no longer respected. The incident with Danny and the bomb threat had only confirmed it.

As Chris intently jotted down some notes on the music stand that he used as a podium, he suddenly sensed that he was not alone. He looked up, and standing in the doorway was Mark, silently allowing Chris to finish writing. The fact that Mark was willing to wait patiently for him was almost more shocking than his stealthy entrance. But Mark's appearance

surprised him just as much; Chris had never seen him unshaven before, and his posture was slumped, his gaze fidgety. He looked nervous.

"Mark?" Chris greeted him cautiously, setting his pen down.

"My son and I talked for three hours last night. He told me everything." Mark started right in, looking up at Chris from the floor.

Chris felt himself growing defensive. Mark wasn't going to try to pin his son's behavior on him, was he? But his voice wasn't mad—if anything, he sounded broken. So Chris remained silent, letting Mark say his piece.

"I had no idea the kind of trouble he was in," Mark continued, his voice beginning to quiver. "Here I was, trying to lead a church, when I didn't even know what was going on in my own house."

Chris had worked with Mark for five years; he'd never once heard him so vulnerable, so real. His heart actually went out to his hard-nosed boss as he watched him struggle to find the right words.

"My son didn't think he could call me. But he could call you," Mark marveled. He shoved his hands in his pockets, then looked directly at Chris. "I realize we don't always see things eye-to-eye, but for what it's worth, I just wanted to stop by and say thank you, Chris."

Chris remained planted on his stool, speechless. In all these years, Mark had never thanked him for pouring his life into anyone, much less Danny. He could literally feel his anger toward Mark begin to drain away.

"I think I finally met the Jake Taylor you've been telling me about all this time," Mark added.

Chris was confused. "I actually introduced you to him several months—"

Mark interrupted, "I know, but I *really* met him last night. He's a good kid. You've done a great job with him."

Chris smiled, still speechless.

Mark looked around uncomfortably, then added, "I've decided to take a leave of absence. If I can't lead my own son, I'm sure not in a place to lead the whole church. I wanted you to be the first to know." With that, he turned around and walked out of the room.

Chris simply stared at the now-vacant doorway, where the man he had resented so much had just left in submission. He wanted to say so many things, but no words came to his mouth. Instead, he pulled his resignation letter out of his Bible and ripped it up.

47

THREE WEEKS LATER, Jake, Amy, and both of their moms sat expectantly in the Vaughn's living room. Chris had explained the process to them several times before, but now that the time had actually come, the magnitude of their decision weighed heavily. Amy fidgeted nervously with her long blonde hair, listening attentively to Chris.

"Frank and Jan are really an amazing couple," he reassured them, sitting on the edge of his seat. "They've been our friends forever and have struggled so long to become parents. So, they've been dying to meet you ever since I told them." Chris' smile was full of sympathy and understanding. "And they are really excited about an open adoption, so the child will grow up knowing who you are," he added.

Jake turned to Amy tenderly, taking her hand in his. "Are you sure this is what you want?"

Amy's lips twitched into a faint smile, and she nodded resolutely. Her mom reached over and rubbed her daughter's back.

"Well, Cari's with them outside." Chris stood up from his seat and moved toward the door. "Let's do this."

Jake inched closer to Amy on the couch, lightly placing his hand on her trembling knee. Chris opened the door, and a cute couple in their mid-thirties tentatively entered the room and approached the nervous teenagers.

"Jake and Amy, this is Frank and Jan."

Jan smiled and bashfully handed Amy a pink gift bag. "This is for you."

Amy slowly stood up, still getting used to her increasing weight. "What? Why?" she puzzled, completely taken off-guard.

"Oh, it's nothing, really." Jan wrinkled her nose. "Just a little something to express our gratitude for your amazing gift." Her eyes grew watery as she eagerly watched Amy open it. "We want to keep you a part of the family."

Amy pulled out a beautiful baby book. Inside the front cover, they had handwritten, "Amy, you're our answer to a lot of prayer. We love you already." Jan shyly reached out to hug Amy, and tears flowed freely down both their cheeks.

Frank looked at Jake and shook his hand, "You have no idea what this means to us." He erupted into a smile and pulled Jake into a huge bear hug.

"Oh!" Amy grinned through her tears, placing Jan's hand on her stomach. "Feel this! The baby must know who you are. It just jumped!"

There were smiles all around.

CHRIS PREACHED to the entire church three weeks later. Mark had publicly announced a three-month leave of absence the week before, and he'd asked Chris if he would take at least the first two weeks of preaching. Chris had accepted wholeheartedly. Now he looked out into the crowd of familiar faces, each one an incredible story of how God changes lives. In the front row sat Jake, Amy, Andrea, Jonny, Billy...and Danny. They had promised Chris to sit there every Sunday he preached, just so he'd feel more at home with the "old people." Behind them sat Frank and Jan, the anticipation of parenthood radiating from their faces.

Chris smiled peacefully. This was home. "Faith is a journey," he began. "The journey is not so much about a destination but a transformation..."

Out of the corner of Chris' eye, he spotted Pam Taylor walking through the auditorium entrance. She stood uneasily at the back wall, until Marv-the-bowling-pin usher jovially helped her find a seat next to a friendly single woman. Chris looked at Jake, who was listening intently as always.

"...Looking back, sometimes don't the richest times come right in the midst of our hardest times? That's because God made us to live in community—to laugh, cry, hurt, and celebrate with each other, no matter what we're going through..."

As Jake sat there, his fingers lightly touching Amy's, he smiled contentedly. Chris was right. Through the good and the bad, one thing was for sure: He had been transformed. He had gained so much along the way, and it felt so good not to dread, but to actually look forward to where the journey would take him over the next few months.

✦ ✦ ✦

"Graduates, please move your tassels!" the Pacific High principal instructed the celebratory group of seniors. Jake jerked his head sharply, propelling the tassel to flop sides by itself. How quickly the last month of his senior year had flown by! He glanced up into the packed beach band shell, knowing that scattered in the masses were numerous people who had helped him get here, to this moment.

He turned toward Amy standing next to him on his right, her pregnancy showing even in her billowing black graduation gown. She had never looked more beautiful as her slender fingers demurely lifted her tassel.

"Then, by the power vested in me by the State of California, I now pronounce you graduates of—" Before he could finish, pandemonium erupted as seniors and spectators cheered wildly and 600 green-and-white caps soared into the early evening air.

"Oh my gosh, ow!" Amy flinched, pushing the side of her stomach.

"Are you okay?" Jake turned in alarm, suddenly oblivious to the raucous celebration all around them.

Amy looked up at him, her entire face beaming. "I think the baby is celebrating, too!" she giggled, grabbing Jake's hand and placing it over her belly.

After only a second or two, he felt a soft but sturdy thump on the center of his palm. He looked at Amy, his face aglow. "I just felt my baby kick!" Jake shouted, blending in with the thousands of other chants and cheers. A roving photographer clicked their picture as they hugged in exhilaration. While this was far from how either of them had originally pictured their Graduation Day, they had made it, and it couldn't get much better.

✚ ✚ ✚

If graduating from high school was a transforming event, then standing by Amy five months later, through seventeen hours of labor, seriously rocked Jake's world. "AAAHHHH!" Amy screamed almost demonically as she pushed with a contraction. "Where's my epidural?!" she shrieked, grabbing Jake's shirt and yanking him toward her face.

Jake nodded, petrified by the moment and what she would do to him if he didn't obey. He spun around to the nurse, who smiled calmly and handed him a cold washcloth. With one hand in Amy's tenacious grip that was causing his hand to turn blue, Jake placed the washcloth on her forehead and whispered in her ear, "Almost there, keep pushing." He was pretty sure he had never been more proud of her.

After much more blood, sweat, and tears, Amy's body finally collapsed in exhaustion as the doctor lifted up a crying baby girl. Jake honestly thought it more resembled a tiny E.T. The doctor cut the umbilical cord and handed her, draped in a white hospital blanket, to Amy.

Jake watched Amy cradle the precious life in her arms and leaned down to kiss her tiny forehead. A tear rolled down Amy's cheek and plopped onto the IV tube in her arm. To think that he and Amy were somehow responsible for making this perfect little girl was almost unfathomable, and he was overwhelmed. And then it was time to invite Frank and Jan to meet their new daughter.

The delivery seemed almost easy compared to handing baby Emily over to her new parents. Jake had never considered

how hard it would be to give her away. Frank and Jan walked in delicately, smiling infectiously, but remaining sensitive to the moment. Amy offered them their child, and they scooped her up with trembling arms, radiating joy. Amy sobbed as she let her go, and Jake squeezed her hands in his, mourning their loss together. But the enormous smiles plastered on Frank and Jan's faces and the tender way the couple caressed their infant's soft skin was more than enough proof that Jake and Amy had made the right decision. In that moment, Jake took a deep breath and renewed his commitment to wait until he was married. Whatever brief physical pleasure they had enjoyed was nothing compared to the weight of the aftermath.

✚ ✚ ✚

The final step of the journey, and the ultimate evidence that God had somehow been there with Jake throughout all the highs and lows of senior year, came two months later as he stuffed his last box into the bed of his truck. Surrounding him were all the people he cared about most in this world, all there to say good-bye as he embarked on a whole new adventure.

When Jake had called the coach at Louisville to say he couldn't accept the scholarship, the coach had been so impressed with his maturity that he was willing to work out a special deal. Jake would red-shirt his first season and delay his enrollment until spring semester, at which time he'd dive right into college basketball life. Jake still couldn't believe how God had let him keep all of his dreams alive, despite everything.

He approached his mother at the top of the driveway first. Their extra time alone together had turned into an amazing opportunity to get to know her better. She had even started coming to church with him, a habit she had promised would continue even after he left.

"It took an extra semester, but you made it." Pam tearfully rubbed her hand through Jake's sandy-blonde hair. "I'm so proud of you."

Jake reached out and hugged his mother. He'd never thought leaving her could be this difficult. "I love you, Mom." He smiled.

Pam smiled back and kissed his cheek. Something across the street caught her eye, and she quietly requested, "Then don't be mad at me."

Jake turned to see what she was looking at. Looking more disheveled and less fit than usual, Glen stepped out of his Porsche with a small travel bag. "What's he doing here?" Jake looked back at her, annoyed. After they'd exchanged a cold handshake at graduation, the only other time Jake had seen his father since he left had been the obligatory holiday dinners with the Taylor side of the family up north. He shuddered as he remembered how Jake-the-all-star had become Jake-the-irresponsible-teen-dad-and-loser, and he had driven himself home early when he couldn't endure any more of their disapproval.

"Jake, no matter what, he's your dad," Pam urged.

Glen stopped at the sidewalk in a pair of khakis and a Louisville T-shirt, a far cry from the usual power suit. "I'll pay for gas if you've got a seat open," he awkwardly offered.

As much as Jake wanted to refuse and punish his father, everyone was watching, and he didn't protest. Maybe a couple thousand miles on the open road together would be a good thing—at least that's what Chris would say. *It's not so much about the destination, right?* Jake reminded himself. So Glen secured his travel bag amidst Jake's belongings in the truck bed while Jake walked to the other side of the truck.

The lineup was waiting. First, there were Jan and Frank holding six-week-old Emily. She was dressed in the infant Lakers jersey he'd given them as a going-away gift—to encourage her into sports at an early age, of course. Jake carried a picture of her in his wallet, proud that she'd gotten her mother's looks. "She's growing up so fast." He shook her pudgy little fingers and hugged her new doting parents.

Next was Andrea. "Thank you," he whispered, reaching down to give her a huge hug.

Andrea peeled off one of her Wonder Woman bracelets and handed it to Jake. "I heard the gangs are pretty rough in Kentucky," she kidded.

Jake slid the silver band over his wrist and raised it above his head. "Pichew pichew!"

Billy was waiting next.

"Tell your mom I'll miss her," Jake joked.

"She's right there, bro." Billy pointed to his mom, waiting in her car. "Do you want me to introduce you to her?"

Jake smiled back and gave him a one-armed basketball team hug.

Jonny stood a few feet further down the driveway. He pulled out an envelope from his back pocket and handed it to Jake. "This is for you, man. Thank you for everything," Jonny said with a serious tone. Jake embraced his best friend.

Chris, Cari, and Caleb waited in line next. "Can I go with him?" Caleb asked, clutching tightly onto Jake's leg.

"Maybe next time, Polar Bear," Chris laughed, struggling to detach his son.

Jake hugged Cari. "Thanks for all the advice."

"Anytime," she promised.

Jake made his way to Chris, locking eyes with his mentor for a brief moment. "You remind them that I won't be around to cuss them out if they start slacking off," Jake warned as the two men embraced.

"Jake," Chris said softly. "Go change the world!"

Jake nodded.

Finally, standing at the door of his truck was Amy. As much as he loved all of them, this was without a doubt the most difficult goodbye. As they kissed, Amy whispered, "Thanks for staying with me these past few months."

Jake nodded. "I wish you were coming."

"I just need some more time. I want to make sure this is my dream, too."

As bummed as Jake was about Amy staying behind, he was equally proud of her decision. "Well, figure it out quickly, then." He grinned, pecking her one last time on the forehead.

Amy threw her arms around Jake, and they squeezed as much as they could out of each other. "Call me tonight!" she ordered with her cute, stern face.

"I'll call you every night," Jake promised.

Jake hugged his mom tightly one last time and got in the truck. Sitting next to him was his dad, a man he hadn't spoken more than ten words to in the past few months. This would be quite a ride.

49

EVEN BEFORE THE SEPARATION, Jake couldn't remember the last time just he and his dad had spent this much time together. The drive began with uncomfortable silence, and then his dad tried to initiate sporadic, safe, shallow conversations about things like the weather, the Louisville campus, and the Lakers' chances to repeat. At first, Jake felt like he was betraying his mom with every word he spoke, but then he reminded himself that she was the one who had orchestrated this in the first place. And if he could make things work with Danny Rivers, then surely he could give a little effort to his dad.

Somewhere toward the end of Nevada, he decided he'd allow the conversation to go a bit deeper. He started asking his dad a few questions of his own and offering honest answers back to his queries. Before long, Jake was telling his dad all about his new friends from church, about Chris, and about the events from the past six months. Oddly, his dad listened without judgment, and a couple times Jake thought his grunt or sniff seemed laden with emotion as he gazed away from him out the passenger window.

One thing they'd always had in common was their border-line addiction to coffee. Even when Jake was a young boy, Glen would top off his son's glass of milk at the breakfast table with fresh brew. So when they saw a quirky coffee shop shaped like a bright red mug four hours into middle-of-nowhere Arizona, they pulled over without even discussing it.

Glen jumped out to grab the drinks while Jake walked around the lot to stretch his legs. The hot Arizona sun beat down on his face, and he was glad that he'd rejected the scholarship offer to play for the Wildcats. As he stretched, something stiff in his back pocket poked him, and he pulled out Jonny's envelope. It was decorated with Jonny's famous cartoon figures engaged in a variety of activities, from dancing a jig to eating spaghetti. In the center was Jake's name written in big block letters and a warning to read it in private. Jake glanced through the coffee shop window at his dad, still standing in line, then ripped open the envelope.

Inside were two pieces of paper, each labeled with a number. Jake unfolded the one with a "1" written on it and began to read Jonny's familiar chicken-scratch.

Dear Jake,

I'm sorry if this paper smells like roses. I got it from my mom's room and I didn't realize the scent until I was almost done. Anyways, I wanted to say this in person but it's weird... Thanks for being my friend. I know you are like super popular and have tons of friends, but they have always been harder for me to come by. With my mom being in the Marines, we've always had to move every couple years and it just didn't seem worth it anymore. So, remember that time you asked me if I had ever felt the way Roger did? I said I didn't, but I lied. I thought about taking my life all the time. I even wrote the letter explaining why to my mom.

Jake clutched to the letter tightly with both hands and weakly leaned up against the back of the truck to read the rest. His heart started beating fast.

But then out of nowhere YOU came up and invited me to eat with you guys. I mean who does that? And then, when I hit very bottom, you threw yourself in front of the car to save me. I don't want to think about where I'd be if you hadn't done that. I just wanted to say thank you.

P.S. Here's the letter I never had to leave for my mom.

Jake frantically flipped to the next page to read Jonny's suicide note. He pictured Jonny writing, sitting in his trailer alone, thinking this world would actually be a better place without him. Just the thought sent Jake collapsing to his knees. What had he really done but invite him to eat lunch and give him a ride home from school? Jake remembered his own nervousness the day he first approached Jonny and how close he'd come to turning away. And then Jake cringed, thinking about that morning he had taken out all his problems on him. He had almost given up trying to make things right—what if he had? Jake shuddered at what could have been.

Glen returned with two tall iced mochas, jogging over with concern to his son, now on his knees in the middle of the dusty parking lot. He set the iced mochas on the truck and squatted down next to him. Jake looked up with tears in his eyes and spontaneously hugged his father. Taken aback, Glen froze for a moment, then he slowly wrapped his arms around his son and held him close. Cars flew by them on the busy highway, but there in that parking lot, time waited.

Life was too short, and Jake was done playing games. Jake had screwed up with Roger, but in spite of all his failures and mistakes, God had still used him to save a life.

TO SAVE A LIFE:
DARE TO MAKE YOUR LIFE COUNT

A powerful, inspirational book for teens, based on
the message in the movie, *To Save A Life.*

✚**DEVELOP** friendships that really matter

✚**ANSWER THE QUESTION:** what is your life going to be about?

✚**TOUCH LIVES** of other teens who are hurting and lonely

✚**SEE THE RIPPLE EFFECT** your life can have on others

ACKNOWLEDGMENTS

To Jesus Christ, our best friend, Savior, and Dad. You're our ultimate motivation and inspiration for everything we do.

To our amazing editing team of Jennifer Dion, Brenda Josee, and Toni Ridgaway. Thanks for challenging us to be better every step of the way.

To Scott Evans and the rest of the Outreach team, for empowering us to live this dream.

To our New Song church family, for inspiring so much of the story.

To the whole *To Save A Life* production and marketing team, for your passion for getting this story to every teen who needs to hear it.

To our incredible families, for all your amazing support.

ABOUT THE AUTHORS

 Jim and Rachel Britts share a passion for serving God and impacting the lives of teenagers. The Britts met as undergraduate students at Biola University, where Jim received his degree in film and Rachel her degree in English. They both also completed master's degrees—Jim in general ministry at Western Seminary and Rachel in education at Biola.

Today, the Britts are living the dream in Southern California. Jim is a seasoned youth pastor at New Song Community Church in Oceanside. He's well-known among his students for his wacky sense of humor, his likeness to Jim Carrey, and his passion for helping students live out their faith authentically. Rachel teaches English at Oceanside High School, where she hates grading essays but loves greeting students at the door with a smile and pushing them to do their best.

The characters in the film *To Save A Life* are drawn from the couple's real-life experience with their students, and the story reveals a compassion for teens and an understanding of the challenges they face. If you watch the film carefully, you'll even see Jim and Rachel's church, kitchen, and cool black Jeep!